WAR ZONE PRESS, LLC

STORIES ABOUT AND BY THOSE WHO'VE *BEEN* THERE!

PRIMARY CANDIDATES

A Novel

By

Mike Sutton

Khark and Kharko Islands images courtesy of and © 2015 DigitalGlobe, © 2015 Google, Data SIO, NOAA, U.S. Navy, NGA, GEBCO (see http://www.google.com/permissions/geoguidelines/attr-guide.html)

Library of Congress Control Number: 2015914442

ISBN: 978-0-6924-8327-5 Primary Candidates hardcover
ISBN: 978-0-6924-8328-2 Primary Candidates softcover
ISBN: 978-0-6924-8329-9 Primary Candidates e-book
All are registered to:
War Zone Press, LLC
P.O. Box 549
McLean, VA 22101-0549
Phone – 1-703-847-8771
FAX 1-703-991-7127

http://www.WarZonePress.com

Inquiry e-mails should be sent to: Staff @WarZonePress.com.

Because of the dynamic nature of the Internet, any web addresses or links contained in this book may have changed since publication and may no longer be valid.

The views expressed in this work are solely those of the author and do not necessarily reflect the views of the publisher, and the publisher hereby disclaims any responsibility for them.

Any people depicted in stock imagery provided by Thinkstock are models, and such images are being used for illustrative purposes only. Certain stock imagery © Thinkstock.

Lulu Publishing Services rev. date: 10/06/2015

ACKNOWLEDGMENTS

The list of those who have been instrumental in this project is too voluminous to complete here. But I would be completely remiss if several people who went out of their way, and in some cases their *minds*, in an attempt to be of assistance were not singled out for thanks. In this time of Islamic Terrorism, sadly, it is unwise to list the names of current or recently retired members of the military. In those cases, only their call sign is mentioned. However, that in no way diminishes my incredible gratitude for their time, knowledge, and service to our country.

☆ **HAMMER** – Is on active duty with the U.S. Air Force flying AC-130 gunships. As a member of U.S. Special Operations Forces – "The Quiet Professionals" – the descriptions of the unclassified elements of an incredible weapons platform were key in writing those scenes. Hammer also reviewed and corrected passages to ensure their accuracy in terms of the air to ground communication players and sequence of events in firing missions.

☆ **SCARY** – U.S. Air Force Lieutenant Colonel (Retired) and former F-16 pilot with numerous tours overseas. He provided great insight into close air support, particularly B-52 target acquisition, clearance, and bombing runs. In fact, some of the dialogue in those scenes was his suggestions . . . which I used verbatim.

☆ **MOWGLI** – Former member of the U.S. Air Force with AC-130 crew experience. He provided great insight into the makeup of the aircraft, describing its sections, their nicknames, and firing sequence communications between the various crew members on these awesome aircraft.

☆ **TRPLSTCKS** – Is one of the very few U.S. Army Green Berets to become a Navy SEAL and later return to the Army, achieving the rank of Command Sergeant Major. His insight and experience were a tremendous help in developing some of the black op scenes.

☆ **SPEAR ONE** – Master Sergeant (Retired), U.S. Army Special Forces. He was a tireless asset in terms of the black ops scenes. He is also a military Explosives Ordnance Disposal expert with many tours "down range," under fire. Spear One provided excellent tactical, communications, and movement input, *vis-à-vis* the Green Berets and SEAL scenes.

✳ **DANIEL GENIS** – Is an extremely gifted writer. I read an article of his in the *Washington Post* concerning Islamic activities and hierarchies in prison systems. I sent him an e-mail saying how interesting and well written I thought it was and mentioned this project, never expecting to get a response. Daniel answered within hours with an offer to assist and answered numerous questions. I believe he will enjoy a *very* successful writing career.

✳ **JIM GEIBEL** – Detective/Bomb Technician (Retired) Baltimore County Police Department. I met Jim while researching *High Order*. He answered many technical questions and provided input for a number of scenes in this work as well. He continues his work to protect America. Jim was the basis for one of the major characters.

✳ **DON HEALY** – Major (Retired) Baltimore City Police Department. Don introduced me to the following two resources who not only contributed to this and other works, but have become great friends as well. His extensive knowledge of the inner workings of terrorist organizations allowed me to hopefully create an interesting narrative of their nefarious activities. He is now a Program Officer with the Diplomatic Security's Antiterrorism Assistance organization. Don was the basis for one of the main characters.

✳ **PAUL DAVIS** – Sergeant (Retired) Baltimore City Police Department. Paul has been instrumental in a variety of ways. First, his incredible knowledge of ballistics allowed for a fact-based description of the sniper's choice of weapon. Second, Paul's advice on police tactics, equipment, and communications was outstanding. Finally, his in-depth knowledge of courtroom proceedings was extremely valuable. Paul was the basis for one of the main characters.

✳ **JOE COSTANTINI** – Retired from the Baltimore City Police Department as its Bomb Squad's Lead Technician. He has gone out of his way to ensure the narrative and dialogue relating to explosives and render-safe procedures were accurate. Joe's input regarding search and seizure operations were a mainstay of accuracy in this work. Joe also continues to man the Thin Blue Line by training domestic and international police forces in render-safe procedures. He is currently one of the instructors of the T4 – Transit Terrorist Tools and Tactics – course. Joe was the basis for one of the main characters.

☆ **JIM MILLIGAN** – A dear friend and fellow Vietnam-era vet who served in the U.S. Air Force in Thailand loading ordnance on fighter jets. Jim is a private pilot who provided great assistance on all the scenes and dialogue, *vis-à-vis* airports, flight and air traffic control instructions.

☆ **ROBERT STANTON** – Retired Detective Colonel, Chief of Detectives, Baltimore City Police Department. Bob's input and reviews served as the backbone of the homicide investigations scenes. He provided great insight into the inner workings of the BCPD Homicide Squad he led.

☆ **DICK WEBER** – Retired FBI agent and former Marine helicopter pilot in Vietnam. Dick's assistance in the federal activities following some of the scenes was a great addition to their accuracy and clarity. Dick also continues to man the Thin Blue Line as an instructor for the T4 – Transit Terrorist Tools and Tactics – course, as well as other background work.

☆ **TAD WILSON** – Retired Marine Mustang Officer and head of a family with multiple current and prior service veterans who turns my manuscripts into "publisher-ready" Microsoft Word files. Tad does in a matter of hours what I wouldn't accomplish in multiple lifetimes!

☆ **BARBARA CARLSON** – AKA Ms. G! Barbara continues to amaze me. She is a tireless and invaluable resource – on this and my other writing projects – who always slips on her kid gloves before pointing out my outrageous spelling and/or grammar errors. A retired educator, Barbara currently makes her home at a beautiful place affectionately known as Butterfly Landing, where she is involved in many aspects of her friends' and families' lives, providing support and counsel across a wide range of subjects. Ms. G is not a mere passenger on the train of life; she is in the cab with her hands on the controls.

AUTHOR'S NOTE

Primary Candidates is a novel inspired in part by historical events. It contains fictional characters, places and circumstances set during in the 2008 time frame. The characters in it are completely fictitious, as are the airport bombing and military scenes. However, America's "soft targets" remain a major exposure in these troubling times.

I decided that Henry Small Deer – a primary character in my Vietnam War novel, *No Survivors* – didn't have to end his fictional career with one book. So, you'll meet him again in *Primary Candidates*.

All of the characters in *High* Order have returned, some in different roles. Beyond Hunter and Sam however, the other *Primary Candidates'* first responders are based on the real people as mentioned on the "Acknowledgments" page.

I would be remiss if I did not mention two faceless resources that were of great assistance in this work: Wikipedia and Google Earth. The former offers a galaxy of information on virtually any topic imaginable. The latter enables the writer to do research at the street level on the other side of the planet without leaving the office. The detailed descriptions in *Primary Candidates* were possible because Google Earth took me to almost any spot on the planet and let me look around. Simply incredible technology.

The men and women who man the Thin Blue Line – my son, Brian, among them – are people with amazing courage, dedication, and a tremendous sense of altruism – you don't become a police officer for the high pay and steady hours. In this time of increased tension – particularly racial – let us not cast these heroes aside based on insufficient evidence and the microscopic percentage of them who are less than honorable.

By the same token, those who wear – or wore – military uniforms deserve much praise on many levels. There is some dispute over the origination of the following *paraphrased* quote: "We sleep safely in our beds because rough men *and women* stand ready in the night to visit violence on those who would harm us." There is no debate over their courage, sacrifice, and dedication to our Great Nation!

And finally, to my many friends who agreed to let me use their names and descriptions in this work! Thank you, all!

In an attempt to make *Primary Candidates* as reader-friendly as possible, a glossary of common terms has been included in the back of the book.

As a measure of my incredible appreciation and respect for all those who contributed their time, knowledge, and names to *Primary Candidates*, I am donating fifty percent of the proceeds to a variety of military and first responder support organizations.

Mike Sutton
MikeSutton@WarZonePress.com

FOR:
MARK CHRISTIAN LAVEY
AND
JAMES CASSELLS MILLIGAN

PROLOGUE

Shortly after the conclusion of Operation Desert Storm, on February 28, 1991, a group of military and CIA operatives presented a bold plan to the President of the United States (POTUS).

The U.S. Embassy in Iran had been taken over by a mob on November 4, 1979 in an unprecedented diplomatic infringement. Soon afterward, Iranian support for, and their direct export of, terrorism became apparent around the globe.

If Saddam Hussein could boldly invade Kuwait and Iran could operate covertly – or overtly – with impunity, what might the future look like in ten, twenty, or thirty years? Could quiet preparations be made for some future hostile action in the Middle East, and be maintained and updated over time with current technology?

The president reviewed the plan, code-named the Diogenes Agreement, so named because the drafters were all world-class cynics. Following the invasion of his country, and its defense by a coalition of thirty-four countries, led by the United States, the king of the State of Kuwait – without the knowledge of the National Assembly, other staff members or his deputies – agreed to the plan and signed it during the emir's visit to Washington, D.C.

For security reasons, the Secretaries of Defense and State became the only cabinet level members informed of Diogenes.

★ ★ ★

On April 19, 1995, a bomb blast outside the Alfred P. Murrah Federal Building in downtown Oklahoma City killed 168 people and injured nearly 700 others.

In early June, an amendment to the anti-terrorism bill, sponsored by Dianne Feinstein of California, was approved by a 90 to 0 vote in the U.S. Senate. The amendment established a requirement that dynamite and other commercial explosives contain tagging agents, also known as taggants, designed to help investigators trace where the materials used in an improvised explosive device (IED) had been manufactured and to whom they had been sold.

PART I

THE ACTORS

"Misinformation and/or misfortune can divert any person's or group's life course in an opposite direction for good or . . ."

ONE

March, 2008

"Targets, large and small, with a thousand times the impact of September eleventh," the strategist said bluntly.

"What could that possibly be?" the bearded man asked quietly.

"Something to paralyze the Great Satan financially and turn it against itself," the strategist replied, keeping his leader at bay for the moment. "Targets to spread panic and play on the prejudices and hatreds cultivated in America since 1619."

"And they are?" the bearded man asked, a slight edge in his voice this time.

"Targets that require care in planning, but little effort to execute." The strategist knew he was beginning to annoy his leader, but at the moment he didn't care. The enjoyment of meting out the information a few words at a time far surpassed the threat of the other man's wrath.

"Play this game no longer, Asad."

The leader's voice remained calm, but the strategist knew the emphasis on his name shouted a clear message: His leader's patience threshold had been exceeded.

*** *** ***

Everyone said – even her husband, the former president – that the Texas and Ohio primaries were her last best hope. Newspaper, radio, and television pundits had almost unanimously laid Jeannette Freddo Reynolds into a political casket, cloaked in the shattering disappointment of a warp speed transition from presumptive presidential nominee less than ninety days ago to an almost also-ran status today. Oh, sure, she'd won big states – California and Massachusetts – on Super Tuesday, and Thaddeus Tasman had won states the Democrats couldn't carry in November, like Georgia and Alabama. But the bottom line was he had more delegates, and that was the key to the nomination, regardless of where they came from. Thaddeus Tasman now not only enjoyed a lead in the delegate count, he was also running ahead of her in the national polls by enough percentage points to be outside the margin of error.

Mrs. Reynolds' campaign manager, Rose-Marie Santos, had stepped down, following the Super Tuesday debacle. Of course, the media pounced on that saying Santos had been fired, which didn't do anything to bolster the Latino vote. The fact that Jackie Beaudro – a black woman – had replaced Ms. Santos might help a little. But the chances of Mrs. Reynolds picking up the majority of the black vote while running against the first black man asking for the nomination was considered a remote possibility at best.

Mrs. Reynolds had certainly paid her political dues, working her ass off getting Benjamin into the Alabama Governor's Mansion and the White House. Then she'd put in eight hard years standing in his shadow, being subjected to the humiliation of *all* of her husband's romances – culminating with the little pie-faced intern, which led to his impeachment. She'd run for the Senate from New Hampshire . . . and won . . . twice. And this *kid* in his forties, with less than half a term in the Senate came out of nowhere to challenge her. What dues had he paid? One good speech at the Democratic Convention four years ago? Where was his political scar tissue? Promising *change*!

Well, there'd been a change all right! Yesterday! When the voters shoved the polls saying Thaddeus Tasman was leading in Texas and running neck-and-neck in Ohio right up his tight ass! She was still running in second place, but once again it was the Reynolds campaign that had reason to celebrate at the end of the night. And again, T-squared showed his inability to win the big states that had to be won for *any* candidate to get into the White House! Even Thaddeus Tasman's charm wouldn't put him in the Oval Office if he couldn't win *Ohio*!

"How's that for change, T-squared?" she muttered, shaking her head.

Sometimes the bullshit of politics became too much even for a seasoned spreader of it like Senator Reynolds. "Anybody in a voting booth who believes the election of me or Tasman or Robert Fox will make any fucking difference in Washington is a *naïve* moron! Change we can believe in, my *ass*!"

Senator Reynolds knew Winston Churchill had said it perfectly: "The best argument against democracy is a five-minute conversation with the average voter."

✦✦✦

TWO

"T-squared can beat her. He's got the momentum," the campaign's communications director said.

"Yeah? Everyone had a toe tag on the Ice Queen yesterday morning. In the media's eyes, she was dead and buried. The only group that didn't seem to know that were the voters in the Texas and Ohio primaries. If T-squared has so much fucking momentum, how come he lost?" The campaign manager, John Mallard, sat back in his chair, crossed his arms, and then continued.

"I'm telling you right now, and this doesn't take a rocket scientist to figure out. This will be a see-saw battle for months. This primary campaign is going to wind up in the hands of the superdelegates. You mark my words."

The communications director smiled. "Then we better start jockeying for position."

"No *shit*! Why didn't *I* think of that?" Mallard snarled.

The communications director ignored the outburst. "Everyone has a little dirt in their lives that would best be swept under the carpet. Superdelegates are no exception. We need to make sure that any of them who've announced their backing for the Ice Queen have a nasty *political* accident before the convention. That is, if the replacement would be likely to line up behind T-squared."

"And who would that be and what kind of 'accidents' do you have in mind?"

"I've already started the ball rolling. And for your own protection, you don't need ..."

★ ★ ★

". . . to know that. And trying to trace this prepaid burner cell phone will be a waste of time. What you *do* need to know is that the governor of Pennsylvania likes his women young, built, and beautiful," the caller said. "Take a look at Satans-Sweeties-dot-com if you want to get an idea of where his tastes run."

"I need your name, sir," the FBI duty agent said, a slight tone of irritation in her voice.

"No, you don't, *honey*! Here's what's important. The governor routinely moves money across state lines for the purpose of paying for prostitution. Not only that, here's the icing on the cake. Satan's Sweeties operates out of Philadelphia. His Honor has women shipped to Washington, New York, Miami, etc., in violation of the Mann Act. I believe that felony could get him about ten years in a federal license plate factory, per *count*."

"Sir, we don't accept anonymous tips," the agent lied.

"Bullshit! Now, just so you know, this same information is going to the FBI Director by mail mentioning your name, Agent. So, if you just disregard this phone call, it won't be long until you're taking a shit-shower."

✸ ✸ ✸

The Roadrunner Railroad passenger line runs between Los Angeles and New Orleans, with stops in California, Arizona, New Mexico, Texas and rural Louisiana along the way. The Texas and Pacific Freight Railroad Company's tracks parallel the Roadrunner's between Houston and the Port of Los Angeles. The dual railroad tracks cross the north-flowing San Pedro River just east of Benson, Arizona. At that point, passenger and freight movement schedules overlapped only three times a month and only once at night – at 1:47 a.m.

T&PFR train number 641 consisted of 191 heavily loaded freight cars of various types. Towed by four General Electric ES44DC diesel-electric locomotives, each producing 4,400 horsepower, it traveled at 57 mph toward the West Coast. RR's eastbound Red-Eye Express – consisting of a locomotive, baggage car, dining car, four coach and three business class cars – sped toward the bridge spanning the now bone-dry San Pedro Riverbed and its next stop – El Paso, Texas – and at nearly 70 mph.

Forty-five seconds before the trains crossed paths, T&PFR 641 hit a cracked left rail. The first forward-facing locomotive veered off the tracks, slamming into the steel framework of the bridge trestle, then plunged into the dry riverbed. The remaining three rear-facing engines piled on top of it like playful children, the last of which rolled into the path of the oncoming Red-Eye Express.

The REX locomotive smashed into the obstruction, sending tons of steel and other debris onto both sides of the track. Its passenger cars folded like a concertina behind the locomotive, littering both sides of the rail bed. Several piled into the San Pedro, each smashing the car below it.

Each freight locomotive contained a little more than three-quarters of its 5,000 gallon fuel supply. The impact of the crash ruptured and ignited three of the four tanks, sending a huge ball of flame and thick black smoke into the night sky. The burning fuel also rained onto the passenger cars west of the bridges, igniting many of their interiors and other flammable parts. Only the last few RR cars were spared this deadly shower.

For the few lucky passengers still alive in the demolished RR cars in the San Pedro, their luck was about to run out. A freight car in the riverbed on the north side of the tracks blocked the flow of burning diesel fuel, causing it to pool and back up to the south. Within three minutes the fire spread beneath them.

The screams of the few survivors west of the river and those being cremated alive pierced the flame's moving shadows into the dark desert night.

*　＊　
＊　＊
　＊*

THREE

Very rarely is the President of the United States – POTUS – *ever* seen waiting for anyone, especially on camera. Mere mortals wait for POTUS. But, today offered an exception, and the gaggle of cameramen and reporters in the Rose Garden bore full witness and seemed to be enjoying it.

Outside the Oval Office, President Rodney Thatch paced, left, came back and paced some more, waiting for Senator Robert Fox to arrive for the press conference. Today, the senator, AKA the Desert Fox, would receive POTUS' official endorsement as his party's presidential nominee.

Finally, a black limo rolled to a stop amid several Secret Service vehicles, and Senator Fox hurried to the Rose Garden and the waiting President.

"*Jesus*, Bob!" Thatch said in a whisper, his southern drawl slightly masking his displeasure. "I been out here lookin' like a fool waiting for ya!"

The senator leaned in close to Thatch's ear. "Sorry, Mr. President. There *was* a traffic jam coming back from the Senate. Didn't anyone call your office to tell you we were running late?"

"Would I be standin' out here with my thumb up my ass if they had?"

"Sorry, sir. I'll have someone drawn and quartered as soon as this is over!"

☆ ☆ ☆

"Now that their Treasury Department has closed the spigot of donations from America to our causes by bullying the international banking community, there is no reason not to proceed with our grand scheme.

"However, the idea is dangerous at best. The Americans will immediately believe we are responsible. Then, even their most liberal legislators will have to fall in line, either willingly or because of political pressure. The fact that they have failed to extend their phone surveillance act has been to our advantage, but even their trial lawyers' lobby and the Civil Liberties Union won't be able to argue Americans' privacy rights are being threatened. America's response will be immediate and devastating." The bearded man paused, his grey eyes boring twin holes into the strategist's face.

"What you say is very true. However, any military response will be viewed by the rest of the world as unjustified, especially if there is no clear connection to us."

The strategist continued. "We have discovered an asset that offers a vast array of possibilities. One who can deliver a deathblow that will appear to come from within America. Our hands will be stained with no apparent blood and it will further confuse the issue of who was responsible for the first plan."

"And how will you obtain the tools for your larger blow?"

The strategist smiled broadly. "There are many willing participants who will gladly martyr themselves for Allah – The Most Merciful – and our cause. Men who feel betrayed by America. There is nothing more dangerous than a person who feels that everything has been taken from them, *including* their dignity. Not a lion protecting her young. Not a cobra ready to strike."

"That is true. But even the most dangerous man on the planet needs tools to be effective. How will you put them in his hands?"

"Some will be provided by our supporters. Others, purchased legally in the broad light of day," the strategist smiled and waited for the leader's obvious question.

"Explain."

"To create the greatest amount of confusion, there can be no traceable signature that implicates us. We can take credit when it suits us, but delaying doing so will only confuse and further cripple our enemies.

"All evidence needs to either point nowhere, or inward toward America itself. To do so, we will use their own tools against them." The strategist straightened on the small three-legged stool and became silent.

The reflected candlelight in his eyes made them seem to sparkle. He didn't need any outside influences to provide this simulated pyrotechnic display. The excitement in his belly made them gleam all on their own.

"How will you obtain these tools for Allah?" the leader asked quietly. He'd known his advisor long enough to understand this type of exchange was an erotic release for the other man. So long as he had time, the leader was willing to play along.

"Buy or steal them. The American military is notoriously underpaid. Many of them have to ask for food coupons to feed their families. There is always someone in need of money and willing to betray their country for a price, monetary or otherwise.

"Their borders are like sieves. The weapons we have captured in the two theaters of war here can easily be smuggled across either the Mexican or Canadian border. Finally, we have many eyes and ears within America's defense industry. These agents provide information on shipments of weapons from the manufacturer to the various military bases and ports. Intercepting one of these deliveries would not take much effort.

"Obtaining the tools to execute the plan is not difficult. Putting the right *people* in place is a very delicate task. Our new American asset solves that problem. And there are other actions we can take to increase confusion and alarm."

"Yes?"

The advisor smiled broadly. "To confuse the infidels, we should take responsibility for things we don't have any involvement in . . ."

"Such as?"

"A plane crash, a bridge collapse, a train wreck, brush fires across America, especially in the western part of the country where drought is blamed on global warming, or 'climate change,' as they have renamed it. Anything that gains national news coverage, or even just in large population areas – New York City, Los Angeles, Dallas. For these events, as we choose, we take immediate responsibility. If the Americans claim there was no such involvement, it will simply cause them to be doubted, since it is impossible to prove a negative."

The leader smiled slightly.

"And for our own actions, we say nothing, if it serves our greater purpose. Of course there are many of our jihadist brothers operating independently or in small groups. We have no direct control over them;

however, we can make efforts to pass this strategy onto them where possible.

"Look at all the changes put in place to protect America. If they are seen as ineffective, America's stupid politicians will answer by spending more money and time implementing additional safeguards. We should take credit for every unnatural disaster that happens in America. Our power and reach will appear unstoppable, resulting in even more wasted time and money."

★ ★ ★

Nearly a dozen investigators from the National Transportation Safety Board combed through the thousands of tons of wreckage they could access in and near the San Pedro Riverbed. As a result of the two trains' interstate commerce involvement, FBI agents worked with and independently of the NTSB staff at the crash site.

The rescue aspect of the disaster ended a few hours following the first responders' arrival on scene. Police, firefighters and medics pulled a relatively small handful of passengers, nearly all critically injured, from cars at the end of the RR red-eye express. Now in the recovery phase, the same exhausted men and women worked through the debris as best they could, filling body bags.

The passenger and freight cars piled in the riverbed presented a very difficult obstacle. Their removal required rough terrain heavy cranes due to the location and sheer tonnage involved. The nearest crane company to the wreck site, in Sierra Vista over thirty miles south of Benson, had cranes with the muscle to lift the railroad cars, but could not meet the terrain requirement. This left the closest alternative in Tucson, which would not arrive by truck for another twelve hours.

One fact was certain at this point. Even if the dual tracks hadn't been destroyed for several hundred yards in each direction, it would take months to replace the two bridges, both damaged beyond repair. East-west rail traffic through the area faced detours in excess of 300 miles for the foreseeable future.

★★
★ ★
★

FOUR

Near midnight, the FBI surveillance team sat outside Washington, D.C.'s Hay-Adams hotel in a standard issue Ford Crown Victoria sedan – black, of course.

"This sucks! He's not comin'!" the agent behind the wheel said in a low voice.

"Well, if he is, he's takin' his sweet-assed time about it," the agent in the passenger seat responded, lowering a pair of night-vision binoculars to his lap. "That little black-tie *soirée* was over at ten."

The first agent squirmed in his seat, in a losing battle with discomfort. "This poor dumb schmuck's just lookin' to get his rocks off while he's on the road. Who cares?"

"First, he ain't poor. Second, he ain't dumb. He's a fuckin' governor and ex-attorney general, for Christ's sake. He *is* seriously fuckin' arrogant though. You can't be an attorney general of a state like Pennsylvania and not know that the Patriot Act has banks watching almost every nickel that moves from one account to another."

"Patriot Act? Are you fucking kidding me? The Patriot Act has nothing to do with this. Someone dropped a quarter on the Gov."

"Yeah? Who would do that?"

"Anybody with a political ax to grind. Who knows? You don't believe all that bullshit that the Executive Branch throws around about somebody watchin' every nickel that moves in this country, do you? Someone set this guy up."

"Well, regardless of how they found out, Governor Big Dick transferred forty large to a shell company that fronts for this stable of high-priced hookers. These babes go for five K an hour!"

"Swell!" the agent behind the wheel said. "But, how can you say he's not dumb? He knows how the system works! He'd be safer stickin' his dick in some crack-whore in an alley and hopin' not to get AIDS."

"Can't argue with ya there," the agent in the passenger seat answered, chuckling. His cell phone chirped and he reached into his inside jacket pocket for it. "Eade," he said quietly, and listened for several seconds. "Okay, thanks."

The agent snapped the phone closed and looked at his partner. "We're done. He took the 11:30 train back to Harrisburg. Maybe he's not so dumb after all."

"Hope he's luckier than those poor bastards in Arizona. That's a first class catastrophe."

✹ ✹ ✹

At the railroad disaster site, two CR046 Liebherr, LTM 1250-6.1, 300 ton all-terrain cranes had inched their way from the low-boys they arrived on to the scattered cars west of the river. An additional Liebherr had yet to arrive on the east side of the San Pedro to move and upright scores of freight cars.

The three RR business class cars and one of the coach class cars lay scattered on and beside both sets of tracks. The baggage, dining, and remaining three coach cars smoldered in a pile in the San Pedro Riverbed.

The Liebherr cranes had no problem lifting any of the cars, ranging in weight from 57 to 67 tons. However, the General Electric locomotives weighed in at 216 tons each, meaning the cranes had to be virtually on top of them to have the capacity to lift them out of the riverbed. This would entail removing what remained of the steel railroad trestle still standing after the T&PFR locomotives' impact.

As the cranes worked their way toward the riverbed on the west side of the San Pedro, NTSB and FBI agents combed through the debris field left by the T&PFR on the east side.

Harvey Stone, a thirty-year veteran of NTSB crash site investigations, and FBI agent Don McGuire measured the length of piece of rail lying south of the track bed.

"Twelve feet, eight inches," Stone said, more to himself than McGuire after measuring the rail's length. Before getting to his feet, he examined the end of it closest to him. "Well, that's not good."

He turned to the north, toward the track bed and held out the end of the tape measure. "Just out of curiosity, let's see how far this piece got thrown, Don."

McGuire took the tip of the yellow Stanley forty-foot tape and pulled it to a spot on the ties that had obviously been covered by the steel rails. "What's it say?" he asked Stone.

"Twenty feet, nine inches," Stone responded, pushing the retract button and writing the specifics in his notebook. "So, let's see. Three feet of 139-pound rail weighs a little over forty-six pounds per foot. So this weighs almost 560 pounds. But that's not really the important factor here, Don. Come take a look."

McGuire walked back to the spot where Stone stood, pointing to the end of the length of track.

"What do you see?"

The FBI agent bent and examined the track. "That looks like it's been cut."

Stone nodded. "Exactly. We can take this catastrophe out of the 'accidental' category. You guys will have to figure out if it was a terrorist's attack."

✷✷✷

FIVE

Dusty Rhodes sat at her desk in the *Baltimore Mirror's* Lutherville office. Although a few months shy of the half-century mark, Dusty looked far better now than she had a decade earlier. Her round face suggested she could drop a few pounds, but in fact, Ms. Rhodes was in very good shape due to her dedicated use of a local health club and her husband's getting her interested in jogging.

Dusty absent-mindedly scratched her left ear with a pencil eraser through her short dark hair. Her deep blue eyes, along with everyone else's in the *Mirror's* bullpen, watched the solemn swearing-in ceremony on a TV monitor mounted on the far wall. The Lieutenant Governor of Pennsylvania – a black man – was being sworn in as the state's fifty-fifth chief executive after his law-and-order boss was indicted on a variety of charges associated with prostitution.

The phone on Dusty's desk rang and she reached for it without taking her eyes from the screen. "Rhodes here."

"You're the crime reporter?" a woman's husky voice asked.

Dusty's first reaction was the woman was a phone sex pro. She glanced at the Caller ID screen. The display read: "Blocked."

"I like to think so. Who are you?"

"That's not real important right now. What I have to tell you is."

Dusty rolled her eyes. *Another hot tip*, she thought.

"What would that be, Ms. . . .?" But, just in case, she pushed the "Record" button on an answering machine she had attached to the phone. Recording someone's voice without their consent is illegal in the State of Maryland as Dusty well knew. But this technique had served her well for years in making sure she quoted people accurately – a professional trait more and more of her colleagues seemed to have lost interest in.

"You know about the Governor up north getting his dick in a wringer, right?"

"I'm watching his replacement get sworn in right now," Dusty answered.

"What would you think if one of the presidential candidates was puttin' his dipstick in someone else's wife? Would that make the news?"

Dusty's eyes abandoned the TV screen and swung her full attention to the caller. "Yes. That would probably make the front page, if it were true and could be proven. Who are you talking about?"

"Well, it's not the senator from New Mexico. That only leaves one possibility."

Dusty didn't know how seriously to take the caller. She'd seen more than a few wingnuts come out of the woodwork in search of fame, fortune, or just to get noticed, in her time as a reporter. "I'd need to know what kind of proof you have."

"I'm not giving you that on the phone. That's a face-to-face discussion."

"Okay, where and when?"

✷ ✷ ✷

Former California Governor Justin Cunningham sat on the couch in the corner of the small hotel conference room. The curtain covering the floor-to-ceiling window next to him filtered the early afternoon light. Cunningham pulled the almost gauze-sheer curtain back a few inches and gazed out at Washington, D.C. In the distance he could see Lafayette Park and the north side of the White House.

"This time next year, I'll be visiting you in the Oval Office," Cunningham said to Thaddeus Tasman. "That is . . . with my help."

Tasman, standing near the wet bar in an opposite corner of the room, dropped two ice cubes into a crystal tumbler and added three fingers of Johnnie Walker Blue Scotch whiskey. Walking toward Cunningham, he held the out glass to the other man.

"And what is your help going to cost me, Governor?"

The handsome Californian looked up, smiled and took the drink from Tasman. His dark face would have given George Hamilton a run for his suntan money. "I'm easy to get along with, Thaddeus. When Bob McKenna takes the Stygian ferry, I want his job."

"People have survived liver cancer, Governor."

"Some people have, but Chief Justice McKenna won't. He's got one foot in the grave and the other on a banana peel. If he makes it to the election in November, it'll be a near-medical miracle."

"And what can you deliver for me, Governor?"

"Enough superdelegates to get you within a red cunt hair of the nomination."

"Getting within an RCH doesn't do me any good. I need 2,025 or more."

"Okay. Here's what I'm willing to sign up for. I'll guarantee you enough delegates to take you over the top, regardless of the number needed after the Pennsylvania primary. And, I'll make the announcement that the number needed, plus some small safety factor of five or maybe ten, have pledged their votes to you the day after the PA primary."

"You sound pretty confident, Governor."

"I have reason to be. Here's the only condition: If the Ice Queen drops out of the race between now and the Pennsylvania primary, our deal is still in effect."

"Why don't you just make the announcement now and take me over the top? That would probably get Senator Reynolds to bail out immediately and give me a chance to start campaigning against Senator Fox now, rather than waiting for Reynolds to see the light sometime in the future."

Cunningham stood and turned toward the window. "Because I don't know how many delegates you really need."

"Come on, Governor! Subtract the total number of delegates I have, pledged and super, from 2,025. It's not that you can't do simple math. The real reason is you don't have that many in your pocket."

"I can bring this to an end for you on April twenty-third, after Pennsylvania. If I promise to do that, is the Chief Justice job mine?"

Tasman thought for several moments without answering or looking at Cunningham. Finally, he turned and walked back to the wet bar. He poured a splash of the Johnnie Walker into a glass and lifted it in Cunningham's direction. "It will be if the Senate confirms you."

★ ★ ★

On New Mexico Highway 180, near its intersection with Memory Lane in Silver City, a Hispanic man pulled into the parking lot of a small body shop. The battered, green, 1974 Chevy pickup he drove pulled an empty, black, auto transport trailer behind it.

He left the truck. The tail of a long sleeved, blue flannel shirt flapped outside faded blue jeans as he walked to the front door of the Ravens' Auto Body Shop and pulled it open with a worn, leather work glove.

Inside, the office showed no more class than the business' shabby exterior. A stained, gunmetal gray, Formica countertop, scarred and torn in several places held an old style manual cash register, a spindle with a number of receipts of various sizes impaled on it, a plastic Ravens business card case, and a silver bell to ring for service. A rickety looking black swivel chair sat between the counter and the wall, which sported a very busty model on an auto parts calendar. The man slapped the bell and waited. He absently-mindedly picked up one of the cards and read it.

Ravens' Auto Body, Rico Ferrari, Owner
Free Estimates and Towing
6115 Memory Lane
Silver City, NM 88061-9737
1-575-ROAD

The man chuckled, looking around the room. "Don't look like no *Ferrari* lives here."

The door to the shop opened and a tall Caucasian man also dressed in jeans and a Rolling Stones t-shirt entered the office.

"Hey, you must be Rico. *Qué pasa?*" The man said slipping the card into his left hand and extending his gloved right hand to Rico.

Rico glanced at the offer to shake, ignored it and continued using a shop rag to clean his hands. "It's finished. Follow me," he said, turning back to the door to the shop.

The Hispanic man looked down at his empty right hand in embarrassment, moved the card back to it and shoved it into his right front jeans pocket before following Rico toward the three-bay garage.

Two late model sedans occupied the closest and middle parts of the business in various stages of repair. On the far side, a beige car cover concealed the third. The Hispanic man followed Rico past the first two overhead doors.

As Rico rolled the car cover back, beginning at the front bumper, a freshly painted new vehicle came into view.

The Hispanic man whistled. "*Mi amigo,* that looks like the *real thing*."

"It *is* the real thing, right down to the electronics. Now, give me the rest of my money. Then back your trailer up to the overhead door. Does it have a winch on it?"

"*Si*, a hand winch. But why don't we just drive it on?"

"Because, this beauty ain't leaving my shop without a cover on it that's tied down securely. I don't want anyone to see it between where it sits here and wherever you're takin' it. Got it?"

"*Si*." The Hispanic man pulled a thick white #10 business envelope from a rear pocket and handed it to Rico. "Count it, if you want to."

"You don't need to ask 'cause you're not goin' anywhere till I do. That doesn't look like enough." Rico pulled a wad of cash from the envelope. "What the fuck! These are all hundreds. I told them nothing larger than *fifties*!"

"What can I say, *amigo*? That's what they gave me. I didn't even look inside."

"Go pull the trailer up. I'll open the door when you're in place."

Without a response, the Hispanic man walked across the shop and into the office. Outside, he maneuvered the back of the trailer to within inches of the third bay's door.

Rico rolled up the door using a chain hoist, and the Hispanic man lowered the trailer's ramps, which extended almost three feet into the bay.

Lifting the car cover enough to make the driver's side window accessible, Rico reached in and turned the ignition key, starting the engine. He then slipped the gearshift lever into neutral and turned the key off.

The Hispanic man unlocked the hand crank winch and pulled the hook on its cable to the front of the vehicle where Rico secured it to the frame.

"You crank, I'll push," Rico instructed.

"*Si, mi amigo*." After walking to the front of the trailer he began turning the winch's handle. It rotated easily until the slack was out of the cable. As the tension tightened, he had to use two hands to turn it, even though Rico began pushing on the covered trunk lid. When the front tires started up the trailer's ramps, he could no longer move the handle.

"Hey, Rico. You got to help me turn this crank!"

Rico walked from the back of the vehicle to the man's side. "Get out of the way and go push," he ordered. As the man walked away Rico muttered under his breath, loud enough for the Hispanic man to hear: "Fuckin' candy-ass wetback."

With assistance from the rear, the much stronger and heavier Rico pulled the car onto the trailer within minutes. He set the lock on the winch and began using tie-down chains to secure the load. Finally, he retrieved almost a dozen bungee cords from the shop, and then worked his way around the trailer ensuring the car cover wouldn't come off in transit.

"Rico, that car will fall off the trailer before the cover comes off."

"That's the idea. Now haul ass. I don't want this thing anywhere close to my shop anymore."

"*Sí, amigo*. I just need to take a piss first."

"Make it quick."

Rico rolled the overhead door down while the Hispanic man went to the restroom.

Inside, he removed his gloves and pulled the zipper of his jeans down. He listened to the noise of the chain pulley lowering the overhead door as he relieved himself. When he finished he shook himself several times, zipped his jeans and pushed the flush handle on the right side of the toilet's tank. He heard the door to the office bang shut outside the lavatory. After pulling on his right work glove, he lifted the back tail of his flannel shirt and pulled a suppressed 9mm Glock from his jeans waistband. Pulling the slide back and releasing it loaded a hollow point round into the chamber.

Concealing the weapon behind his back in his right hand, he opened the restroom door. He walked to the office, pushing the door open with his left hand.

"Okay, *mi amigo*. I'm outta here," he said, walking toward the counter.

"Yeah, fine. Hit the road." Rico didn't look up from the cash register as he emptied it into a white bank bag and dropped the envelope he'd just received in it as well.

From less than five feet away, the Glock spit a hollow point bullet toward the right side of Rico's head. He fell to the floor like an anvil dropped down a well, as most of the left side of his head erupted across the floor and counter with a few flecks of skull, brains and blood decorating the auto parts calendar as well.

"Fuck you, *gringo*."

The Hispanic man walked to the counter, lifting the bank bag from the spot where it had fallen when Rico could no longer grip it. There were only a few small specks of blood on it, testifying to Rico's departure from this world.

When the Hispanic man reached the door of his truck, he tucked the bag under the driver's seat and climbed into the cab. After starting the engine, he checked to make sure the brake lights and turn signals were working on the trailer via the oversized, outside rearview mirrors. A traffic stop in New Mexico would cost him a lot more than mere money at this point.

★ ★ ★

Dusty sat in a Starbucks on Pratt Street, in the Gallery at Harbor Place. She had been there less than fifteen minutes when an attractive white woman approached her table.

"Dusty Rhodes?"

"I am. And you are?"

"Anonymous, for the moment. Who I am will come out soon enough, if I feel I can trust you."

"Fair enough. Have a seat. Can I get you a cup of coffee?" Dusty pushed a chair to her right away from the table.

The woman pulled it out even farther and sat down. "No thanks. I'm allergic to caffeine."

"Wow! Don't think I could handle that. I need it to get my heart started, at least in the morning."

"I get my rush other ways." The woman lips moved ever so slightly into a momentary, coy Mona Lisa smile. Her almost azure suit was clearly off the rack, but nonetheless well-made and expensive. Her auburn hair was not quite shoulder length. She crossed a long right leg over her left. The tip of a stiletto heel, dyed to match the color of her suit, scraped the floor lightly.

"So, what can I do for you?" Dusty asked, sipping her latte.

"It's what I can do for you. I read all your stuff about that old man who went nuts and started making bombs. How would you like another Pulitzer?"

Dusty eyed the other woman a little suspiciously before answering. "I guess you can't have too many of them. What's the story?"

"I am . . . *was* . . . Thaddeus Tasman's mistress."

Dusty frowned, shaking her head. "How would that be possible? He has TV cameras on him virtually everywhere he goes. Why would he risk a chance to plop his ass in the Oval Office's big seat to . . ."

". . . bang a white whore?"

"I wasn't going to say that."

"You have to pay better attention, Ms. Rhodes. I said 'was' his mistress. He broke it off the day before he announced his candidacy."

"And why are you coming to me with this now?"

"I see people lining up to throw money at the Governor's extramarital squeeze." The Mona Lisa smile returned for a moment before the woman's face turned rock hard. "I was good enough for T-squared until his galactic ego pushed me out of the way on his way to being a presidential candidate. I was put out like last week's trash. So, *fuck* him. If the Governor's chick can cash in, a presidential candidate's – especially one with a damn good chance of getting elected – should be like a winning Power Ball ticket."

Dusty leaned in and spoke quietly. "I need proof."

The blond reached into a small handbag and produced a 5" X 7" glossy photo, placing it face down on the table. She pushed it toward Dusty's latte cup with the tips of her fingers.

Dusty reached for it, but a French nail landed in its middle like a schoolmarm pointing out a spelling error to a slow child.

"You can see this, but you can't keep it. Not until we have a deal. Clear?"

Dusty nodded and the woman lifted her finger.

Dusty used a far less elegant index fingernail to turn the picture over, then picked it up. Thaddeus Tasman had clearly been captured in a sexual encounter with a white woman. January 27, 2007, 9:41 p.m. was printed in the lower right corner of the photo – automatically captured at the time it was taken by the camera. The slightly oblique shot revealed a muscular back glistening with sweat. His eyes were closed and his head angled slightly to the left and down.

A set of long, very shapely legs, wrapped in black fishnet stockings, pointed toward the ceiling, rested on Tasman's shoulders. Stiletto heels decorated the feet.

The woman's face was hidden by Tasman's shoulder and her own leg, but her large right breast was clearly visible. On it, just above the nipple was a tattoo – a small horseshoe and a rose.

"I can't tell this is you," Dusty said quietly, looking up at the woman.

Without a word, the woman unbuttoned her blouse, pulling it and a black lace bra aside far enough for Dusty to see the same tattoo, and a small, tan crescent of areola.

"This is just an *hors d'oeuvre*. I have high quality video of the senator in several of our encounters. Lots of it on a DVD in my safety deposit box. Interested?"

"What is it you want me to do, Ms. . . . Can I have a name, please, even if it is just your first?"

"Jordan."

"Okay, Jordan. What is it you think I can do for you?" The idea crossed Dusty's mind that this woman could blackmail her way into any number of plum jobs, if she cared to.

"I want you to write my story from a sympathetic angle. Sexually abused as a child, raped as a teenager, exploited as a woman." Jordan smiled broadly. "Sympathy always ups the ante."

"Who else knows you're talking to me?"

"Just my husband."

"Ms. . . . Jordan. This kind of claim can make a nuclear explosion look like a Fourth of July sparkler and cause even more collateral damage. You realize that, don't you?"

"I do. And . . . I have insurance."

* * *

Silver City Detective Cletus Ursic pushed the door from the shop to the office open with a latex gloved hand, Officer Maggart followed him.

Ursic walked to the end of the counter and surveyed the bloody scene behind it carefully. "Who called it in?"

"His girlfriend. He didn't come home on time and she found him when she brought his dinner," Maggart answered.

"Where is she now?"

"At the hospital, with his mother. The girlfriend was hysterical. We had the ambulance that showed up take her there since the ME had to remove the body. I called dispatch and asked them to send an officer to the mother's home for the notification and he drove her to the hospital.

"The cash register is clean, except for the small change. I'd say it's a simple robbery homicide."

Ursic knelt near the body. "This guy took a bullet in the right side of his head. If someone was holding a gun on him while he took money from the register, why would they shoot him before he turned to hand it over?"

Getting to his feet, he studied the open register drawer and the counter next to it. Both showed blood spatter, but the counter's spatter increased moving away from the cash register. "I think this guy was here, following instructions, and when the shooter knew he was done loading the cash, he popped him while the victim's head was turned."

"Could be," Maggart said.

"That would suggest that the shooter knew everything was in the bag and there was no reason to keep the vic alive any longer."

Ursic walked around the counter and surveyed it closely from the customer's side for nearly a minute. "Take a look at this."

Maggart moved to Ursic's side.

"See how the spatter gets more concentrated down here away from the register?"

"Yes, sir."

Ursic returned to the open register drawer bent and studied it closely. He pointed to a portion of the drawer and made a circular motion with the index finger of his left hand. "There's no spatter on the left side of the drawer." Lifting his gaze, Ursic studied the register's buttons and display. "There's spatter here above it, but none below on the cash drawer. Something was in the way.

"And who the hell holds up a body shop? Those two torn down cars sitting in the shop are going to cost hundreds, if not thousands, of dollars to repair. This isn't a cash business. People pay with checks – they probably even have to be certified – or credit cards.

"Have the crime scene guy study the spatter and dust the place for prints."

"All of it?"

"Yeah, Randy, *all* of it!"

✶ ✶ ✶

A few minutes before dawn, in Tucson, Arizona, a dark blue Kenworth t660 tractor hauling a trailer with no markings or advertisements pulled up to the closed main gate of the Roswell Corporation. A guard left the air conditioned comfort of a cinderblock building and walked to the cab. He made a checkmark on his clipboard next to vehicle's USDOT identification number – 74761945, and destination – Fort Hood, Texas. After doing so he looked up at the driver. "This load must be going by truck because of the train wreck," the guard said. His English carried a very slight Spanish accent.

"Yes, sir. The Army didn't want to wait for 'em to be repaired."

"Yeah. That'll be a long time comin'. GPS tracking turned on and functioning properly?"

"Yes, sir. Roger that," the driver said.

The guard smiled at the driver's military response. "Let me check the seal and you'll be ready to roll." He turned and walked to the back of the trailer and inspected the numbered, steel security closure on the rear doors and then returned to the cab.

"Okay, you're all set. Your security is waiting outside the gate. You do a radio check yet?"

"Yes, sir, five by five with both cars, sir."

"Seems odd that you don't have a military escort."

"I guess the Army didn't want to have them drive all the way from Texas," the tractor driver responded.

"Fort Huachuca is only seventy-three miles away," the guard pointed out.

"Yes, sir. But they'd have to drive back from Texas."

"That's true. Okay then. Safe travels."

The guard returned to the cinderblock building and pressed the switch opening Roswell's main shipping gate. A black Ford sedan pulled out of a small parking lot to the right of the shipping entrance in front of the truck. A second, similarly colored sedan pulled in behind the trailer and the three vehicles set off for eastbound Interstate 10.

✳ ✳ ✳

Secret Service Agent Ayo Amoako looked into the Ford Crown Victoria's rearview mirror. "Good morning, Senator."

Thaddeus Tasman smiled back at the young man, as he adjusted his seatbelt. "Good morning, Ayo. How are ya today?"

"So far, so good, sir."

"Let's keep it that way," Tasman said, looking down at the pile of papers in his lap.

"Yes, sir."

Ayo – an African Yoruba name meaning "Joy" – put the black sedan into drive and pulled away from the front of the hotel. The local police detail on motorcycles and the rest of the security detail moved out as well – two cars in front, one in the rear.

"How long to Harrisburg?" Tasman asked, shuffling through the inch-thick sheaf of memos and notes.

"About twenty minutes, sir."

★ ★ ★

Two time zones west of his identical twin brother, Dayo Amoako stood in the security line at Denver's International Airport. His destination: Washington, D.C. Dayo – an African Yoruba name meaning "Joy Arrives" – looked around nervously, though he had no need to. Leaving Colorado would violate his parole, less than forty-eight hours after walking out of the Kit Carson Correctional Center in Burlington, but there was no system in place to alert the authorities to his departure.

The Amoako brothers had traveled very different life roads. Had either of their parents still been alive, Ayo would indeed be their "Joy," while Dayo would certainly have provided great disappointment. The brothers hadn't seen or spoken to each other since their parents' double funeral due to smoke inhalation and burns in their home almost five years earlier to the day.

Of course, as a guest in one of Colorado's Graybar Hotel's for "possession with intent to distribute," Dayo's communications options had been rather limited. This lack of contact between the brothers had protected – and possibly saved – Ayo's career . . . for the moment. The Secret Service would certainly have expected to be informed if one of their agents became aware of having a close family member being convicted of a felony. But, so far, what Ayo didn't know hadn't hurt him.

However, the Secret Service doesn't leave much to chance. Every five years, all federal employees holding a top secret clearance go through the reinvestigation process. Of course a lot can happen during half a decade, and the Amoako brothers were nestled firmly in that time frame crack.

Ayo's last reinvestigation had taken place nine months before his brother's Class 3 felony conviction. Arrested with fourteen ounces of cocaine – a Schedule II substance in Colorado – Dayo received the minimum four-year sentence.

With good behavior and prison overcrowding, Dayo served barely twenty-four months. The math proved simple – it would be more than two years before the Secret Service checked Ayo's background again.

✯ ✯ ✯

A cell phone chirped in the dark bedroom of a rented Deerfield Park RV near I-10 East's exit 62 in New Mexico.

A man fumbled to find the phone on the nightstand, knocking a glass with a quarter inch of bourbon in it to the floor in the process. The glass crashed onto a .45 caliber automatic pistol with a SWR HEMS2 suppressor mounted on it.

"Hijo de puta!" his deep voice said at the sound of shattering glass.

Finding the phone and flipping it open, he answered, *"Este es Jesús."*

"Número de camiones 74761945 es el I- 10 va a Fort Hood. Mantenga 12 paquetes, enviar el resto. Cuenta con una escolta de civil, no militar. ¿Entiendes?"

"Sí. Entiendo."

Jesús closed the phone and turned on the nightstand's lamp. He walked to the RV's bedroom closet, carefully avoiding the broken glass on the green shag rug. In it hung a complete uniform of a New Mexico State Policeman – District 12. Jesús removed it, plucked the .45 from the glass debris field, walked to the living room area where he dressed quickly.

Within five minutes, two vehicles crunched to a halt on the gravel in front of the RV's self-contained cab. Moments later, the recognition signal – three quick raps, followed two seconds later by a fourth – came from the front door.

Checking himself in a full-length mirror mounted next to the booth-style dining area, he adjusted the epaulet on his left shoulder – slipping its point under his collar – then went forward, opening the door.

Outside, in a parking space next to the RV, four men, dressed in dark business suits, waited for him at the rear of a trailer with a covered vehicle on it.

"No te quedes ahí, se mueven rápidamente. La caída de las rampas y descubrirlo," Jesús snapped as he stepped to the ground and walked behind the trailer.

The men quickly followed his order, dropping the ramps and uncovering the car, revealing an exact replica of a New Mexico State, Ford Police Interceptor sedan. Jesús slipped on a pair of leather driving gloves, stepped up onto the left side of the trailer, opened the door and seated himself behind the steering wheel. After starting the cruiser, he turned on the radio and tuned it to the NMSP dispatch frequency.

The vehicle's backup lights came on before it rolled noiselessly down the trailer's ramps. Once on the gravel drive, Jesús shifted into "Drive," turned and drove slowly toward the RV park entrance. The four men got into identical, black Chevrolet Suburbans – two in each – and followed the counterfeit NMSP sedan.

★★
★ ★
★

SIX

Dusty Rhodes' desk phone rang and she fumbled for the handset while saving her computer notes on the potential Thaddeus Tasman story.

"Rhodes."

"They killed her," a man sobbed.

The words and tone of the voice snapped Dusty's attention to the phone. She pressed the record button before responding. "Excuse me? Who was killed, sir?"

"You met her yesterday. My wife, Jordan." A whimper followed the name.

"What happened?" Dusty asked as a thousand tiny pin-pricks ran down her spine.

"She was going to the neighborhood bank near our house. He ran her down with his car. They murdered her to steal her purse!"

"Wh . . . *What*?"

"The driver got out of his car and grabbed Jordan's purse and took off!"

Dusty's mind raced. This was probably just an accident, but she didn't want to be insensitive to this man. A man who probably had the evidence Jordan had promised.

"Sir, could it have just been an accident?"

"*No*! The driver was wearing a ski mask and gloves. He *took her purse*! They meant to kill her." The emotion in the caller's voice snapped to anger. "You don't *understand*. These people don't fuck around when the White House is the prize. I told her that, but she wouldn't listen. This was a hit!"

"Where did this take place?"

"Down the street from our *house*! I saw it *happen*! He hit her and she flew in the air for . . . *Oh God*!" The man's sobbing interrupted the narrative momentarily. "Then he moved the car to where she landed. He got out and walked over to her like he was on a summer stroll – cool as you please. He bent over her and did something, then pulled her purse off her arm. He walked back to his car, looked around, got in and drove away!"

"What did he do when he bent over?"

"I couldn't tell. I saw all this happen from our balcony on the second floor half a block away."

"Could you identify him?"

"I *said* he had on a ski mask. He was short, that's all I can tell you."

"How do you know he was short?"

"Because when he got back to the car he looked to be the same height or shorter than the car's roof.

"All right." Dusty had trouble believing that this was a conspiracy, but if it wasn't, it was a major escalation in the purse snatching profession. "Did Jordan tell you where we met yesterday?"

"Yes, at the . . ."

"*NO! DON'T SAY IT*!" Dusty barked. Several reporters and staff nearby looked at her, surprised by the outburst.

"Are you calling me from the same phone Jordan did yesterday?"

"No, my cell phone. Why?" A tinge of fear crept into the last word.

Dusty could hear the growing sound of wailing sirens forming an audio backdrop behind the man's voice.

"Leave right now and meet me at the place your wife and I met yesterday. Do you understand?"

"Do you think our home is . . .?"

Dusty didn't give him a chance to finish. "I don't know. Just do what I'm telling you. I'm on my way."

✳ ✳ ✳

Cletus Ursic pushed the speaker button on his desk phone. "Ursic."

"Cletus, this is Ortega. I've got some info for you on the body shop murder," the Silver City lab tech said.

Ursic reached for the handset and lifted it to his ear, making the conversation less public.

"What's that, Juan?"

"What you'd expect from the ME's report on COD, gunshot wound to the head. Looks like what you thought. He was killed standing in front of the register. No GSR, so the shooter was a few feet away."

"Any prints of interest?"

"There were prints all over the place, most of them smudged or pretty much useless small partials. The vic's were everywhere and a few from his girlfriend. The guy apparently worked alone. I lifted one usable thumbprint from the handle on the toilet that didn't appear anywhere else and ran it through AFIS and got no hits.

"But yesterday afternoon, the Grant County Sheriff's Office responded to a 911 call. It turned out to be a burned-out pickup on the dirt road northeast of Separ on I-10."

"You mean where that trading post is, out in the middle of nowhere at the continental divide?" Ursic asked.

"Yeah. There's a dirt road that goes off to Hachita, which is even *more* in the middle of nowhere.

"There was a body in it . . . a male. The guy had been popped twice in the head, mob style. The corpse was lying on its right side. The guy had been wearing leather work gloves, one of which protected his right hand and the front pocket of his jeans. The ME discovered minute traces of GSR on the palm of the glove remnant and part of a business card that hadn't burned completely in the guy's pocket. The only thing legible on it was 'Raven.'

"I sent our toilet thumbprint over and it looks like a match to the dead guy, also due to the position and glove he wore. But they have to hydrate the thumb to make a positive determination. They don't know who he is yet 'cause any ID he was carrying got cooked."

"How long will that take?"

"We should know by later today or tomorrow morning, if the ME doesn't get a rash of business all of a sudden in between."

"How 'bout the tags on the vehicle?" Ursic asked.

"They were removed before the fire, along with any registration info in the glove box. They even removed the VIN number plate from the dashboard."

"Well, there are vehicle ID numbers on other parts that wouldn't have been destroyed."

"That's true, but it will take time to track 'em down, Cletus. And, who knows if he owned the truck or it was stolen to start with. But here's the kicker."

"Yeah, what's that?"

"The vehicle was towing a trailer. I spoke to one of the on-scene deputies. She said it must have had a load on it based on the tracks. Whoever popped this guy turned it around, hooked it up and drove off with it."

"Did they get any tire track molds?"

"We're not talking about *CSI Miami* here, Cletus. It's the Grant County Sheriff's Department in the middle of nowhere."

"I'll take that as a 'no.'" Ursic was silent for a moment. "So the question is, was the guy killed for whatever was on the trailer, or some other reason, like a robbery, and the trailer and cargo were just a bonus?"

"Good questions, Cletus. One thing looks like a strong possibility at the moment. The crispy critter in the pickup was likely also in the toilet at Ravens' Auto Body."

"And I assume there was no sign of the money, either."

"That would be correct, Detective."

"Okay, Juan. Let me know when you hear something definite, please."

"Will do, Cletus."

✳ ✳ ✳

In Baltimore's fashionable Federal Hill neighborhood, Homicide Detective Hunter Morgan looked down at the body of a once very attractive woman, sprawled akimbo on East Churchill Street.

Morgan's partner, Detective Andrew Hermann, stood opposite the body.

"Well, this is a new one on me," Morgan said, shaking his head. "It's the first 'hit, stop, maim, and rob' case I'm aware of."

"Man, that's cold," Hermann responded.

Morgan looked down the street. A block away, Federal Hill Park overlooked the inner harbor.

Sergeant Paul Staron of the Baltimore Police Department's Traffic Investigation Unit approached. "Detectives. Based on the shoe in the street down there," Staron said, jerking a thumb over his right shoulder, "it looks like she was hit about thirty meters from where her body wound up."

"Any indication that the vehicle tried to stop, Paul?" Morgan asked.

"None that I can see. No skid marks. In fact if anything, it looks like a vehicle – maybe the one that killed her, maybe not – burned rubber, trying to speed up."

✦✦✦✦✦

SEVEN

Dusty looked at her watch and saw it was ten minutes north of 5 p.m. She had already drained the last of her coffee. She knew drinking it this late in the day wouldn't help her sleep pattern, but she needed something to do with her hands. She didn't know where Jordan's husband was coming from, but the fact that she'd been here for nearly forty minutes without seeing anyone who seemed to be looking for someone they didn't know had her as keyed up as the java juice.

Her cell phone began playing Pachelbel's *Canon*, a ringtone she'd set up for her husband, Jim Grabowski. Dusty's long standing byline had prevented her from taking Jim's name. But, even if she didn't have a built-in excuse, love him as she did, she couldn't ever see herself using it.

"Hey there!" said a friendly voice. "Is this a bad time?"

"No, I'm waiting for a possible source. I'm glad you called."

"Of course you are, but why?" The humorous tone in Grabowski's voice brought a smile to Dusty's face.

"Can you check the last few hours for a hit-and-run victim, first name Jordan. She's a young woman in her mid-thirties, very attractive."

"Hey, I'm a bomb tech. I don't do *traffic*."

Dusty could hear the chuckle in his voice. "Do you have any thoughts of *doing* me in the near future, Mr. Bomb Tech?"

"Hey! Using sex as a reward is bad policy."

"Yeah, bad for you."

"Excuse me, but I get the impression you enjoy our encounters."

"Oh, I do! But I'm a woman, the stronger gender who can go without sex like a camel without water. I should know, I did it long enough before I met you. Now, will you check this out for me? If you can find it, I need her address and last name."

"I could get my ass in a crack for this," Grabowski said quietly.

"I can guarantee you won't be getting anything else in a crack if you don't." The play on words, off color as it was, made her chuckle at her own quick response.

✳ ✳ ✳

Joe Costa looked across the small Baltimore City Bomb Squad office at his partner scribbling on a piece of paper, a telephone handset squeezed between his ear and shoulder.

Following his testimony in a court case earlier, Grabowski sat at his desk in civilian clothes – slacks, shirt, tie, and sports jacket – rather than his police uniform.

"Okay. She was a Signal 32," Grabowski said, referring to the code used for a fatal traffic accident. "Did you ID her?" Grabowski questioned and sat up ramrod straight at the answer. "*What*?"

Making another quick note he said, "*Jesus Christ*! Did you run her prints?"

Grabowski scribbled another note. "Got it. Last known address?" He wrote down one final piece of information and leaned back from the desk. His swivel chair squealed a brief protest. "Oh, no, nothing official. Dusty heard the 32 on her police scanner. She has a source that lives in the neighborhood."

Grabowski listened for a moment. "Don't worry. I'm not going to tell her anything that the PIO doesn't announce. Thanks, Paul. I appreciate the info."

Grabowski set the phone in its cradle. He tore a piece of paper out of his notebook, folded it and shoved it into the left breast pocket of his jacket with his wallet. Amid another squeal of protest from his swivel chair, he turned to see Costa staring at him.

"So, what did you discover, Sherlock?" Costa asked, smiling.

✳ ✳ ✳

Jesús sat in the counterfeit New Mexico State Police car in the parking lot of I-10's eastbound rest stop at mile marker 53. He scanned the oncoming lanes of the interstate to the west with powerful binoculars while monitoring the police dispatches and responses on the radio. Two black Chevy Suburbans idled next to the car, their air conditioners keeping the business suited occupants cool.

In the distance, Jesús spotted a blue tractor-trailer led and followed by black sedans. He watched the trio for nearly a full minute. Then, without lowering the field glasses, reached across the console to the right passenger seat, lifting a yellow, Motorola walkie-talkie to his face. "*Aquí vienen. Vamonos.*"

Jesús laid the radio and the binoculars on the passenger seat and put the police cruiser in drive. He drove slowly toward the road leading back to I-10, waiting for their target to pass the rest stop's exit. When the chase security vehicle had done so, he continued to I-10's eastbound on-ramp.

No other vehicles traveling east were in sight when Jesús flipped on the cruiser's lights and siren. Behind him, seconds later, both Suburban's grills displayed red and blue flashing lights.

The Ford P.I. sedan's powerful engine quickly accelerated the vehicle to 75 miles per hour. The drivers of the Suburbans had the gas pedals of their respective SUVs on the floor in an effort to keep up.

As soon as the second security sedan passed the off ramp for exit 55, Jesús and the first Suburban sped up and quickly passed the three vehicles ahead. As Jesús passed the tractor, he used the PI's loudspeaker. "Pull over! New Mexico State Police and Army CIC! Pull over!"

The second Chevy slowed and followed the rear security sedan.

It took well over a quarter mile for all six vehicles to come to a stop on the side of I-10. Jesús was the first out, followed by the man in the first Suburban's passenger seat.

The Suburban passenger reached into his left, inside suit jacket pocket, removed a leather credential wallet and flipped it open, displaying an Army CID badge and picture ID card to the driver and passenger in the lead security sedan.

As Jesús walked back to the tractor, the lead security car's driver window lowered. "What's goin' on?" the man behind the wheel asked.

"We intercepted a satellite phone conversation that this shipment is going to be hijacked outside of Deming. We're going to escort you to Gage, exit 62. When we get to the bottom of the ramp, we're going to turn left and go back under the highway. We'll lead you to a place where the tractor can turn around to head back. When we get the all clear, you're on your way to Ft. Hood again."

"How old is this information?" the security car driver asked.

"Less than an hour. My partner and another CIC team were out here investigating a weapons theft at Fort Huachuca when we got the call to meet the State Police at the rest stop back there."

"We'll need to contact our dispatch about this," the security driver said.

"You'll have plenty of time to do that after we get off the highway. Let's get going. There's no time to waste."

Jesús and the passenger in the second Suburban repeated the same story to the drivers in the tractor and trail security sedan. In less than four minutes, the now six-vehicle convoy got underway again, eastbound.

★ ★ ★

The young sergeant set a large, covered, plastic storage box into the trunk of her car outside a nondescript building at Aberdeen Proving Ground. Dressed in her desert camo BDUs, she didn't stand out from anyone else in sight with the exception of two Army officers walking toward her – dressed in desert camo as well.

Aberdeen, Maryland has two distinctions: It's the home of the Army's oldest proving ground and the birthplace of baseball legend Cal Ripken, Jr. Not listed in any of the city's promotional information is the sad fact that Aberdeen is apparently the home of several very stupid criminals who – on separate occasions, and apparently by different people – kidnapped Cal's mother, Vi, from her home and attempted to carjack her outside her bank. No arrests were made and Mrs. Ripken was released unharmed each time after the criminals apparently discovered who she was.

Closing the trunk, she turned toward the two officers.

Sergeant E-5 Aamina Al Yami offered evidence of the U.S. Army's diversification programs. Named after the Prophet Mohammad's mother, "Aamina" is generally thought to come from the Arabic word "amina" meaning "safety." Sergeant Al Yami's Military Occupational Specialty (MOS) belied her first name. As an Explosive Ordnance Disposal (EOD) specialist – 89D – the work Aamina did could be called a lot of things, but certainly not *safe*.

"Morning, sir," Sergeant Al Yami said, snapping off a perfectly rendered hand salute as the officers passed. She couldn't have sounded more American, but her Southern drawl seemed completely out of place coming from a woman of apparent Middle Eastern ancestry. The youngest offspring of Saudi immigrants, Aamina – a devout Muslim –

owed her faith to her father's own pious beliefs following her mother's death from breast cancer in the mid-nineties. An engineer with an Atlanta-based defense contractor, her father had also lit and stoked Aamina's interest in electronics and explosives.

After 9/11, while in her first semester as a Georgia Tech junior, over her father's objections, Aamina dropped out to enlist in the U.S. Army with a "guarantee" to be trained as an "89-Delta."

Misinformation and/or misfortune can divert any person's or group's life course in opposite directions for good or . . . In Sergeant Al Yami's case, both forces formed a perfect storm of alteration.

✳ ✳ ✳

On April 1, 2002, the West Bank's Jenin refugee camp became a target of Israel's Operation Defensive Shield. Based on allegations it had served as a launch site for numerous terrorist attacks against Israeli civilians and towns, the camp remained sealed until the Israeli troops began withdrawing on April 18. During the operation, the Palestinian Authority claimed that thousands of innocent civilians were being massacred as armored bulldozers destroyed homes.

Booby traps set by militants caused the Israelis to use heavy equipment to destroy the suspected launch sites and the homes of those refugees suspected of being involved. Subsequent investigations showed no evidence to substantiate the claims of mass killings. But, like so many news stories, those facts were buried in the back pages of various news outlets, if they appeared at all. The news phrase, "If it bleeds, it leads" was clearly in play. No need to cloud the issue with the facts by placing them in the same bright light the original story enjoyed.

If the story of the Battle of Jenin had any "legs" left in the non-Muslim world by early July of that year, they were amputated when a Saudi spy was discovered stealing weapons secrets at an Atlanta-based defense contractor. Though the subsequent investigation produced no evidence of involvement by Abdullah Al Yami, he was nonetheless terminated for "cause" by his employer.

Contrary to what has become a common western belief due to attacks before, on and after 9/11, Islamic and other Abrahamic religions view suicide as a great sin and certainly no way to accelerate one's spiritual journey. "And do not kill yourselves, surely God is most Merciful to you," is one of the Quran's instructions on the subject.

Then Private E-2 Al Yami was ending her twentieth of thirty-nine weeks of Advanced Individual Training (AIT), at Elgin Air Force

Base in western Florida when she received a call from her brother in Atlanta on a Thursday. Her father had been found dead. By the following Monday morning, she was back in class at Elgin AFB, wearing the same uniform, but newly recruited to a very different force.

* * *

"You're a fuckin' moron! You know that?"

The huge hand of the very muscular black man held a much smaller white man against the wall, the tips of his running shoes barely providing any support. The ham-like paw's two fingers and thumb wrapped around the throat prevented any response.

The bigger man wasn't interested in one.

Gasping and gagging, the smaller man used both hands in an unsuccessful attempt to pull the vice-grip, deformed hand off his windpipe. His lungs were about to explode and the lack of oxygen had already diminished his strength.

Finally, the larger man released his captive and watched him slide down the wall into a squatting position, coughing for breath and holding his throat.

It took several seconds for the smaller man to recover enough to speak. "God damn, Harley! You almost killed me!"

"No shit, asshole! I *will* cap your ass if you don't clean up the mess you made. Where's the tape?"

"It wasn't there, Harley! We tore their place apart. It must be in the safety deposit box."

"Then you really fucked up when you ran her down in the fuckin' street! Didn't you?"

"You said take her out before she got back to that reporter. I did what you said."

"And that was the only thing you could think of to do? Run her down in broad daylight?"

"That wasn't smart, Harley, I get it. But we know where the bank is. Angela will clean out their box. I'll make this good. I swear!"

* * *

In Tucson, Roswell Corporation's head of security answered his desk phone. "Simpson."

"Sir, this is Al Murphy in dispatch."

"What can I do for you, Al?"

"The GPS on truck number 74761945 with a load of Stinger missiles went dark."

"En route to where?"

"Fort Hood, sir."

"Did you contact the security detail?"

"Can't raise them either, Mr. Simpson."

"Where and when was their last check-in?"

"Near Deming, New Mexico."

"What's close to Deming?"

"Puerto Palomas, Mexico, twenty, maybe thirty miles to the south."

"Have you alerted the New Mexico State Police?"

"Not yet."

"Then do it now. I want an update every thirty minutes or when you learn anything."

"Yes, sir."

★ ★ ★

"He's going to do well in Philadelphia. The black population there is about forty-four percent." Jackie Beaudro looked up at Senator Reynolds from the map of Pennsylvania on the hotel room desk that she had been studying. "You're going to do well in Pittsburgh. It's mostly blue collar and pro-union."

Beaudro made a sweeping motion over the map between Philadelphia in the lower right-hand corner of the state and Pittsburgh near the western border. "You've got to do well in the 'T.' That's this area between the two cities. It doesn't look much like a 'T' but that's what it's called. These small-town Democrats tend to be God fearing, more conservative, and have a strong sense of community. This is your oyster, Senator."

Mrs. Reynolds glanced down at the map and nodded. "Where's Benjamin today?"

"The President is in Philadelphia. If anyone can sway, or at least mitigate, the African-American vote there, he can." Beaudro's heavy black face broadened into a grin, flashing enough high-end crowns to put a lazy student through Harvard. "We black folk be lovin' Massa *Ben*!"

Mrs. Reynolds smiled and shook her head. Just out of the shower, without any makeup, and in her ratty but comfortable bathrobe, she didn't create even the palest reflection of a presidential candidate. She removed a shower cap to reveal short blond hair that looked like she hadn't brushed it since getting out of bed. The dark circles under her eyes said Mrs. Reynolds and her bunk didn't spend much time together. "Jackie, don't even do that when it's just us. God only knows if there are cameras and bugs in these rooms. A comment like that could be on *YouTube* or *Coyote News* in a matter of minutes and then every media outlet in the world before sundown, with *Coyote News* airing it at ten-minute intervals. We've already got one hell of an uphill battle. Let's not make it any steeper."

"Senator, we sweep all our hotel rooms three times a day for electronics. There are no bugs or cameras. So relax. I'm telling you, I have a very good feeling about this election. It's going to turn out just fine and in the end you are going to smash the *ultimate* glass ceiling. Trust me on this."

"I wish I had your confidence." Mrs. Reynolds reached out and patted the taller woman on the shoulder. "Just be careful. We can't afford any more gaffes."

An impish grin spread across Beaudro's face. "Yessum, Senator, I sho be doin' *dat*. Now, if you 'cuse me, I be fetchin' you a drink whilst you be gettin' ready fo dis evenin's speechifyin'!"

* * *

Within hours of the discovery of rail sabotage near the San Pedro River, the word spread through various law enforcement channels across the country. The Arizona Terrorism Information Center posted an item almost immediately to its law enforcement only access website. Soon afterward, the Joint Terrorism Task Force, DOT and NTSB sent reports to the airlines, rail companies – especially AMTRAK – and large and small metropolitan areas in an attempt to alert as many first responders as possible. The primary intent being the discovery of other attempts through the idea of "See something. Say something," before any more carnage could take place.

* * *

Instructions in English and Spanish hung below a large STOP sign at the U.S. – Mexican border. "Until CBP Officer Arrives," "*Hasta Que El CBP Oficial Llegu.*"

The Suburban ahead of the tractor-trailer stopped under the large canopy on the U.S. side of the Puerto Palomas Mexico crossing. A US Customs and Border Patrol agent approached the driver's side window as another agent and dog circled the vehicle, even though little chance existed that drugs, weapons or other dangerous or hazardous materials would be smuggled *into* Mexico. When the dog didn't sit down, an "alert" to something suspicious, the first CBP officer waved the vehicle onto the Mexican side of the border.

Next, the tractor pulled to the stop sign. "Let's see your bill of laden, manifest and Shippers Export Declaration," the CBP officer said.

The driver handed down a blue, pocket folder.

The CBP officer opened it as the handler and dog made their circuit of the vehicle. The folder's left pocket contained the required U.S. documents to move cargo into Mexico. The right pocket held import documents required by the Mexican government. After a short inspection of the U.S. documents, the officer handed the folder back to the driver, then made a note of the U.S. DOT number and time on a clipboard log sheet. "You're good to go."

"Thanks," the driver said as the tractor rumbled toward the Mexican customs stop a hundred yards away.

When the tractor driver handed down the blue folder on the other side of border, the right pocket contained a thick, white #10 envelope in addition to the Mexican customs forms. After a quick glance at the envelope's contents, a Mexican agent nodded to a fellow officer and the red light-green light inspection indicator turned green. The truck entered Mexico uninspected and without any record of its crossing.

The second Suburban made the crossing as easily as the first.

★ ★ ★

Grabowski's round, wire-rimmed glasses always gave him the look of a school teacher or professor, especially in candlelight. The flame's reflections danced in orange and occasional blue streaks on the convex surfaces.

Dusty looked across the table and lifted her wine glass toward her husband. Jim's hair was a little grayer and a little thinner than it had been when they'd met almost a decade earlier. Other than that, he was the same handsome guy she'd fallen for. So far he'd eluded the wrinkle-fairies, or at least their magic hadn't made any real difference on his tanned, narrow face. "Where did she live?"

"Who?"

"Jim, I'm not talking about the *Duchess of Windsor*!"

"You know I can't share anything that the Public Information Office hasn't put on the street. It's an ongoing investigation," Grabowski said. "Dusty, if he'd wanted to talk to you, he'd have shown up."

"He did want to talk to me. I could hear it in his voice." Dusty took a sip of her wine, keeping her eyes on her husband. "Doesn't this strike you as a little suspicious? The wife is run down. The killer takes the time to get out of the car – wearing a ski mask I might add – walks over to her body and then leaves with her purse? The husband calls to say she was murdered. Oh, by the way, from the same place Jordan probably called me from the day before. Then *he* doesn't show up at a place that was never mentioned in the conversation."

"It was mentioned the day before," Grabowski pointed out.

"*Exactly*!" Dusty moved her chair closer to the restaurant table, scraping its legs loudly on the floor in the process.

"I specifically told him not to repeat the location. But, if someone listened in on Jordan's call to me the day before, they already *knew* where he'd be going."

"If someone listened in on the wife's call, why didn't they clip her before *she* could meet with you? Why would they let her get you involved?"

Dusty didn't miss a beat. "Maybe they weren't in a position to stop her before she met me."

"True, but just because her husband didn't show up doesn't mean anything happened to him. Maybe he was embarrassed. What was he doing, anyway? Letting his wife screw another man and just sitting by? Watching?"

"I don't think he was. I think he was photographing and videoing the encounters. They were in it together.

"The one photo I saw was well lit, and clear. It wasn't taken by some cell phone from the corner. And, the subjects were positioned so that it was clear that Thaddeus Tasman was making love to a woman who definitely was *not* his wife. Jordan's face was hidden so they could blackmail Tasman and never reveal her identity if they didn't want to. The horseshoe and rose tattoo on her breast was the only proof they needed if they ever wanted to prove it was she.

"I think they got greedy. They saw the hooker the Governor was screwing become a millionaire overnight, with all kinds of modeling and movie deals being thrown at her. They knew they could only get so much out of Tasman and they changed course."

"Changed course and headed where?" Grabowski said.

"Headed for people with a lot more money than T-squared," Dusty shot back in a whisper. Then, in a normal voice, she said: "Probably all of the following and more: Hollywood, the major networks, *Playboy*. All those organizations could transfer a load of money into her bank account and not bat an eye. Politicians and their supporters weren't the only game in town and politicians had to employ stealth with any payoff.

"That's clearly why Jordan called me. I'm sure she was smart enough to have tried the political option first. They didn't bite, bite enough or bite fast enough. I'll bet her political threat started the clock running on her eventual demise. As her husband said to me on the phone, 'These people don't fuck around when the White House is the prize.' The only question is: How high did the decision to kill her go?

"You got the address, right?" Dusty asked.

"Christ, Dusty! Have you been on another planet for the last few minutes? I can't tell you anything."

Their waiter came to Grabowski's side of the table. "Can I get you anything else?"

"No, thanks," Grabowski answered. "Just the check."

"Then I'll leave this with you," the waiter responded, setting a black folio with the American Express logo embossed on it in front of Grabowski.

"You can take it now," Grabowski said, pulling his wallet from his breast pocket. He flipped it open, pulled out a VISA card and laid it on the folio.

"Very good, sir. I'll be right back."

Grabowski stuffed his wallet back into his jacket pocket and pushed his chair back. "I'm going to hit the head. Be right back."

As her husband walked away, Dusty noticed a small piece of folded paper on the opposite edge of the table. She reached for it, opened and read the handwritten note:

Jordan Moses
231 East Churchill St.

Wow! Pricey neighborhood! she thought.

Her cell phone rang as she refolded the paper and replaced it. The *Sweet Home Alabama* ringtone indicated the phone's "Contacts" contained the caller's name and phone number. The display read: "Call from Jack Reigle."

"Hey, Jack. What's up?"

"You know the hit-and-run you told me about this afternoon?" Reigle asked.

"Yeah?"

"I was talking to my brother in the ME's office just now. She's missing some parts."

"What? You mean she had a hysterectomy or something?"

"No. I mean whoever hit her took her purse and her *thumbs*!"

☆ ☆ ☆

"Mr. President, the Secretary of Homeland Security is on the phone."

POTUS, seated at the *Resolute* desk, pushed a blinking light on the phone. "Hello, Bob. You're working late."

"I'm afraid we're all going to be working late, Mr. President. I just got off the phone with the Chief of the New Mexico State Police. A shipment of FIM-92B Stinger missiles was hijacked outside of Deming, New Mexico, a little over six hours ago. It was equipped with GPS tracking and the data stream stopped."

"Are you telling me there's a truckload of MANPADS loose in New Mexico?"

"Well, sir, I'm telling you they're missing, but I wouldn't count on them still being in the U.S. My guess is they headed south to Mexico. I'm going to call the Secretary of State and Justice to see if they can make some discreet calls to the Mexicans for assistance."

"No, don't do that yet. I don't want anyone to know about this outside of us for the moment. Jesus fucking Christ! Don't those shipments have security details?"

"Yes, sir. When the Roswell Corporation lost the GPS signal from the tractor, they called the New Mexico State Police and gave them the last location they had. The NMSP went to those GPS coordinates and discovered the lead and trail security vehicles on a dirt road north of I-10's exit 62 at Gage. They were both burned out with five bodies inside – burned beyond recognition. They're probably the four security guards and the driver of the truck.

"The NMSP Chief told me they suspect that a patrol car was counterfeited and . . ."

"Counterfeited?"

"Yes, Mr. President. It's not that tough to do. Any number of paint shops could make that happen. Especially if the job paid well and or someone was sympathetic to a given cause. All you need are a few pictures of a real patrol car and *voilà*.

"In fact, New Mexico's Silver City Police and Grant County Sheriff's Departments are working a couple of related murders. The owner of a Silver City body shop and another burned out vehicle north of I-10's exit 42 at Separ. The dead man in it had been killed mob style. His pickup was towing a trailer. The thumbprint of the body in the pickup turned up in the body shop's lavatory. The trailer had been taken, presumably by whoever murdered the man."

"So, why does the NMSP think there's a counterfeit cruiser involved?" POTUS asked.

"Because they checked their inventory and all of their cars are present or otherwise accounted for.

"There's an Exxon station and a Dairy Queen at exit 62. The NMSP looked at the security camera data from both for the timeframe before and after the GPS signal was lost from the tractor. The DQ camera caught an NMSP cruiser leading a black Suburban, followed by the three Roswell Corporation vehicles and another Suburban down the eastbound off-ramp at exit 62. The six vehicles turned left, went back under the highway and out of the camera's view. About thirty minutes later, five SUVs, of various makes, models and colors came back under the highway and turned onto the eastbound ramp. A few minutes after that the tractor-trailer emerged, led and followed by the Suburbans, and went up the eastbound on-ramp as well. There was no other sign of the cruiser, but it probably went west on I-10. That on-ramp is out of the camera's view."

"Any other surveillance cameras to the east on I-10?"

"No, sir, not that we know of. An NMSP helicopter checked the highway east of exit 62 and thirty miles east of Deming with no results. But, by the time it got to the scene, they could have gone virtually anywhere."

"Was the surveillance camera able to capture the plates on the SUVs?"

"No, sir. It didn't have that kind of resolution. But we're sure we have a correct list of the makes and models and colors of them. If they were carrying parts of the Stinger shipment, going east, we have to assume their destinations are major metropolitan airports. That would be DFW, ORD, ATL, IAD or DCA in Washington, BWI in Baltimore, and JFK. And if five vehicles went east, we believe at least one went west on I-10, out of the camera's view.

"The DOJ has had its appropriate agencies, the ATF, FBI, U.S. Marshals' Service, even the DEA, put out APBs nationwide, with particular communications to the jurisdictions in the path of likely routes to the cities just mentioned. Of course Homeland Security has done the same thing, including state highway commissions."

"How many Stingers were in the shipment?"

"Forty-eight, sir."

"God in heaven! Why take them into Mexico, if that's where they went?"

"Couple of reasons, Mr. President. First they're probably a lot easier to hide there. Second, they may want to ship them to other groups inside and out of this hemisphere. Getting them out of Mexico would be a sight easier than the U.S.

"But there's something else you need to know, sir. These aren't your garden variety Stinger missiles. They're the FIM-92B or POST model."

"Meaning what?"

"That POST stands for 'Passive Optical Seeker Technique.' It has a dual-detector seeker, infrared and ultraviolet. That allows it to distinguish between the target and any countermeasures the aircraft might employ.

"You've heard pilots talk about 'puking flares,' like the AC-130 gunships do to confuse surface-to-air missiles?"

"Yes, I've seen pictures of them too."

"We've developed flares that have IR signatures that very closely match those of the engines' exhausts. However, the UV signature of the *flare* is easily discernible from that of the engine exhaust. If those Stingers find their way into Afghanistan or Iraq or anywhere else friendly aircraft fly – especially ours – their aircrews are going to face significantly higher risks."

POTUS was silent for a moment. "Okay, Bob, make sure we quietly – and I mean *very* quietly – beef up security at every U.S. airport. I don't want word of this cluster fuck getting into the media before we're ready and hopefully have recovered those missiles."

"I understand, Mr. President. However, beefing up security is going to be much easier said than done."

"Meaning . . ."

"The stinger can be operated by a single individual. The missile and launcher only weigh 34 pounds. So, you put one in an SUV or van, drive to the perimeter fence around an airport – probably in a heavily populated area like JFK, LAX or ORD and park. If you're smart, and want to create the maximum death and damage, you dial in the airport's

ATC radio channel – 120.95 or 133.9 megahertz – and listen for a carrier and aircraft type that represents a departing wide-body aircraft – preferably to a foreign destination so it has a large fuel load, maybe even with national significance.

"Let's take LAX for example. On one of the ATC frequencies you hear 'El Al, 123-Heavy, you're cleared for takeoff, Runway 7 Right. Turn right to heading . . .'

"'El Al" says it's got a load of Jewish passengers on it. 'Heavy' says it's a wide-bodied aircraft. Boeing 747, 777, Airbus A330 and so, on carrying a ton of fuel to get to Tel Aviv. Runway 7 Right says it's taking off toward the city rather than the Pacific. You want it to come down in a populated area. Now, you'd have to be patient because LAX rarely takes off to the east, only when the Santa Ana winds are really blowing.

"So when you hear that transmission, arm the Stinger and wait for the plane to get overhead with a heat signature like a toaster for your missile to lock onto. Then you squeeze off your shot. You hop back in your vehicle and haul ass while the Stinger chases down the aircraft traveling at up to Mach 2.2 – hardly a fair race, like a snow leopard *versus* a sea slug. A few seconds later the three kilogram, penetrating, hit-to-kill warhead takes out an engine or shears off a wing. A whole lot of people die instantly, the rest on impact, not to mention all those individuals covered in burning jet fuel on the ground. Not a pretty picture."

"*Jesus*, Bob! Do you have any *good* news?"

"Not today, Mr. President."

EIGHT

"You still haven't told me how you found out about her thumbs, Dusty," Grabowski said as they approached the front steps of the East Churchill Street row house near Federal Hill Park.

"Remember how you couldn't share any info that the PIO hadn't 'put on the street'? Well, I can't reveal my source."

Dusty used the brass door knocker to announce their arrival. After a minute without a response, she knocked again, harder.

"He's not here; let's go, Dusty."

"Try the doorknob."

"No, that's puts us in the B and E category."

"We're not breaking and entering if the door's unlocked."

Grabowski shook his head. "You got here because I looked into a case I had no reason to and the information I got inside the system fell into the wrong hands . . . *yours*!"

"Jim, I found out about her *thumbs*," Dusty said in a hoarse whisper. "Do you think figuring out her address would have been that tough?"

Grabowski shook his head. "Just remember, one of us is a cop, who could not only lose his job *and* his pension, but wind up in the joint with some people he *put* there. *Not* an appealing proposition."

"Come on, Jim!" Dusty reached for the doorknob. "For Christ's sake! Where's your sense of adventure?" The door swung inward from the simple pressure of her hand. "See? It was already open."

"Don't . . ." was all Grabowski managed to get out before Dusty was through the door.

"Hello?" Dusty called into the dark room in a moderately loud voice.

Getting no response, she found a light switch inside the front door. The apartment had clearly been ransacked. Books covered the floor. Drawers had been opened and dumped helter-skelter. The cushions of an expensive black leather couch lay sliced open, its quilted Dacron filler pulled out and discarded in piles.

"Gee, Jim. Do you think maybe there's some foul play involved here?" Dusty said quietly, stepping into the living room. "Jordan is dead, Mr. Moses is missing, and somebody did an excellent job of tossing their house."

✭ ✭ ✭

In Fayetteville, North Carolina, John Mallard felt the burner phone vibrating in his breast pocket. Conversations on this phone weren't for public consumption. Mallard stepped quickly into a small alcove off the hotel's lobby and answered the call.

"Yes?"

"We got what we need."

"The card and access codes?" Mallard's knuckles went white, squeezing the phone.

"We have the card and two codes. One of them will work. We got the password last night."

"And the package?" Mallard asked.

"It will be retrieved tomorrow when the bank opens."

"Excellent. Call me as soon as it's in your possession," Mallard said, ending the call before the caller could respond.

✭ ✭ ✭

"Do you have the latest polls?" Senator Tasman asked. Two Secret Service agents followed a respectable distance in his wake, scanning the area for potential threats.

"Yes, Senator. We've got a comfortable lead. The fact that we're spending five dollars to every one of Reynolds' should give us the edge. But, this primary can't get here soon enough for me," Mallard answered.

✭ ✭ ✭

"Dusty, if whoever tossed this place didn't find what they were looking for, what makes you think we will?" Grabowski said to Dusty's derrière.

On all fours, looking under the leather couch, the reporter didn't answer. She got to her feet and switched on a brass lamp on an end table between the couch and the wall. The light didn't come on.

"Dusty, we have to get the hell out of here. You've left your prints all over this place and that won't go unnoticed if the lab rats wind up here. Jesus! What are you doing?"

"I want to see if they opened the bottom of the couch and I need light."

"The bulb is burned out."

Dusty looked down through the glass end table top at the outlet. "Maybe it's not plugged in. Maybe they pulled it out during the search."

Reaching under the table top, Dusty pushed the plug into the outlet. When she pulled her hand back, her wrist caught the cord against one of the table's legs, pulling the plug away from the outlet. A second later the entire outlet fell out of the wall onto the floor – *sans* any electrical wires.

"A poor man's safe," Grabowski said.

Dusty picked it up and pulled the plug from it. On the back was a small, round latch. Dusty turned it slowly and the back of the *faux* outlet opened. A small, black answering machine cassette tape dropped onto the floor.

Dusty looked up at her husband. "I don't know if this is what they were looking for, but I can't *wait* to hear what's on it," she said reaching for the cassette.

"*No!*" Grabowski snapped. "Don't touch it! It could be evidence with prints on it and the last prints I want on it are *yours!*" Grabowski reached into his sport coat's side pocket, pulled out a latex glove and slipped it onto his right hand. Bending over his wife, he picked up the cassette by its sides with as little pressure as possible.

Straightening, he looked at the cassette closely. A white adhesive label simply said: Tasman Calls. He set the black cassette on the end table and looked down at Dusty, still on her knees. "Don't touch! I'm going to see if I can find a plastic bag in the kitchen."

"Do you want me to look?"

"*No,* Dusty. I'm the one with the glove. The last thing I need is more of your prints in what may be a crime scene."

"What *may* be?" Dusty said to Grabowski's back.

Getting to her feet, Dusty reached into her purse, removed a small digital camera and turned it on. Moving the camera and using its zoom feature to get a close-up of the cassette, she snapped a photo and returned the camera to her purse.

In less than a minute, Grabowski returned with a plastic sandwich bag. He deposited the cassette in it, then grabbed Dusty's arm. "Let's get the hell out of here," he said, ushering his wife ahead toward the front door. As she exited he picked up the faux outlet and then used his handkerchief to wipe it clean.

On the front stoop, after wiping down the switch Dusty had used to turn on the light when they entered, Grabowski used the index finger and thumb of his gloved hand to gently pull the door shut and wipe the knob clean of his wife's prints. As he moved toward the sidewalk, the smartphone on his belt rang.

"Grabowski," he answered. "Okay, what's the location?" He listened to the caller momentarily, then said, "Got it. I'm on my way."

Dusty stood by the driver's side door of her gray BMW 530i. Looking over its top at her husband, she asked, "What's up?"

"Suspicious package outside a synagogue. B'Nai Israel, 27 Lloyd Street. You can drop me off there," Grabowski said, pulling the front passenger door open and getting in. He set the sandwich bag containing the cassette on the console between the bucket seats, reached for his seat belt, buckled it, stripped the latex glove off his hand and dropped it on the sandwich bag.

Dusty started the BMW and pulled away from the curb, driving down one-way East Churchill Street. She turned right on Battery Avenue, then right again on Warren, headed for Light Street. At Light Street she turned right again. In seconds, they passed the other end of East Churchill. There, on the corner of Light and East Churchill, she saw the glow of a bank's neon sign. A temporary canvas banner restrained the majority of the light, but what penetrated the material made the wording easier to read.

CORNERSTONE BANK
IS NOW
FREEPORT BANK

✳ ✳ ✳

"What news do you bring me, Asad?" The bearded man asked quietly, without looking up from his Quran.

"Wonderful news, Praise Allah. We have secured more tools to bring the great Satan to his knees."

"Yes . . ."

"We have secured a number of their military's own anti-aircraft weapons. A truckload of what they call 'Stinger' missiles."

"How many and what have we done with them?"

"Forty-eight. Most are in Mexico. We will disperse them to our brothers and affiliates around the world. A dozen of them were unloaded before the truck crossed the border. They have been broken up into smaller groups and sent to major cities with airports."

"And what is our plan, Asad?"

"We will quietly offer to give them back for two hundred million U.S. dollars."

"And if our offer is not accepted?"

"Then we will leak the facts of the situation to *Al Jazeera America*. The word will spread quickly to the other media outlets and panic will bring air travel to a near halt."

"And if our offer is still not accepted?"

"The public outcry over exploding aircraft will drive their politicians to make the payment."

✶ ✶ ✶

With little traffic on the road, just before the midnight shift change at the Will Rogers Turnpike toll booth on I-44 near Vinita, Oklahoma, Georgina Dunlap fought to keep her eyes open. The widowed mother of two, the younger only four months old, didn't get much sleep between the time her Oklahoma Turnpike Authority job ended and her grocery store checker employment began at 8 a.m.

As she looked around the small booth to make sure her belongings were gathered, a sheaf of papers caught her attention. She had glanced at it when her supervisor delivered it at the beginning of her shift, but the heavy traffic hadn't allowed close inspection. Now she picked it up and read through the description of the several vehicles the Turnpike Authority had asked toll takers to keep an eye out for. Several sheets showed color pictures of five SUVs. The last image in the list – a dark green, 1987 Chevrolet Suburban – put a lump in her throat.

Georgina's late husband had restored and driven the same color '87 model until he lost his battle with cancer a few months before their son entered the world. Now, it waited for her in the parking lot less than fifty yards away.

A blaring horn snapped her attention back to the present. A bearded, Caucasian man sat at the wheel of the same vehicle in the photo and nearby parking lot.

"Let's go, honey!" The man said, holding out a five dollar bill.

Taking his money, Georgina quickly made change and handed it back to him. Before the vehicle pulled away, she noticed another bearded man in the passenger seat wearing dark sunglasses. Behind the men, the Suburban's back seats were folded down and a gray moving blanket covered something occupying nearly all eight feet of the cargo bay.

The driver took the money and sped off into the night toward the Missouri state line.

Within seconds she picked up the phone handset, a direct line connected to the nearby supervisor's office.

"Yeah, Georgina? What's up?"

"Bill. What was the license plate number on that green Suburban that just went through my lane?"

"Wait a minute." After a few seconds of computer keyboard clicking, the supervisor pulled up images of the vehicles front and rear bumpers. "Colorado tag. George Adam William 6624. Why?"

Georgina wrote the information down before she answered. "It matches the last page of that alert flyer you gave me at the beginning of our shift."

"Oh! Want me to call it in?"

"The driver was an asshole. I want to do it, even if they aren't the right people."

"Okay, all yours."

"Thanks."

Georgina's right hand dove for the cell phone in a hooded sweatshirt pocket under an orange safety vest as she retrieved the flyer with the other. After punching in 911 and the "Send" button, Georgina listened to several rings before a male voice answered.

"Craig County 911, what is your emergency?"

"This is Georgina Dunlap. I'm a toll taker here at exit 283."

"Oh, hey, Georgina. It's Bob Spalding. What's up?"

"The last page of the flyer we got today has a green, '87 Chevy Suburban listed. One just paid a toll going east."

The sound of shuffling papers at the other end of the line preceded Bob's response. "Are you sure it was an '87 Suburban, ma'am?"

"I drive one, Bob. I'm sure."

"Can you describe the driver?"

"A white man with a long black beard."

"Age?"

"I'd say mid to late twenties, maybe early thirties."

"Anything else you can say about him?"

"Yes. He was rude."

"Was he alone?"

"No. Another man, bearded like the driver, was in the passenger seat wearing sunglasses. Kind of odd at this time of night."

"Anything else you can tell me about them or the vehicle?"

Georgina repeated the tag number.

"How long ago and what direction are you working tonight?"

"Within the last five minutes, eastbound. They had something big in the back covered up with one of those padded moving blankets. It looked like it was gray."

"It's less than forty miles to the Missouri state line. Of course they could get off at the Vinita exit here or the Miami exit." Bob did some quick math in his head. "If they don't, that just gives us a little more than half an hour, if they do the seventy-five mile speed limit, till they're over the line. Anything else?"

"Just this. If it's one of the vehicles mentioned in the flyer, you're lucky they didn't invest in a Pike Pass. If they had, I'd have never seen 'em."

☆ ☆ ☆

The 911 operator thanked Georgina and ended the call, immediately dialing the Oklahoma Highway Patrol dispatch number. After passing on the information to the OHP, he dialed the NCIC number and did the same.

☆
☆ ☆
☆

NINE

Dusty held out the sandwich bag – shrouded in a latex glove several sizes too big for her hand – and said, "I need you to make a copy of this quickly. Then some advice. And . . . we never had this conversation. Okay?"

Peter Liu, the *Baltimore Mirror*'s senior photographer, looked up from his desk. "Oh! Another one of *those* conversations. You had to drag me back to the office in the wee hours of the morning. This couldn't have waited until normal business hours?"

"No, Peter. Jim's on a call at the B'Nai Israel Synagogue. When he gets home, he's going to expect to see this bag where he left it in my car and from there, it'll go into that black hole known as 'the BPD evidence locker' at 601 East Fayette Street."

"Okay," Liu said, shaking his head.

"Do you have gloves? I have to get this back without any fingerprints on it that weren't there to start with."

Liu pulled open a drawer and removed a box of blue surgical gloves. "I'd say a hundred or so. That enough?"

"Smart ass! I think one will do."

"So you're adding the theft of evidence to your string of recording phone conversations without the other party's knowledge or consent offenses?"

"I didn't *steal* it. Jim got called for a suspicious package and left it in the car. I'm just making sure it's *safe*."

Liu slipped his hands into the blue gloves and took the bag. He removed the cassette and slipped it into the throat of a portable recorder on his desk. After plugging a jack into its line-out female connector, he started a recording program on his computer and pushed the recorder's "Play" button. After a moment, green sound wave forms danced on his monitor, as the cassette's audio moved from one device to the other.

"Okay, Dusty, what kind of techno-geek advice do you need today?"

"Do you know anyone who can do a voice analysis quickly and keep their mouth shut?"

"I might be able to do that for you. I do some work on the side, mostly for private investigators in divorce cases. Photographs, voice analysis, stuff like that. I've built a little lab in my basement with some fairly sophisticated equipment in it. Whose voice are we talking about?"

☆ ☆ ☆

The only OHP Troop L cruiser in the area at the time of the report traveled southwest on I-44. Fortunately, it had not passed the only break in the Jersey barriers separating the east and westbound lanes – nine miles southwest of the Miami exit – allowing Trooper Shelia Gibson to reverse direction. She responded to the call with red and blue bar lights and siren at high speed. At the break in the barrier, Gibson turned her black and white cruiser in the opposite direction. With virtually no traffic on the road, she soon sped through the night at 105 mph toward Missouri.

Two miles from the Missouri state line Gibson saw the Suburban ahead. Apparently, the driver noticed the OHP cruiser as well and increased speed. In seventy seconds, the Suburban crossed into Missouri, with the OHP cruiser 100 feet behind it.

Interstate 44's exit 1 for Baxter Springs is a little over a tenth of a mile into Missouri. The exit ramp dead-ends in less than two tenths of a mile on an access road to Downstream Boulevard in one direction and the entry ramp to eastbound I-44 and Outer South Road in the other.

Crossing into another state apparently gave the Suburban's driver a false sense of security. Gibson watched as the vehicle ahead of her unexpectedly veered onto exit 1. Having used this spot to return to Oklahoma many times, she well knew the ramp's short length and made no attempt to continue the pursuit.

Continuing east, lights and siren still on, Gibson radioed her dispatch, advising them to contact the Missouri State Police with an alert of a possible serious automobile crash at the end of eastbound exit 1. She continued to exit 4 where she reversed course.

Back at exit 1, she could already see what looked like a fire on the opposite side of the highway. At the bottom of the ramp, she turned left toward South Outer Road. Beyond the highway's overpasses, another vehicle's emergency flashers alternated between on and off.

Clearing the eastbound overpass, the pile of burning wreckage came into view. The Suburban's impact had virtually buried the vehicle in the berm after tearing out a traffic light and the concrete pillar it stood on.

Gibson pulled to the side of the road fifty yards from the crash site and called the situation in to her dispatch. She popped the car's trunk, got out, grabbed a handful of road flares and ran toward the vehicle stopped on the other side of the crash site.

The driver lowered his window as she approached. "What happened . . ." was all he got out before Gibson yelled at him.

"*Get out of here!*"

"*Where am I supposed to go?*"

"*I don't care! Back up and go somewhere else! This place isn't safe! Go!*" she yelled and turned back toward the crash as the driver backed up and turned onto the I-44 on-ramp, eastbound.

Gibson placed flares on either side of the bottom of the exit ramp and ran back to her car.

Less than five minutes later, two MHP cruisers, from Troop D, approached her vehicle. The first MHP car stopped behind Gibson. The second, seeing the situation, passed the other police cars and slowly drove up the off-ramp, on the shoulder with its light bar flashing red and blue, to stop any traffic attempting to exit.

Gibson stood near the trunk of her car as an MHP trooper approached. "I'm Carlson. What do we have here?" he asked.

"I'm Gibson. Have you guys seen the APB on the Stinger missile hijacking?"

"We have."

"I was in pursuit of a vehicle matching the description of one of the suspected SUVs. We got a call from the Vinita dispatch. A toll taker said two bearded men were in it with something big covered up in the back. When I approached them running hot, they took off. We crossed into your jurisdiction and the driver suddenly swerved onto exit one. I guess he thought he was home free in Missouri. Traveling at ninety-five, I knew I'd have to lock up the binders and might not be able to stop, so I kept going toward exit four. I know I'll catch shit for that from some of the old timers, saying I didn't want to be the first on the scene."

Trooper Carlson nodded. "Yeah, you probably would if you'd been in Oklahoma, but you're not."

"Well it has nothing to do with jurisdiction. Some in the old boys club don't think women are aggressive enough. And some aren't, but neither are some men. Anyway, if this is one of the Stinger SUVs, you might want to call in your bomb squad, hazmat team and . . ."

Two loud explosions a few seconds apart, followed by a huge fireball, interrupted Gibson's suggestion. Both troopers ducked behind her car.

Still squatting, Gibson said, "I guess that confirms who they were."

"Yeah, I don't think we need the bomb squad anymore. I'll call it in. We need to get a message board put up at the state line saying that the exit is closed and a priority zero call-out to the coroner. I don't think anyone in there is in need of emergency medical attention," Carlson said, tilting his head toward the crash scene.

* * *

"I can't get there before ten," a man's familiar voice said.

"That's okay. You're worth the wait," a woman countered with a husky response.

"Bring something from Victoria's Secret and high heels."

"Have I ever disappointed you?" There was a slight giggle in the woman's voice.

"No, baby! Never. I'll see you then."

A metallic, computer-generated voice followed the click, signaling the end of the call. "Recorded at 10:20 p.m., January 18, 2007."

"That's Tasman's voice on the tape," Dusty said, barely containing her excitement. "The woman is Jordan Moses. She was run down and killed the other day, shortly after she told me about her affair with the senator."

Peter Liu looked up at Dusty from the equipment covered desk. "This would never hold up in court, but the voice pattern matches Tasman's pretty closely. Of course, comparing a *copy* of a phone answering machine tape to a sample from the Internet certainly leaves room for error. But, I'd say there's a ninety-plus percent chance that a certified voice stress analysis would confirm my comparison."

"What about a comparison of my answering machine tape and the one we found? Could that confirm Jordan Moses' voice?"

Liu smiled. "I'd say that would be a lot closer, but you'd still need a certified lab to run the test to make it legit."

★ ★ ★

TEN

"Emergency Services Unit, Grabowski."

"Hey, Jim, it's Paul Staron. You got a minute?"

"Yeah, sure. What's up?"

"You know that hit-and-run you were askin' about the other day? Well, her old man turned up dead too."

"Yeah . . .?"

"We pulled a stiff out of a Dumpster up near North and Pennsy yesterday. Neighbors complained about the smell. He'd been whacked mob style – two twenty-two rounds in the back of the head."

"They left his ID on him? That's pretty sloppy work," Grabowski said.

"Well, sloppy or stupid. They didn't leave his wallet or anything, but he had a safety deposit key card in his *sock* and car keys in his pocket with a remote lock/unlock fob on it. Looks like whoever clipped him made him drive his own vehicle. We just pressed the unlock button on the fob and a Toyota Camry chirped around the corner.

"The card's from Cornerstone Bank. The registration in the glove box says it belongs to Gordon R. Moses."

"Did they work him over?"

"No. He had a couple of scrapes on his face. The ME says they happened postmortem. But, other than that, he was in pretty good shape – if you discount the holes in his head."

"Did the medical examiner recover the slugs?" Grabowski rubbed his forehead. Now he had some tall explaining to do.

"Yeah, one of them. In good shape too. The other one went out his ear hole wherever he got hit. But the weapon is probably at the bottom of the Patapsco River."

"Who caught the case?" Grabowski asked.

"Morgan and Hermann."

"Thanks for the update, Paul! I appreciate it. *Ciao*." Grabowski replaced the phone handset in its cradle slowly as if it were filled with nitroglycerin. *Shit*!

✶ ✶ ✶

The phone rang on a desk at Baltimore's 601 East Fayette Street Police Headquarters. "Homicide, Morgan."

"Hunter, Jim Grabowski."

"Hey, Jim! How the hell are ya?"

"That depends."

"On what?" Morgan said, putting down the autopsy report on Jordan Moses.

"On how you react to what I'm about to tell you," Grabowski said. "I hear you caught the Moses case."

"*Cases* now. Yeah. Why, do you know something about them?"

"I do. Dusty got a call from Jordan Moses the other day and met with her. She claimed to have been Thaddeus Tasman's mistress. She showed Dusty a picture of her and Tasman in the sack."

"No *shit*?" Morgan fumbled for a pad and pen. "That could throw a hitch in his political giddyap."

"Sure could," Grabowski agreed. "Anyway, they were supposed to meet the next day and Jordan Moses was going to bring video of the good senator. But, her husband called Dusty and said his wife had been murdered."

"So was this another case of the jilted lover? Is that why Ms. Moses called Dusty?"

"Yeah. There's some of that, but mostly she wanted to cash in like the governor's hooker is right now."

"Okay. So the husband . . ." Morgan shuffled through several reports on his desk, then continued. ". . . Gordon Moses, calls Dusty."

"Correct. Dusty and the husband arranged a meeting, but the husband never showed. I got their address from Paul Staron, and Dusty and I went to the Moses' house. The door was unlocked and someone had tossed the place like a pro."

"Jim, I don't like where this is going."

"Well, I want you to hear it from me rather than the lab rats. They may find Dusty's prints in the apartment. And there's something else too."

"Yeah . . .?"

"Dusty found a mini-audio cassette in one of those poor man's electrical outlet safes. It may have been what they tore the place apart looking for. Based on what Jordan Moses told Dusty, it probably has recordings of her talking to Tasman, making arrangements to meet."

"Jesus, Jim! You didn't remove evidence from the scene, did you?"

"I took it into my possession and I still have it. You'll have it in the next thirty minutes."

"And the chain of evidence is unbroken?" Morgan asked.

There was silence on the other end of the phone line. After several seconds, Grabowski answered. "Yeah. Let's go with that."

ELEVEN

Morgan hung up the phone and looked across the desk at his partner, Andrew Hermann.

"*Fuck!*" Morgan muttered.

"'Sup?" Morgan's tall, black partner asked, adjusting a flame red tie near the white collar of a deep blue, long-sleeved shirt.

"A damn good bomb tech may have ended his career."

"Yeah?"

Morgan recounted most of Grabowski's story for Hermann, then added, "He's bringing the tape in."

"Has the scene been processed yet?" Hermann asked.

"I think Proffitt's crew is over there now," Morgan answered. "How do you think we should play this?"

"Grabowski's a good man, and I like his old lady too, even if she *is* a reporter. Dusty has been good to us. Let's see what the lab rats come up with. If they find Dusty's prints and ID her, we'll have no choice but to give up Grabowski."

"And if they don't ID her . . .?" Morgan asked.

"We play it by ear. As long as we have the evidence, and the chain of custody isn't broken, we're in pretty good shape."

"And if it gets out that we covered up what Grabowski did, we could all go down," Morgan pointed out.

"Yeah, we could. But look at it this way. A lot of people will talk to a reporter before they'll spill their guts to a cop. Like the Simington case, for example. That old man told Dusty stuff he'd never have said to anyone wearing a badge. And if it hadn't been for her giving Simington the information we asked her to, we might never have closed the case."

Morgan looked uncertain. His brown eyes swept the ceiling for a moment, then returned to Hermann's face. "Okay. No guts, no glory."

☆ ☆ ☆

"In the Name of Allah, Most Gracious, Most Merciful," the *imam* finished.

"In the Name of Allah, Most Gracious, Most Merciful," the group of men repeated, in almost perfect unison.

"*Allahu Akba*," the *imam* said.

"*Allahu Akba*." Again the men echoed the *takbīr* as if they had rehearsed it together.

Dayo Amoako rose from his prayer rug and began rolling it carefully. His conversion to Islam in prison – known as "*Prislam*" by some detractors – had been primarily spawned out of a need for protection. Muslim communities in the "joint" are highly structured. Every prison has its *imam*, Chief of Security, Treasurer, Secretary, Piety Inspector and soldiers. Members actually pay dues into the treasury. The Security Chief negotiates with the leaders of various prison gangs. If a Muslim runs up a debt that can't be repaid or some other offense, the Security Chief is approached and in the case of a debt, it is paid out of the treasury. The offender is then dealt with by the community. Rarely did the infidels – black, white, Asian or Hispanic – decide any reason was important enough to engage in hostilities.

In the vast majority of cases, his brother Ayo's occupation would have been a huge negative for Dayo. When it came to light, well along in his process of taking *shahad* – meaning "witness" – Dayo came under serious suspicion until the *imam* began to conjure up the many possibilities the young man could serve, once released. The fact that a considerable amount of time would pass before the next background investigation of his brother put icing on Dayo's cake.

Another plus, Muslims were allowed to pray five times a day. Christians were limited to Sundays!

As he became more familiar with the teachings of Muhammad, the void in Dayo Amoako's soul – created over decades of playing second banana to his brother but expanded exponentially after causing the deaths of his parents – began to feel a little less cavernous.

The Amoakos' deaths were ruled accidental; the result of a fire which started in their family room trash can as they slept upstairs in a home with one faulty smoke detector. The fact that the source of ignition came from Dayo's carelessly discarded cigarette as he exited to score drugs never came to light – one of the few cases of a cocaine habit saving a life.

Though he and Ayo Amoako shared very similar DNA, the two children, adolescents and men, could hardly have been less alike. Ayo – the good child – had always minded their parents, gotten good grades, gone to USC, graduated with honors and become a Secret Service agent. Ayo was the light of their parents' lives.

Dayo – the disappointment – seemed rebellious almost from his time in diapers; he became potty trained months later than Ayo. Dayo went through three pre-schools on his way to Kindergarten, dismissed for acting out and fighting with other children. In middle school, Dayo managed to get suspended often enough to be held back a year, although his teachers were almost violently opposed to the idea of having to deal with him again.

In high school, Dayo limped along academically and administratively until his senior year. The final straw came when he smashed the very popular baseball team captain's head with a bat. His expulsion began before the end of the school day.

In prison, he studied Arabic in order to read from the *Quran* and attended the regular classes on Islamic culture and beliefs taught by the State's paid *imam*. Dayo quickly learned that his fellow inmates held the inside *imam* in much higher esteem than the state employee. After the sessions, in the exercise yard, at his job in the laundry and in his cell, Dayo was introduced to a different flavor of Islam.

Imam Mustafa Kamel Mustafa's name prior to his own religious awakening had been U-Dell Washington, AKA 187. U-Dell/Mustafa had acquired his street name – the California penal code for murder – because of his position in Los Angeles' Queen Street Blood street gang, in Inglewood. U-Dell took care of the gang's "problems" so to speak. Sometimes quietly, but generally in a way that sent a loud, clear message to other gangs, business owners and or members of the community: "Those who trespass on, or disrespect the Queen Street Blood territory or commit any other offense will soon have homicide detectives familiar with their names."

U-Dell left all that behind when he was given room and board at one of California's Convict Colleges for savagely mugging a wealthy real estate developer in Los Angeles. In San Quentin State Prison, U-Dell discarded the tattered remnants of his Catholic upbringing and converted to Islam for much the same reason Dayo Amoako did later –

safety – but also because the Muslim structure inside closely mirrored that of the Bloods. Soon U-Dell embraced the teachings of his *imam*: The black man's plight was due to the rich white establishment and had been since the first slaves had arrived in America in 1619. The Negroes' emancipation in the mid-nineteenth century had provided the white establishment with a *different* set of opportunities to exploit them.

U-Dell's *imam* taught and repeatedly reminded his students that the Human Immunodeficiency Virus which leads to the Acquired Immunodeficiency Syndrome had been engineered and introduced by the white-dominated U.S. Government for the purpose of eradicating blacks *worldwide*. The *imam* never allowed the issue to be clouded by the fact that the first casualties of HIV and then AIDS were homosexual *white* males.

U-Dell Washington's religious migration to Mustafa Kamel Mustafa didn't exorcise his violent nature, but did severely exacerbate his hatred of "Da Man."

Upon Mustafa's release from the joint, he joined a new organization: The American Muslims for Unity. The name, purposely picked to suggest an organization seeking peace and harmony, couldn't have been more dissimulating. The AMU wanted worldwide Muslim unity – meaning the elimination of all the infidels who followed the teachings of anyone other than Muhammad.

Mustafa continued his Islamic studies as a member of the AMU while working on their various "causes." These included activities such as scamming the State of California out of millions of dollars in educational aid. The overworked, underpaid and rarely appreciated state officials responsible for ensuring that the state's contribution was actually being used for its intended purpose still hadn't gotten around to visiting the AMU's schools. Had they, they would have discovered the fact that there was only one school instead of the four for which the AMU had requested assistance, and it had only five students – a little shy of the 492 kids California's taxpayers were being scammed for.

The money the AMU received, minus operating expenses, traveled a rather circuitous route to the Middle East in an attempt to avoid its discovery by the Departments of Justice, Treasury and other Federal watchdogs. Nonetheless, it wound up in the hands of al-Qaeda and other Islamic terrorist groups.

Mustafa attained the title "*imam*" himself and shortly after doing so, he was sent on a very special recruiting mission. Like the *imam* who taught him in San Quentin, Mustafa got himself sent back to prison by robbing an old man in Boulder, Colorado. The location of the crime wasn't randomly picked. The thought was that a judge in Boulder would be less harsh on a poor, misguided black man by virtue of the city's liberal leanings. The plan paid off. Mustafa received a one- to three-year sentence.

And so, Dayo's conversion to Islam followed much the same path as Mustafa's. Dayo's violent nature couldn't begin to rival his teacher's. But, where he could send a thousand young men to violently martyr themselves, Mustafa would never even consider carrying out the act himself. Dayo embraced the concept of martyrdom, wrapping himself in it like a blanket on a cold night.

Standing in the Shrine of *Hazrat Ali* Mosque in Northern Virginia, just a few miles from Washington, D.C., Dayo was prepared to carry out his mission – an opportunity provided by Allah – to begin the shredding of the Great Satan.

✷ ✷ ✷

In Texas on eastbound I-20, a black, 1998 Ford Explorer took exit 42 for U.S. Highway 285 in Pecos. At the bottom of the ramp, the driver turned left toward the small town. A mile later, it pulled into a Shell gas station and convenience store on the right side of the road, parking next to the outside pump island. Two men, the driver of Middle Eastern descent, both bearded, got out. The dark-skinned driver stood between the SUV and the gas pump as the passenger walked to the convenience store.

Inside he stood in line behind a fat woman in a green muumuu and a tall black man beneath a well-worn cowboy hat with a gallon of milk in one hand. When he reached the counter, he handed four $20 bills to the clerk. "Pump five. Where's the men's room?"

Without comment the acne-faced, young clerk pointed to the right-rear corner of the store and the man threaded his way through the aisles of merchandise in that direction.

Outside, the driver saw $80 appear on the pump readout, removed the nozzle and began to fill the 21-gallon tank. On the other side of the pump island, two Texas Rangers from Company E drove toward I-20.

"Hey, Bob. Pull in here. I need to get a pack of gum."

The driver glanced at his partner. "Still got the cancer sticks urge?"

"Yeah. I'm startin' the third week. Pull in."

"Okay."

The unmarked, gray Crown Victoria PI pulled into the Shell parking lot and stopped facing the pump island closest to the street. Ranger Harvey Crane – at 6' 4" known as "Big Bird" – opened the passenger door and walked toward the store. On his way he noticed a bearded, dark man looking in the opposite direction, pumping gas.

Texas Rangers have no official uniform. Inside, with his back to the restrooms, Crane looked like an ordinary big man dressed in typical Texas garb: tan hat, cowboy boots, Western cut shirt, pants and brown leather belt. If the SUV passenger had seen Crane from the front on his way back outside, he would have noticed the Ranger badge pinned over his heart.

Crane picked up a package from the display in front of the counter and laid down three dimes.

The clerk looked at the change and then up at the Ranger. "There's no charge, sir."

"Well, I appreciate that, but I have to pay. We can't accept gifts." Crane said, turning slightly to his left, moving his sidearm out of view.

"Sir, it's just a pack of gum."

"Makes no difference, son. Take the money."

"Okay." The clerk opened the register, removed three pennies and held them out.

"Put 'em in the pot for the next guy."

The bearded SUV passenger passed behind Crane toward the door. As he pushed it open, the clerk cocked his head to the right slightly, subtly nodding toward him.

Crane looked over his shoulder at the man's back. "Somethin' wrong?"

"Naw, he just don't look like he's from around here."

Outside, the passenger walked to the pump island and took over filling the tank. Crane watched the driver walk toward the store. When he neared the door, Crane turned his head back to the clerk. The SUV driver entered the store and walked directly toward the restrooms.

"Thanks," Crane said as he turned toward the exit. Outside he approached the SUV's open passenger door. The Explorer blocked the view of the man filling the tank as Crane glanced inside. Trash littered the floor from what looked like a long road trip. In the back, a patchwork quilt covered something running from the back of the front seats to the rear cargo hatch.

Crane walked to the driver's side of the Crown Victoria, glancing at the rear tag on his way. Ranger Robert Kennedy lowered the power window. "What's up, Bird Man?"

"I think we need to question the two guys in that Explorer over there."

"Why?"

Crane repeated the clerk's comment.

"I think they call that 'racial profiling.'"

"I think that Stinger APB takes profiling off the table. Besides, their Kansas plate says they're not likely to stop and file a complaint. There's one inside. You question the guy at the pump. I'll talk to the other one."

Kennedy shook his head but opened the door and got out. Near the back of the Explorer he said, "Good afternoon, sir. How are you doin' today?"

The gas nozzle clicked off automatically in the bearded Caucasian's right hand. He removed it and turned toward Kennedy.

"What do you want?"

"What do you have in the back of your vehicle?"

"That's none of your business."

Well, sir, I'm going to have to make it my business. I need you to put that gas nozzle away and open the back."

"Do you have a warrant?"

"Sir, put the nozzle away and *open* the back," Kennedy said, putting his hand on his Texas DPS issued Sig Sauer .357 automatic.

The bearded man stepped toward the back of the Explorer and began to reach for the hatch's handle, averting his eyes from Kennedy momentarily.

The Ranger kept his eyes on the man, standing his ground, until the hatch began to open. Inside, under the bottom edge of the quilt, he saw the end of two olive drab green cases similar in shape and color to the photos in the APB. The bearded man's initial reaction had instinctively warned Kennedy of a hostile situation. The sliver of green under the quilt set off all his alarms. He began to lift the .357 out of its belt holster.

The bearded man didn't give him a chance. He squeezed the handle of the gas nozzle covering Kennedy's face and the left side of his body.

Kennedy began to yell for his partner, but only got out "He . . ." before gasoline filled his mouth.

Inside the store, the clerk saw Kennedy being drenched and falling to the ground, still in the hose's spray. "Oh! Shit! That guy needs help!" he said, pointing outside.

Crane turned to see what was happening and ran for the door, drawing his Glock 9mm. Outside, he saw the gasoline pool spreading around the other Ranger and ran around it.

Kennedy rolled over, coughing and wiping his eyes with gas-soaked fingers.

The bearded man came into Crane's view, smiling and staring at Kennedy on the ground. He casually dropped the nozzle, stopping the flow of fuel and reached into his pocket.

Crane saw his hand come out holding a red butane lighter and squeezed off three quick shots without any words of warning. The hollow point 9mm rounds impacted the bearded man in the center of his chest and just above the bridge of his nose with enough force to drive him back into the gas pump. He bounced off it and fell next to the Explorer.

"Watch out!"

The Ranger turned to see the dark man charge out of the store, raising a .45 automatic in his direction. Again without warning, Crane fired three times. The man flew backwards like a charging angry dog at the end of its chain. His body came to rest sprawled on the concrete step, one leg bent at the knee. His head served as a doorstop.

The clerk's head poked up from behind the counter inside.

"*Call 911 for an ambulance! Then start bringing me bags of cat litter!*" Crane shouted, running toward the second man.

"Yes, sir!"

After picking up the .45 and stuffing it inside his belt, Crane holstered the .357 and returned to his partner.

"*BOB! YOU OKAY?*"

Sputtering and propping himself up on his right elbow, Kennedy tried to look up at Crane but the gas burning his eyes forced him to close them. "*Give . . . me your . . . handkerchief!*" he said, groping skyward with his left hand.

"Let me get you out of this gas puddle first," Crane said reaching under Kennedy and pulling him backwards toward their cruiser. Once out of pool, he pulled a handkerchief out of a hip pocket. "Keep your eyes closed, Bob. Let me clean your face off."

The clerk pushed the partially open door with an elbow and stepped over the body. He carried two 5-pound bags of Super-Cat clumping litter in each hand and one under his left arm.

"Don't step in the gas!" Crane shouted. "Spread it in the tracks where I dragged my partner out first, then start covering the puddle."

"You want me to move the Ford?"

"*NO*! Just spread cat litter all over! When you run out, go get more!"

"Yes, sir!"

A car pulled into the station's parking lot and screeched to a stop. A man got out yelling, "*What the hell is going on?*"

Crane looked over his shoulder. "Who are you?"

"*I own this place*!"

"Then get your ass in the store and get more cat litter. Give it to the kid, then go call 911 and tell' em you need the fire department to respond to a gasoline spill here. Is there a hose handy?"

"Right around the corner here," the man said pointing to the side of the building. "Want me to pull it over?"

"Yeah, fast!"

The newcomer slammed his car's door and ran out of site beyond the corner of the building. He quickly reappeared pulling a heavy, gray hose.

Crane could hear metal creaking in protest as the hose came off a reel.

"Bob, can you stand up? I need to hose you down."

Kennedy got to his feet slowly, still virtually blind.

"Okay, now let's get farther away from the gas," Crane said, putting his hand under Kennedy's left arm and guiding him toward the station owner and spray nozzle he held.

"Can you stand on your own?"

"Yeah, I think so."

Crane slowly released the grip he had on Kennedy's arm. The other Ranger swayed a bit but after a few seconds seemed steady.

"Give me the hose, then get that cat litter."

"Yes, sir." The man ran to the front of the store but stopped at the body, staring down at it.

"*MOVE!*" Crane shouted.

The owner glanced over his shoulder, then gingerly pulled the fully closed door open, disappearing inside. Within seconds, he emerged with two more bags of litter.

In the distance, Crane heard a siren's wail. "Help's on the way, Bob! Let's start hosing you down!"

⋆ ⋆ ⋆

Yellow crime scene tape fluttered in a slight breeze across each entrance to the Shell station. The bearded men occupied matching black body bags on the store's gunmetal gray, concrete stoop, to the left of the doors, awaiting the coroner's arrival.

A Pecos Police car, Texas Highway Patrol car and a Texas Department of Safety HAZMAT truck sat at odd angles to the scene of the shootings. Their lights all flashed in what looked like a red and blue battle of the bands.

The HAZMAT truck crew slammed the back doors and prepared to leave the scene with the two Stinger missile cases on board en route to Fort Hood. The THP car would provide the truck's security.

After Crane had taken numerous pictures of the bodies and area around the Ford Explorer, it had been hooked up to a wrecker and taken to the Pecos police impound lot for examination by various federal and state agencies. Once removed, the remainder of the store's cat litter had been distributed liberally. Now the clerk used a large shop broom to sweep it up and discard it per the HAZMAT crew's instructions.

The fire department had been on a training exercise a few miles on the other side of Pecos. By the time they responded to the call, there was nothing much to do and seeing that, they returned to their station.

Kennedy sat on the rear step of an ambulance wrapped in a white blanket. Crane stood a couple of feet away next to an EMT.

"We need to get you into a shower, sir," the medical technician said.

"You'll get no argument from me, Doc. That'll beat getting drenched in that cold hose spray."

"You'd bitch if they hung ya with a new rope," Crane said, grinning at his partner.

The station owner approached the group. "How are you doin', sir?" he asked Kennedy.

"I'll be fine. Thanks."

"When do you men think I can get back to business?"

Crane glanced at the man. "In another hour or two, maybe. It's going to take that young man a while to clean up the cat litter in the meantime. We're going to need all the video from your surveillance cameras for the last two hours at least."

"Yeah, okay, not a problem."

"You ought to be proud of him," Crane said, gesturing toward the clerk. "He saved my partner's and my life, yelling like he did. What's his name?"

"Billy, Billy Daugherty, he's a great kid. He's workin' three jobs to help his mom and little sister out."

Crane pulled a pen and small, spiral note pad from his shirt pocket to record the name. "I hope you take good care of him. I'm going to see if I can get him a commendation from the DPS and Rangers."

"That'd be good. He wanted to go in the Army but he has this problem with needles and the sight of blood. Either one makes him faint. Billy was crushed they told him he was unfit for military service."

"He didn't have any problem with the sight of blood today. There was . . . still is a lot of it spread around. He never paid it any attention to it. The Army missed out on a good man."

On the opposite side of the parking lot, a Pecos policeman held the crime tape up allowing the THS cruiser – lights flashing – to lead the HAZMAT truck onto the road toward Fort Hood, a little over 400 miles away.

TWELVE

"Crime Lab, Proffitt. The *Ace* of Trace."

Morgan smiled. "Hey, Ace! Morgan here. How's it goin'?"

"Same effluent, different day. There's still more perps than crime scene technicians and cops combined," Proffitt answered. The head of Baltimore's crime lab chuckled. "Which of your pile of cases are you calling to bitch about?"

"Moses. You find anything at their apartment?"

"Just got a hit on one set of prints."

Morgan sucked in his breath a little, but said nothing.

"Apparently, our good friend Jim Grabowski . . . One second," Proffitt said.

The click told Morgan he'd been placed on hold.

"*Shit*!" Morgan said under his breath. Though less than thirty seconds, the wait seemed like minutes to the homicide detective before Proffitt returned to the line.

"Okay. So, looks like Jordan Moses was popped on a minor drug charge a few years back. Of all the prints we collected, hers were the only set we got a match on in AFIS," Proffitt said.

Morgan breathed a sigh of relief. "What were you saying about Grabowski?"

"Oh. Just that he's interested in the case too. I guess his wife knew the Moses woman."

"Yeah, that's what I hear." Morgan quickly changed the subject. "Nothing else we can use?"

"We found strands of hair here and there in the living room and kitchen and of course all over the bathrooms, as you'd expect. The victims' most likely. The ME is going to send us samples to compare from the bodies. Any strands that belong to another party or parties will be checked for DNA, if the hairs have follicles. We'll run any we get through CODIS. But you know DNA analysis doesn't happen overnight and the chances of getting a hit in CODIS are pretty remote, unlike what the public expects after the avalanche of *Crime Scene Investigation* shows on TV.

"Whoever tore the place apart wore surgical gloves, based on the residue we found throughout the apartment. But, you already knew they'd probably wear some hand protection."

"Yeah. Are there any security cameras in the area of their address?" Morgan asked.

"There's one a couple of blocks away on Light Street. We took a look at four days' worth of the video from it before Gordon Moses' body turned up. We figured it might have taken that long for him to get ripe enough for neighbors to complain.

"Two guys walked around the corner of Light Street and down Churchill in the direction of the Moses residence about seventy-two hours before his corpse was discovered. Both wore wide-brimmed hats and had their heads down – a couple of pros who knew to avoid any surveillance system that might be in the area."

"Was there anything on the tape we could use to identify them?" Morgan wasn't hopeful, but needed to ask.

"We zoomed in as best we could with a low resolution image. One guy appeared to only have two fingers and a thumb on his left hand. And, either he is a very large man or the second guy is a midget, because the two-fingered guy towered over the other person.

"Then twenty-six minutes later, a vehicle matching the one found near Moses' body appears at the intersection and drives away."

"Could you read the tag on it?" Morgan asked.

"The front tag was missing. We couldn't read the rear one because of the direction the vehicle took."

Morgan hesitated a moment. He had to play this next part of the conversation very carefully. "Okay, Ace. I have one more piece of evidence for you to check out."

"Yeah? What's that?"

"An audio tape from an answering machine. We think it has Thaddeus Tasman's voice on it. Looks like he was poking Jordan Moses."

"*No shit*! How'd you come by the tape?"

Morgan cleared his throat. "Keep the following to yourself. Okay?"

"I'll do my best, Morgan," Proffitt said, a dash of caution in his voice.

"Jordan Moses told Dusty she was having an affair with Tasman up until the time he announced he was running for president. Then when the governor up north got popped for all his activities with prostitutes, the Moses woman feeling scorned, decided to go public like the Governor's chick, hoping to cash in the same way. The day after Dusty meets Jordan Moses, the late Ms. Moses winds up on a slab in the ME's office."

"Well, that explains the high-end video cameras and microphones we found in the Moses' master bedroom. There was no computer, but there was a big UPS in the study with the audio and video gear wired into it," Proffitt said.

"UPS?

"Uninterrupted power source. If they lost power, any recording in progress would have continued."

"Okay. Anyway, the next day the husband calls Dusty to say his wife was murdered. They arrange to meet, but the guy never shows. So Dusty and Grabowski go by the Moses' house and find the door open and the place tossed. As they're about to leave, they notice an electrical plug sticking out of the wall at an odd angle. Turns out to be one of those fakes that people put their valuables in. Inside is a mini-cassette from an answering machine.

"Grabowski, not knowing if a crime has actually been committed or, if one has, when your guys will get to the scene, takes the tape into evidence and brings it to me and Hermann."

Proffitt didn't speak for a moment and a chill ran through Morgan. Had he sounded convincing enough to protect Grabowski?

"So, let me guess. You want me to do a voice analysis on the tape."

"Can't slip anything past you, Proffitt!" Morgan hoped the chuckle in his voice made the situation seem like a casual exchange between a detective and the crime lab.

"Well, in order to do that, we'll need a voice sample from the senator. I can't imagine he'll be anxious to provide one."

"Hermann has a call into Celia Gray at the State's Attorney's office. I'm going to bring the tape to you personally later today," Morgan said.

"You realize this could become a political *tsunami* and drown us all," Proffitt said quietly. His usual jocular tone nowhere to be heard.

"Yeah, dust off your water wings."

* * *

The caller patiently listened to the U.S. Department of State's Inspector General Hot Line options to file complaints on-line or via e-mail. Finally, after disclaimers of various types about confidentiality, and the fact that the call might be recorded for training and quality purposes, a live woman's voice answered his call.

"OIG Hotline, Olivia Perkins. How can I help you?"

The man's voice carried a clear accent from the Middle East. "Tell your president the following: We have a number of Stinger missiles spreading across America and will use them if our demands are not met. The cost of their return is two hundred million American dollars. Your president has forty-eight hours, starting now, to agree to these terms by putting the following ad in the *Washington Post* classifieds: 'Yes, Omar. We will meet you for lunch at your convenience. Just tell us where and when.'"

"Sir, could I get your name before we go any farther?"

"No, Ms. Perkins. Did you understand the message?"

"I did, sir. It was recorded."

"Good. Please pass it onto your president immediately."

The line clicked in Olivia's ear. "That was weird," she said to herself.

On the other side of her cubical partition, another employee asked, "What was weird?"

"Oh, just some crackpot wanting two hundred million dollars."

"Yeah? What's worth two hundred mil'?"

"He said they have Stinger missiles and if the president wants them back, he has to pay."

"What are *Stinger* missiles?

"Beats me."

"What are you going to do?"

"Well, I'm certainly not going to waste my time writing *that* call up."

* * *

La Pesca, in Mexico's Tamaulipas State, sits on the banks of the Rio Bravo River near the Gulf of Mexico. The tractor-trailer containing the load of Stinger missiles had been unloaded in an abandoned warehouse to await nightfall. After dark, they would be moved onto small boats and ferried to a cargo ship off shore. Fortunately, the forces of evil are not immune to collisions with Murphy's Law.

The *Angry Panda*, registered in Liberia, inbound from the Port of Havana, currently sat adrift due to a loss of power shortly after leaving Cuban waters, its crew working frantically to get underway again.

Frustrated by the delay of unknown length in moving the hijacked Stingers, the leader of the group in the warehouse instructed a young man to back the tractor-trailer out of the warehouse and deliver it to its new owner at a remote spot outside of La Pesca.

Manuel, barely eighteen, and only slightly over five feet, climbed into the Kenworth cab where the switches were all labeled in English. He had no idea what each did, but he knew that "up" was "on," and proceeded to flip every toggle on the dash that wasn't already in that position.

The engine rumbled and the rig moved backward slowly after Manuel ground the gears several times, causing gales of laughter from the rest of the crew – this being the only light moment the thieves had experienced all day. Even Jesús smiled at the young man's lack of skill in the cab.

After exiting the warehouse, Manuel jumped from the cab to close the large doors, since none of his *compadres* seemed interested in the task. His small frame and weight offered little impetus to start the massive doors moving along their metal tracks. It took nearly five minutes for them to shut amid their creaking protests.

✳ ✳ ✳

Dusty adjusted her headphones, pressed "Play," and continued transcribing the conversations on her copy of Jordan Moses' answering machine tape. There were thirteen exchanges between Jordan and Tasman ranging over nine weeks. She glanced at the tape's rotating spools in her answering machine. Only a couple of minutes remained. The tape hit a blank spot of almost thirty seconds of silence and Dusty reached to press the "Stop" button. Before she could do so another conversation startled her because of its volume and anger.

"*YOU FUCKING WHORE*!" a man's voice screamed. "*YOU DUMPED ME FOR THAT NEAR-NIGGER MOTHERFUCKER?*"

"Calm down. This can work for both of us."

"Yeah? How the fuck is that?" The male voice's volume decreased, but not its intensity.

"It gives us both options."

"Yeah . . .?"

"If he runs for president, and I *know* he's going to, we will have the leverage to get anything we want. Money, cushy jobs, who knows."

"Did he tell you he's going to run?"

"No. He didn't have to. His ego deserves its own orbit. Tasman will run and we'll be in a position to clean up."

"'*We'll* clean up?' What do I get out of this?"

"Leverage. Use your imagination."

Dusty hurriedly finished her transcription, noted the timestamp on the exchange and sat back in her desk chair.

"*Wow!*" she said. The headphones caused the volume of her exclamation to draw looks from her coworkers.

After setting the headphones on her desk, Dusty lifted her phone's handset out of its cradle, paused for several seconds, and then replaced it.

✷ ✷ ✷

On I-10 west, the passenger in a blue, 2001 Dodge Grand Caravan minivan glanced at the printed directions.

> *West on I-10 W through Arizona to San Bernardino California –*
> *643 Miles*
> *Take Exit 73, Waterman Ave (Onto E. Hospitality Ln)*
> *E. Hospitality Ln turns into S. Waterman Ave*
> *Drive to 1706 S. Waterman Ave – .5 miles to Discount Inns &*
> *Suites on left*
> *Reservation under Umarov*

Crossing the Colorado River into California he looked up.
"*SHIT!*"

✷ ✷ ✷

Dusty walked into Peter Liu's workspace and sat heavily in a chair to the right of his desk. "I just discovered something interesting."

"Yeah? Is sharing it with me going to endanger my clean criminal record?" Liu smiled and raised his hands in a "What, me worry?" pose.

"I guess it could, but it's better that you know than not."

"Okay, shoot."

"I just transcribed the answering machine tape. Jordan Moses got an angry call from a very upset man whom she apparently dumped for Tasman."

"Any idea who?"

"No. I started to call Morgan to ask if he'd heard the whole thing and the second man's voice, but I stopped myself."

"Why?"

"Because that question would have let him know that *I'd* listened to it all."

"So?"

"The implication would be that either Jim let me listen to it, or it was not under his direct control at some point before he turned it over to Morgan, and that I'd probably copied it. For it to stand up in court the prosecution has to be able to show no links are missing in the chain of custody. Any way you slice it, Jim would be very exposed."

"Yes, but Jim doesn't know you copied it."

"That doesn't matter. If he has to testify about us finding the tape and asked if it remained in his possession continuously until he turned it over to Morgan he has to either say: 'No,' or perjure himself.

"So *please* don't breathe a word about the tape."

THIRTEEN

Senator Emlyn Keith set her drink on the coffee table in Thaddeus Tasman's hotel suite and looked at the presumptive Democratic nominee across the oval glass.

"How long are you going to let her drag this out?"

Tasman stirred the Scotch on the rocks mixture in his left hand with his right index finger. The remaining ice cubelets in his drink made almost inaudible clinking sounds against the sides of the crystal. Without raising his eyes from the golden liquid, he said, "We're energizing the party."

"*Bullshit*, T-squared! You're letting the Desert Fox build up a lead you may not be able to overcome." Senator Keith leaned forward. "Look at the crowds you're drawing. If that doesn't show the party's energy, then there's not a cow in Texas.

"You have to get Senator Reynolds off the stage and let the country see you alone. You've got an uphill battle at best. You're a black man running for the most powerful position in the world . . . just *forty-four* years after the Civil Rights Act. It took from 1868 to 1964 – damn near one hundred years – for the country to get serious about civil rights. Now, in less than half that length of time, you're asking America to put you in the Oval Office."

"Thanks for clearing all that up for me, Senator. I'd not connected those dots." Tasman took a little of the sting out of his words with a wry smile. "What's your point?"

"My point is that I can put you over the top today – ten days ahead of the Pennsylvania primary. I have the juice to give you the number of superdelegates you need right *fucking* now!"

"And in return . . ."

"In return I want Bob McKenna's chair on the high court," Senator Keith answered.

"That might be tough . . ."

"Why? Because you already promised it to Governor Cunningham?"

"I . . ."

"Justin Cunningham couldn't deliver a pizza much less what you need to give you a fighting chance in the November election. I can."

Tasman thought for a moment and then asked quietly, "And, you'd make this announcement when?"

"Whenever you want. Today, tonight, tomorrow. Your call. Every day you delay shooting this primary fiasco in the head, you give Fox another day to raise money and to run against you virtually unopposed. If you're serious about wanting to get your mail at a Pennsylvania Avenue address, you'll make this deal right now."

"I'd like to think about it."

"You'll have plenty of time to mull over all the things you did wrong after Fox kicks your ass in November. I could just as easily be making this offer to Reynolds right now."

"I can't believe you have the *juice* to put her over the top."

"No, I don't. But I could put her into a dead heat with you. That would mean a nasty fight at the convention with only one guaranteed outcome – that the party would be torn apart. Neither one of you would win. But, it would put her into a position to only have to wait four years to run again rather than eight if you win in November. I think I could sell that to her."

"She'd never do that," Tasman said, getting to his feet.

"You think not? There's only one thing that Jeannette Reynolds wants out of life and it ain't universal health care for the country. Do you think she and her husband became the cornerstone of the Democratic Party by playing nice?

"If you don't take anything else away from this conversation, believe this: Senator Reynolds' knickers are in a nuclear knot over your taking what she considers her birthright to the presidency. She would stab you in the ear with an ice pick if she thought she could get away with it. Reynolds wouldn't think twice about keeping you out of the White House so she could run against Fox in four years. And believe me she won't make the same mistakes the next time if you decided to run again. But . . . that wouldn't happen. Once you've lost, the party elite won't give you a chance to repeat your failure."

✭ ✭ ✭

"Simpson."

"Sir, Al Murphy. The GPS on truck number 74761945 just woke up!"

"Where in God's name is it?"

"*La Pesca*, Mexico, right on the Gulf Coast. Do you want me to call the State Police?"

"No, I'll handle it." Simpson started to drop the phone into its cradle, but paused. "Nice work, Al!"

✭ ✭
✭

FOURTEEN

The shouts of the Pittsburgh crowd and band made it impossible for Senator Reynolds to hear her campaign manager. Jackie Beaudro, wearing a yellow suit, looked visibly shaken – the equivalent of a canary in a political coal mine – as Jeannette Reynolds walked off the stage.

"What's wrong, Jackie?"

"Oh! Jesus, Mary and Joseph!"

"What *is* it?" Reynolds asked.

"We have to find a place to talk! I have good news and *really* bad news!" Beaudro said, taking her candidate's hand and pulling her roughly toward the stage's exit.

"Jackie!"

Beaudro didn't respond as she continued to pull Reynolds toward a hallway outside the stage's door. Several Secret Service agents led and followed the two women into the hall.

Once the heavy metal door was closed, Beaudro turned to the lead agent. "We need a couple of minutes. Make sure no one interrupts us." Without waiting for an answer, Beaudro pulled Reynolds into a small, dark office. After closing the door and flicking on the lights, she turned to Reynolds.

"You're not going to *believe* this!"

"Jackie! What's wrong with you?"

Beaudro lowered her voice to a barely audible whisper. "I just got a call from an old friend in the Baltimore Medical Examiner's office."

"Yeah?"

"A woman was killed there the other day by a hit-and-run driver."

"And . . .?"

"It appears she was having an affair with your opponent up until the time he announced his candidacy."

Jeannette Reynolds' mouth dropped open and she took a step backwards. "Are you shitting me?"

"No, ma'am. They have a tape that they believe has T-squared's voice on it making arrangements to see this woman. They're getting a warrant to get a voice sample from him for comparison.

"And, not only was she killed, her husband turned up dead too."

"Who else knows about this?" Reynolds was still trying to comprehend Beaudro's words.

"I don't know, but it won't be long until the world does, if they get a warrant. Do you want to hear something else? Something that probably doesn't mean much now?"

"Christ, Jackie! What else could there be?"

"There was an avalanche of superdelegates that declared for T-squared this morning. All of them associated with Emlyn Keith."

"That *bitch*! She's hated me since I tried to keep her husband from being appointed to the Assistant Secretary of Defense for Special Operations. What the hell was she thinking marrying a *Republican*?

"How many delegates?"

"Enough to get Tasman to 2,025. But if he was screwing this woman in Baltimore, that count won't last long. His pledged and superdelegates will abandon him quicker than a burnin' dog shedding fleas."

Senator Reynolds took a step back, rubbing her forehead. "What do you suppose Tasman gave Keith?"

"Like I said, it probably doesn't matter now, but Emlyn Keith has made no secret of the fact that she wants Chief Justice McKenna's job after they put him in a box or a bottle."

"God!" Senator Reynolds exclaimed. "This is going to help *me*, but . . . it's not going to help *us*!"

Beaudro arched her eyebrows and shook her head. "What the hell does that mean, Jeanette?"

"I mean, it will help us get the nomination, but it won't help us or the party win in November. The Republicans will shove this up our ass every day from the time the story breaks until November 4. This will be a disaster!"

"Well then, we'll just have to find some dirt on a prominent Republican – preferably Bob Fox. That is, if he isn't too old to get it up," Beaudro chuckled.

☆ ☆ ☆

"Mr. Mallard, there's a detective on the phone who wants to speak to Senator Tasman."

John Mallard didn't look up from the poll results on his desk. "What line?"

"Line six, sir."

"I've got it," Mallard said, dismissing the campaign worker as if he were shooing a fly away from a meal.

He waited for the campaign worker to close the door to his office before pushing a button next to a red flashing light. "John Mallard here. Who am I speaking to?"

"Detective Hunter Morgan, Baltimore Homicide."

"What can we do for you, Detective?"

"I need to arrange a meeting with Senator Tasman."

"Meeting to discuss what? I'm sure I can answer any questions you might have."

"Mr. Mallard, you can help me by telling me when my partner and I can interview the Senator in D.C. – or Baltimore, I don't care which – in the next seventy-two hours. What we have to discuss with him is very personal and I'm not sharing it with anyone but him."

"The senator and I have no secrets. You can tell me."

Morgan's voice took on a flint-hard tone when he spoke. "Okay, we can do this another way. We can get a warrant and march into your campaign headquarters with my partner and half a dozen D.C. cops. With that many people involved, the media is bound to find out beforehand and tag along. So, if you'd like to spend this coming Sunday making the rounds of the talk shows explaining why the police raided the Senator Tasman's campaign headquarters, I'll be watching you tap dance in high definition."

Mallard didn't speak for several seconds. Finally he said, "I'll have to check with the senator's scheduler to see when and where he can speak to you. But Detective, please keep in mind that Senator Tasman is all over the country. Could you grant us at least a week, please?" I'm sure he could speak to you on the phone in the next day or so. Can we do that?"

"No, Mr. Mallard. It has to be in person and it has to be scheduled in the next twenty-four hours for an interview not later than a week from today. Is that clear?"

"Very. Where can you be reached?"

Morgan gave his number and hung up.

Mallard stabbed the button for line six angrily. "*Motherfucker*!" After a few seconds, a smile etched its way across his broad face and he speed-dialed the number for Tasman. After a brief pause, a deep resonant voice filled his ear.

"Hey, John, what's up?"

"I don't know, Senator, but I just got off the phone with a Baltimore homicide dick who insists on meeting with you in the next week, face-to-face."

"Well, I haven't murdered anyone in Baltimore, so I think I'm safe. Why didn't you deal with it?"

"You may be safe from a murder rap, but depending on what this asshole wants, you may not be safe politically. I *tried* to head him off without any luck. He wouldn't talk to me. In fact, he said if he couldn't arrange a personal meeting with you, he'd make life interesting by walking in here with a warrant and a bunch of media maggots. I'll check with Amber to see where and when we can make this happen while keeping it *very* low key."

"Okay."

★ ★ ★

Morgan looked at Hermann and smiled. "Typical political asshole."

"Yeah?"

"Yeah. Let's take a ride down there in the next few days and drop in on him unannounced just to get the lay of the land."

"I'm up for it as long as we can go to Ben's Chili Bowl while we're there."

Morgan smiled. "You talked me into it, you silver-tongued devil!"

★ ★ ★

"Tell me you have some good news, Bob," POTUS said to the Secretary of Homeland Security.

"Well, sir, I have better news than my last report."

POTUS switched the phone to his left hand to allow him to take notes. "Let's hear it."

"We believe we've accounted for six of the forty-eight Stingers."

"That leaves forty-two unaccounted for, but it's a start. What are the details?"

"Two of them exploded in Missouri . . ."

"*What*! You mean someone *fired* them?"

"No, Mr. President. They were in an SUV that crashed while being pursued by the Oklahoma State Police."

"In *Missouri*?"

"Yes, sir. Just over the state line. They took the first Missouri exit at high speed and crashed at the end of it. The missiles' rocket propellant and warheads cooked off in the resulting fire."

"I assume the people in the SUV were fricasseed as well. Anyone else involved?"

"No, Mr. President. The local ME doesn't have anything to work with. It's as if the two men were cremated. We . . ."

"If there are only ashes left, how do we know they were men?"

"Because a toll taker in Oklahoma responded to the APB put out after the hijacking. She called in a tip that two men were driving a vehicle similar to one of those listed. The local 911 operator contacted the OHP and one of their troopers ran them down just before crossing into Missouri."

"And the other four?"

"A Texas Ranger killed two men at a Shell station after one of them soaked his partner in gas and was about to set him on fire. The other man charged the Ranger. Not his smartest move. Anyway, the two they were transporting were recovered and moved to Fort Hood."

"Either Ranger injured?"

"No, sir."

"What about the rest?"

"That may be the best news so far."

"Yes?"

"Two Chechen men in a minivan drove up to a Border Patrol Station on I-10 west just outside of Blythe, California. Apparently, whoever gave them directions didn't consider checkpoints being *inside* the U.S."

"Did they try to run?"

"They did, sir. But, as we learned in Vietnam, there are two things you can't outrun . . ."

"A bullet . . ."

". . . and a radio. The feds at the checkpoint called CHP, who laid down some tire shredders a few miles west. The two in the minivan weren't smart enough to get off the highway and meld into the local background, which was certainly a break for us."

"Have they been interrogated?"

"Yes, sir. Looks like whoever controlled them did so in the blind. They only knew where to pick up their instructions, the vehicle they were driving, the GPS coordinates where they would receive the Stingers, and directions to a hotel in San Bernardino."

"You're sure we wrung out all they know?"

"Yes, Mr. President. They got the same treatment as *Khalid Sheikh Mohammed*. They didn't hold back any more than he did, and with a lot less effort."

☆☆☆

FIFTEEN

"Have the Americans responded to the offer in the allotted time?" the bearded man asked.

"They have not," the strategist answered.

"Are the items properly dispersed?"

"They are on their way to Dallas, Chicago, Washington, Atlanta, Los Angeles, and New York's John F. Kennedy, two to each city. However, I have concerns."

"What concerns, Asad?"

"The men carrying them to Washington have not made contact at the last two scheduled times and those traveling to Atlanta missed the last check in."

"Is there any announcement of them being captured?"

"No. There are reports of automobile crashes along the planned routes, but none specific enough to identify any of our movements."

"Have our agents been instructed to blend in with the people in the Great Satan's belly?"

"They have, but some hold fiercely to their identity and appearance. But I will see to it immediately that they are reminded of the greater importance."

"We can reverse a change in appearance but not a failure of the opportunities offered. Also remember, we cannot concern ourselves about issues outside our control, Asad. We dispersed the shipments because even the best net does not capture all the fish. We will accomplish a great victory if only a few find their targets. Put them to use after our first strike when Americans think they have seen the worst. Start with the middle of their country – Chicago or Dallas – then the other major cities. Save the Washington airport for last – I believe they call it *Reagan* National. Let hell's fire rain down on the Satan's government."

The strategist bowed slightly. "I will pass your instructions on immediately. All praise be to Allah, *The Most Gracious, The Most Merciful.*"

* * *

Dawn behind a thick cloud cover made the scene Dayo Amoako surveyed seem virtually colorless. The green of the hotel's lighted sign offered the only visual effervescence.

Dayo waited in silence in the battered, blue Toyota Corolla. The hotel parking lot on Policy Drive, Belcamp, Maryland, just south of I-95, had little activity in the early hours of the morning, which would make it easier to spot the party he waited for. He had infinitely more information about how to avoid the hotel's security cameras than the person he waited for – none in the latter's case – other than to look for a white Ford Taurus.

Although minor, this was Dayo's first "mission," and he was anxious to show he could follow orders and deliver results. His instructions had come from a man he didn't know on a dark park bench in McLean, Virginia. The irony of the location wasn't lost on Dayo – just south of the Great Satan's CIA headquarters on Route 123.

I will hide in plain sight in the service of Allah, The Most Merciful, he thought.

He unscrewed the cap of a bottle of water and lifted it to his lips. The plastic container distorted the headlights of a car entering the parking lot. Dayo lowered the bottle.

A white Taurus pulled into a space opposite Dayo's and flashed its headlights – two short, one long – Morse code for "U."

Dayo responded with the Toyota's headlights – two short blinks – Morse code for "I."

The driver of the Taurus opened the door and stepped out. To Dayo's surprise it was a woman. As she approached the driver's side of the Toyota, Dayo pressed the power window button and the glass slid into the door with a thump, three inches of it still exposed.

The woman reached the side of Dayo's vehicle and looked down at him. She held a large covered plastic storage container with both hands. On top of it sat a small package about half the size of a shoebox, wrapped in brown paper and secured with heavy rubber bands. Setting the storage box on the ground, she picked up the brown package and extended it toward the Corolla's window.

"Be very careful with these." The soft southern drawl from a woman exacerbated Dayo's surprise.

Handing the small package though the driver's side window, she continued. "Keep them separate at all times from the contents of this box and out of sight. If you're stopped by the police for any reason, and they ask your permission to search the car, refuse. Now, pop the trunk."

"You . . . you're a *woman*," Dayo stammered, taking the small package with both hands.

"You're very observant . . . *numbnuts*! Do you think that only those with *testicles* can fight a war?"

The woman's harsh response surprised Dayo more than her gender. "I . . . No, I don't think that," he said, and added with a tinge of anger in his voice. "I do expect *respect* from a *woman*! You *will show* me that respect!"

"Fuck off, asshole! There's your *respect*! Now, pop the fucking trunk and beat it back to your mosque." The woman's dark eyes flashed with anger as she picked up the plastic container and walked to the back of the Corolla.

Dayo set the package on the passenger seat. Reaching toward the floor, he lifted a lever and heard a lock's "click."

The woman set the large container into the trunk, used her sleeve-covered elbow to force its lid closed, and walked back to the driver's side door. "*Jesus*! Are you *limited*? I said, keep them *out of sight*! Like . . . *under* the front seat!"

Reaching to his right, Dayo took the package – with a gentle touch – and slowly slid it under the back of the front passenger seat.

"Know this, and remind those above you. What I've given you is very special. There is no more left. Use it wisely, in places where the element of confusion would be a major advantage." The woman turned and walked back to her Taurus.

Dayo had no idea what she meant. As he watched her drive away, his anger at her disrespect escalated. *There will come a day . . .*

☆ ☆ ☆

The flashing smartphone in the *Coyote News* White House correspondent's lap told him he had received a new text message. He pressed an icon on the screen to retrieve it. After reading it twice, he raised his hand.

The daily briefing was nearly over when the White House Press Secretary looked over at him. "Yes, Wendell?"

"*Al Jazeera* just reported a few minutes ago that al-Qaeda is claiming to have stolen a number of Stinger missiles and has offered to return them to the U.S. in exchange for an undisclosed amount. Can you comment on that?"

"That's ridiculous. I don't know how they could get their hands on Stingers."

"By hijacking a truck in New Mexico, according to the report."

☆ ☆ ☆

Shortly after 11 a.m., a well-dressed woman, wearing a broad-brimmed hat that matched her plum-colored suit, pulled the front door open and entered the Freeport Bank branch on the corner of Light and Churchill Streets. As she approached the customer service desk to the right of the front door, a woman looked up and smiled.

"Good morning, ma'am. How can I help you?"

"I need to get into my safety deposit box. Has anything changed now that the bank has a different name?"

"No, all the systems are the same. The staff has been changed. The Freeport executives believe that new people will enhance our service level and customers' satisfaction." The woman behind the desk rose, and extended her hand. "I'm Addison Monti."

The woman seemed to recoil from the gesture. "I . . . I never shake hands. It just gives you other people's germs."

The bank's representative didn't miss a beat. "Oh, I understand completely." She came around her desk and started toward the back of the building where a large vault door stood open. "If you'll follow me, please," she said over her shoulder. "Do you have your key card?"

"Yes."

"Isn't technology wonderful? We used to have to keep signature cards and people had to sign in all the time. Now, with biometrics, we save time and trees."

Without comment, the woman followed Addison Monti to a wooden stand next to the vault's door. On it sat a magnetic card reader with a two-inch wide slot across its front and a DigiRead fingerprint reader. Monti took a spray bottle of blue liquid from a shelf above the stand and pulled a tissue from a box on the stand next to the DigiRead. She sprayed the fingerprint cup with a quick press of the bottle's pump and wiped the resulting mist away with the tissue.

"If you'll just insert your safety deposit card in that little slot, please, and put your thumb on the fingerprint scanner when its green light comes on."

"Which thumb?"

Monti gave the woman a quick sideways glance. "Whichever you used when you set up the account."

"It was so long ago, I don't remember," the woman responded.

"Well, most people use their right, since they're right-handed."

"Okay." The woman moved to the stand, turning so her back blocked Monti's view of the scanner. After inserting a magnetic card, the LED turned green and the device made a small "beep." She placed her right thumb on the device and waited. After less than five seconds, the reader made a sound less friendly than the first and the LED turned red.

Monti recognized the sound without seeing the reader. "You need to remove your thumb for at least five seconds so the reader will reset. Then try again, pressing a little harder this time."

The woman complied and after a few seconds the reader beeped twice.

"Okay," Monti said. "You can try again now."

The woman's next attempt was no more successful.

"I think you should try your left thumb," Monti suggested. "However, you only get one attempt with it. If it's not successful, the system will lock you out for twenty-four hours."

"*What*? That's unacceptable."

"It's the three strike security feature that's built into the system. We have no ability to alter or override it."

"Please spray this thing again. Maybe it's dirty."

Though aggravated, Monti didn't show it. "Yes ma'am, if you'll just step back, please."

The woman moved out of the way and Monti repeated the earlier action with the bottle of liquid and another tissue.

"There you go. Please try again."

Again the woman moved into a position that blocked Monti's view of the reader. A few seconds after placing her left thumb on the DigiRead, it made a soft beep and its LED turned green.

"Success!" Monti said in a cheerful voice that masked her aggravation. "Now, please follow me into the vault. You have two minutes to enter your password before the system resets. Would you like a private room?"

"Yes."

✳ ✳ ✳

"Are you *insane* or totally *incompetent*?" The *imam* didn't wait for a response from his assistant. "You used an asset of incredible value as a transport . . . a *mule*? What if he had been stopped and arrested?

"*Go*! Leave my sight, and pray that Allah, *The Most Merciful*, does not punish your incredible stupidity!"

✳ ✳ ✳

"How did you find out about this? Nobody's supposed to know outside of the DOD and Homeland Security," POTUS asked the Secretary of State.

The Secretary stood nervously in front of the *Resolute* desk. POTUS had not invited him to sit down. "An Al Jazeera reporter called our Public Information Office asking if the posting on an al-Qaeda website was true. Have they stolen Stinger missiles?"

"Oh, *Jesus*!"

"There's more, sir."

"What else could there be!"

"Our OIG hotline got a call about this as well."

"The same day?"

"No, sir. The call came in three days ago, Mr. President. I can play the recording, if you like."

"And some moron decided a call about Stinger missiles wasn't important and sat on it?" POTUS said, his face becoming crimson.

"Sir, we get dozens of crank calls every day. She had no way of knowing this was real, especially since her knowledge of our military weapons doesn't cover MPADS. She works for State, not DOD," the Secretary said, a defensive tone creeping into his voice.

"Be in the situation room in fifteen minutes with the recording. I want the National Security team, Defense and Homeland Secretaries, CIA Director, and the JCS to hear it. This is a complete catastrophe."

✦ ✦ ✦

SIXTEEN

The assemblage in the White House Situation Room wore expressions that couldn't have been more serious if each of their families had just been executed as they listened to the recorded conversation demanding ransom for the Stingers.

When it finished, POTUS looked down the long table and made eye contact with every other person there.

"Okay, we know someone stole a truckload of MANPADS. We don't know who for sure, but al-Qaeda is claiming on one of their websites that they have them. It won't take long for the word to spread faster than Europe's black plague in 1347. Fear of American aircraft being targeted like the Arkia Israeli Airlines was in 2002 over Mombasa will bring travel to a screeching halt at the height of the season. It'll be a financial disaster for our air carriers and others flying in and out of the U.S. The demand for their return is two hundred million. Needless to say, we're not doing that. So, what's our next move?"

The National Security Advisor spoke first. "Mr. President, I believe we need to ensure that no one in the U.S. contributes to this theft story, especially not Roswell Manufacturing."

The Secretary of Defense responded. "Roswell won't admit that they *manufacture* Stingers, much less that a shipment was hijacked."

POTUS shook his head. "Yeah, well, that's a moot point now. It's out in the open. *Coyote News'* White House correspondent ambushed the Press Secretary a little while ago with a question about the hijacking."

A collective groan circled the table.

The Secretary of Defense spoke. "Mr. President, we know that the truck's GPS system went dark near a road that leads directly into Mexico. I've ordered extensive Predator surveillance over the Mexican territory we believe . . . ."

The Secretary of State interrupted. "Did you get permission from the Mexicans for these overflights?"

"*Fuck no*, Marge. Why would I ask a corrupt government for permission? First, it might tell them something they didn't already know. Second, some asshole might try . . . in fact, probably would try to line his pockets with the information."

POTUS raised his hand. "Okay, folks. We're all tense, but let's remain civil."

"Mr. President, this could cause an international rift in our relations with Mexico."

"Marge, if that becomes a problem, we'll deal with it. For all we know, a Mexican drug cartel pulled this heist off. If you get a ration of shit from your Mexican counterpart, tell him that our continuation of foreign aid is contingent on their explicit cooperation in a highly sensitive security situation. We've poured a ton of money down that rat hole. Frankly, this may be a blessing in disguise as far as getting the Mexicans back in line and working *with* us for a change.

"So, back to next steps," POTUS said. "Assuming we can find the cargo, then what?"

The Secretary of Defense spoke again. "We dispatch a retrieval team with a *permissive* operation plan."

The Secretary of State looked across the table with a quizzical expression. "*Permissive* operation plan? What does that mean?"

POTUS answered the question. "It means whoever is found with the missiles isn't heard from again."

"So, now you're going to attack a foreign country and murder its citizens?" the Secretary of State asked.

"Marge, do you have the slightest idea what those Stingers could do in the wrong hands?"

"I do indeed, Mr. President. However, starting a war with Mexico will produce another long list of exposures."

The Secretary of Defense chuckled. "I seriously doubt the Mexicans are going to offer any resistance or invade the U.S.. . . . other than the illegal invasion going on every day."

The Secretary of Homeland Defense felt his smartphone vibrate in a breast pocket. After glancing at it and reading a text from a deputy, he cleared his throat. "Sir, I have a couple of pieces of good news."

"Well, we sure as hell could use some of that! What is it?"

"We believe we know where the missiles may be. The truck's GPS system came on this afternoon in La Pesca, Mexico."

* * *

At 2:38 a.m. outside tiny Milliganville, Maryland, southeast of Baltimore, Eastern Railroad's train number 291 rumbled down the tracks. In the darkness ahead of the three engines – in an elephant-style lash up, pulling forty-two freight cars – lay a spur line to the Amalgamated Seed Company. The junction switch at the point where the main and spur lines met had been thrown to the spur the previous evening to allow several Amalgamated boxcars to be shipped. An Amalgamated yard worker would later swear he had thrown the switch back into its normal north-south position after the boxcars departed.

However, at 2:39 a.m., train number 291 veered off the main track at forty-seven miles per hour. Within seconds, it destroyed the steel reinforced terminus near MD State Highway 21 and plowed a thirty-foot gorge across the two-lane road. Finally, all three engines and eighteen of the rail cars lay scattered and smoking in the dark, like giant toys.

The ninth of the forty-two freight cars began to release slightly more than sixty tons of liquefied chlorine gas. The area downwind of the wreck quickly became covered with a deadly, low-hanging, yellow-green cloud as the liquid expanded 450 times.

The impact of the wreck threw an Amalgamated night watchman to the floor of the guard shack a hundred yards away. The surprised man pulled himself to his feet with the aid of a nearby desk. He grabbed a large flashlight and went to investigate. Outside, a pungent, bleach-like odor met him immediately. Within seconds, he stood in the waist-deep fog.

By the time he was able to pull a flip cell phone from a pants pocket, opening it with one hand, his eyes were flooded with tears – the phone's keypad blurred beyond recognition. Dropping his light, he took the phone with both hands running his thumbs over the keypad. Through feel alone he pressed the 9 key with his right thumb and the 1 key twice with his left.

* * *

The *Angry Panda*'s engine finally rumbled to life. Its captain quickly ordered a course be set for La Pesca, in Mexico.

★ ★ ★

"You hear about the train crash this morning?" Morgan asked his partner.

"Yeah. I heard it on the radio comin' into the office. Nine dead and a bunch more in piss-poor shape," Hermann said, shaking his head.

"Milliganville won't be the same for a long time," Morgan commented. "That chlorine gas is going to kill or damage everything it comes in contact with. Electronics, birds, insects, shrubbery, trees, you name it. The area in the immediate vicinity of the wreck is going to be a no man's land for years."

"Wasn't chlorine gas used during World War One?" Hermann asked.

"Yup."

★ ★ ★

The Secretary of Defense ended a call on his secure cell phone. "The advance team is forming, Mr. President."

"How is this going to work?" POTUS asked.

"Three teams: surveillance, forward and hit. The surveillance team will arrive twenty-four hours in advance, set up communications, verify the ground situation and secure a sniper overwatch position that the forward team will occupy upon their arrival. The forward element will receive the hit team, provide the sniper cover and coordinate the assault. They'll pick up vehicles and have them waiting at the landing zone. The . . ."

"Pick up vehicles from where?" the President asked.

"Probably the streets or an auto dealership," the CIA Director answered.

"You mean *steal* them?" the Secretary of State asked, not bothering to conceal her sarcasm.

"Yes, Marge. I guess we could call Hertz and make Gold Reservations, but I doubt they have that service there in the middle of the night!" the CIA Director shot back.

The Secretary of Defense shook his head following the exchange. "Now, if I might continue. The hit team will fly in on two Little Bird helicopters with four men per aircraft sitting on racks mounted on their sides. Once on the ground, they will ride to the site in the provided vehicles and take it down.

"When they've secured it, they'll conduct a quick inventory. If the entire shipment of forty-eight missiles is on site, there's no way to retrieve all of them without a lot of activity and noise. That means destroying them in place."

"Did you listen to the ransom recording carefully?" the Secretary of State asked. "The man said: 'We have a number of Stinger missiles *spreading* across America . . .' If that's true, we already *know* that all the missiles are not in Mexico!"

"I take your point, Marge."

"Won't destroying them create a lot of *noise*?" the Secretary of Homeland Security asked

The Defense Secretary nodded. "Yes, and the noise will serve as a distraction for the teams' departure. The forward team will exfiltrate with the hit team. The surveillance team will have already flown out."

POTUS nodded. "How do you destroy forty-eight Stingers 'in place'?"

"With thermite grenades, sir. Plus, each of the Stingers comes with two thermal batteries. They . . ."

"Thermal batteries?" POTUS asked.

"Yes, Mr. President. They're molten salt batteries. The electrolyte is solid and inactive at normal ambient temperatures, meaning they last *forever*. Which makes the argument that missing or stolen Stingers have a limited shelf life pure bullshit. *All* the stinger components have to be destroyed if we cannot carry them home.

"Anyway, the thermite grenades will cause the thermal batteries to go, the rocket motors to ignite or detonate. The warheads will explode and create an even bigger mess down there, as well as destroy the other important components like the grip-stocks. We'd do that just for spite! But in truth we have to thoroughly destroy every element of that shipment."

✶ ✶ ✶

The phone rang on Joe Costa's desk as he set down a large insulated coffee mug. "Officer Costa."

"Holcomb here. You up to speed on what happened in Milliganville this morning, Joe?"

"I am, Major."

"Well, maybe not all of it," Holcomb said. "Al-Qaeda just claimed responsibility for it."

"*What*? How could those fuckin' ragheads even know about it yet?"

"Careful, Joe! You can get your nuts in a wringer real fast talking like that." Holcomb paused several seconds to let his message sink in. "The story broke within an hour on the radio news networks. A local al-Qaeda operative probably just phoned home."

"Could be," Costa commented. "But still, that's awful fast for them take credit for something, especially when they haven't said *shit* about the Arizona train crash. We know that wasn't an accident."

"That's true, but we have to take this seriously for the time being. Make sure everything is shipshape in case we need to respond within our jurisdiction or assist somewhere else. This may be the *new* war."

"Yeah, everybody learns how to fight the *last* war. Damn few learn the trends, think ahead, and remain vigilant. That's especially true for politically pressured, short-sighted, career ladder climbing, command-type *assholes* . . . meaning no disrespect, Major."

"None taken, Joe. But it's the system we have to work with."

"That's a scary thought. Remember the sulfur-dioxide spill the EVU responded to a few years back?"

"I do. The hose draggers were about to wash the area down when you guys pointed out that $SO_2 + H_2O = H_2SO_4$, AKA sulfuric acid."

"That's right," Costa said, chuckling. "We recovered the bulk of the sulfur-dioxide before they could create a self-inflicted wound. A buddy of mine who owns a bunch of body shops was really pissed that we saved all those cars' paint jobs."

* * *

Baltimore-Washington International (BWI) Airport – once a sleepy, little known and very convenient way to get into its namesake and suburban Maryland outside of D.C. – hummed with Friday afternoon travelers. Business people going home for the weekend, and vacationers trying to get away from home, stood in long lines at every airline check-in counter.

A young black man dressed in Army desert camouflage BDUs and a matching patrol cap – wearing a Specialist 4th class insignia – entered the main terminal building through automatic doors pulling a small wheeled carry-on bag. To his left, a sign pointed to Concourse C. To his right, signs directed passengers to Concourses B and A. Had anyone been paying attention, the fact that he wore black loafers, rather than combat boots, might have aroused curiosity or even a sense of alarm.

Several rows of chrome tensabarrier stanchions snaked passengers back and forth between the man and R&F Airline's check-in counter. Responding to fledgling Rich & Famous' just announced nineteen-dollar promotional fare from BWI to New York's LaGuardia Airport – roundtrip – hundreds of people waited to take advantage of the bargain, including seven children with terminal cancer en route to see *The Lion King* playing at New York City's Minskoff Theater. At least one of each child's parents accompanied the group.

The young man surveyed the people behind the black ribbons closest to him. It only took a few seconds to pick out what he needed to. Near the first turn in the line toward the check-in counter, another black man wearing a Vietnam Veteran baseball cap caught his eye and he walked toward him quickly.

✯ ✯ ✯

Teresa Brewer trotted ahead of her parents and took a position with her back to R&F's snaking check-in line. Norma and Bob – heading to New York City for their fiftieth wedding anniversary – came through BWI's automatic doors a few seconds later. Norma smiled and waved to the video camera in Teresa's hands.

"Look happy, Daddy! This flight is the best deal you're going to get this weekend!"

"Hey! I'm with my best girls!" Norman responded, waving. "Nothing makes me happier than that, even saving a few bucks . . ."

✯ ✯ ✯

"Excuse me, sir. I forgot my wallet at the curbside baggage check. Could you watch my carry-on while I run back to get it?"

"Sure thing, son," the Vietnam veteran said. "Where are your boots, Specialist?"

The young man looked down at his feet and hesitated momentarily. "Somebody stole 'em and my low quarters out of my truck. I know I'm going to catch hell for these loafers, but they're all I had."

"If that's the worst thing you have to face, you'll be in good shape. Go on, get your wallet."

"Thanks!" The young black man started to turn back toward the doors, then hesitated momentarily and faced the older man. "Thank you for your service to our country, sir."

"You too." The older man watched the as the SP4 trotted toward the automatic doors, then turned and moved ahead a few feet in line pulling his own and the adopted bag.

Outside the terminal, the young man didn't stop at the nearest curbside baggage check-in point. He passed it and continued to a double-parked, dark SUV sitting near the front of a line of vehicles discharging passengers and their bags. Once the young man seated himself in the front passenger seat, the driver pulled away slowly.

The SP4 pulled a cheap throw-away cell phone from the cargo pocket on his right leg and began punching numbers into the keypad.

☆ ☆ ☆

At Dulles International Airport, a little less than twenty-seven miles outside of Washington, D.C., all passengers arriving from international locations must be cleared by immigration officials. Once passports and visas have been checked and stamped, hundreds of people collect their baggage from the large, revolving, silver carousels, pass through customs checkpoints and finally into a large hall at the west end of the airport's first floor.

A number of airlines' daily flights arrive in mid- to late-afternoon, ensuring a large crowd of family, friends, drivers, and airport staff in the area between 2 p.m. and 6 p.m. Unlike departing passengers, there is no security screening between Dulles' parking lots and the waiting area for international arrivals. At 4:08 p.m., well over three hundred men, women and children stood shoulder to shoulder straining to see familiar faces emerge from the automatic glass doors sliding open and closed.

Down a narrow hall, to the right of the exiting international arrivals, a locked, metal door of DHS' Customs and Border Protection Global Entry processing point blew inward violently, slicing a CBP officer nearly in half. The blood-splattered small office and an adjoining training room were instantly filled with dust, debris, and a cacophony of anguished screams.

☆ ☆ ☆

Hunter Morgan pulled the door open and stood aside, allowing Andrew Hermann to enter the Tasman for President Campaign headquarters in Northwest Washington, D.C.

Both men stopped inside the door. None of the fifty or more people in the large room in front of them were facing in the detective's direction. Every set of eyes were focused on a large flat-screen TV mounted to the back wall. Several people wept openly.

A local, grim-faced D.C. news anchor occupied the left side of the screen. The other half of the two-shot, screen right, displayed a picture of the front of BWI Airport.

"There are currently no reports of the number of dead and injured. However, Suzanne Martin, of our Baltimore sister station WTCC, was in another part of the terminal when the bomb exploded. I understand we have her on the phone now.

"Suzanne, what can you tell us?"

"Oh, *God, Jim*! *It's a nightmare here*! There are bodies and body parts *everywhere*! The bomb appears to have gone off just inside the terminal, near the check-in line for R&F Airlines. There's a hole in the floor where I think it exploded. I'm standing at least ninety feet from R&F's counter and there are people with injuries all around me. The front windows of the terminal are blown out, and there are people lying on the sidewalk and car alarms going off.

"I've never seen anything like this in my life, including my time in Iraq and Afghanistan! Oh, God! *Oh, God . . .*"

Morgan turned to his partner. "Let's head north. They're gonna need help."

✳ ✳ ✳

Outside the District's Tasman for President Office, a news crew arrived from the local NBC affiliate to get comment from the campaign on the BWI bombing. Shooting B-roll outside the front door, their camera captured the detectives' departure.

✳ ✳ ✳

Within minutes of the BWI bomb detonation, airport police notified Homeland Security, the FBI and ATF. A national communication quickly followed to all transit systems raising the nation's threat level to "Red" or "Imminent."

Officials at Dulles received the notification less than a minute before the automatic doors between the international arrivals hall and the daily parking lot shattered outward, extending the bomb's kill zone across the traffic lanes for taxis and shuttle buses. Glass shards puréed arriving and departing pedestrians in the crosswalk.

Ground stops were implemented at BWI and Dulles freezing all movement on the airports' numerous taxiways. Planes preparing for departure from scores of Jetways received instructions to unload their passengers for security rescreening.

The second blast brought a national emergency alert to all U.S. airports. The FAA quickly suspended departures and ordered in-flight aircraft within U.S. airspace to seek the nearest opportunity and land.

The FBI's Evidence Response teams began rushing to the affected airports. Representatives from the FBI's National Security Branch, Counter Proliferation Unit, Counter Terrorism Division, WMD specialists and, members of the Terrorist Screening Center – all reporting to the Office of the Director of National Intelligence – became engaged, remotely or on-site.

Law enforcement organizations across the nation received situational bulletins. The Joint Terrorism Task Force and all federal agencies received the same threat elevation orders. Airports across the nation were ordered to institute checkpoints and enhanced TSA screening at their facilities' perimeters.

Bedlam became America's byword as the Nation ground to a halt.

PART II
THE ACTIONS
"That must have been like shooting fish in a bucket!"

SEVENTEEN

The Maryland State Fire Marshal's office – a division of the Maryland State Police – maintains one of the state's dedicated bomb squads, though the MSFM stands alone and operates outside the purview of much of the MSP's command and control structure. The MSFM's very well-equipped bomb squad is headquartered at BWI.

Many an hour has been spent arguing over whether bomb squads should ever be part of any firefighting organization or exclusively bonded to the "Thin Blue Line." Pride and prejudice run deep in both camps. However, on rare occasions, one side will ask the other for assistance. This was one of those days.

"Grabowski."

"Jim, Holcomb here. Someone just detonated a bomb at BWI, near the R&F check-in counter. There's no current count of dead and wounded, but the initial reports are that it's *real* bad! I want you and Costa to go down and assist the State Fire Marshal's bomb squad. You'll never get there on the road, it's a complete madhouse. Go to the chopper pad. I'll have a bird waiting for you."

"Yes, sir."

★ ★ ★

The Baltimore Police Department helicopter banked right, offering Grabowski and Costa a clear view of the chaotic scene outside BWI's terminal. Orange, red, and blue flashing lights ran in a string from the front of Thurgood Marshall Airport's misshaped "U" main building, back along I-195 all the way to I-95 North and South. Traffic on I-95 appeared to be stopped in both directions before the afternoon haze curtailed their view.

More first responder vehicles sat on the top floor of the parking lot opposite the terminal. The traffic scene below made Wednesdays before Thanksgiving look like a slow day at a private airfield.

"*Fuck me!*" Costa said into the voice activated microphone attached to his headset.

✶ ✶ ✶

The Sikorsky UH-60 Blackhawk from the Army's aviation battalion hovered almost silently above the Hotel *Desde el Embarcadero* at mid-*siesta* thanks to its specially modified noise reduction rotor assemblies. If anyone had been on the hot streets to see the chopper, it would have drawn little interest since *Ejército Mexicano* – Mexican Army – and a Mexican flag had been painted on its tail.

In less than a minute, a four-man Army Special Forces Team fast-roped down to the hotel's roof with their gear. As soon as the last man completed the transition, the Blackhawk swung to the north toward the tip of Texas.

From their vantage point, the men had a clear view of the buildings surrounding the GPS coordinates received from the stolen truck. Only one seemed capable of holding the forty-eight Stinger cases.

After setting up a secure radio SFC Hanrahan, the team's senior NCO and Commo sergeant, phoned home. "Gallant Jester, Gallant Jester, this is Gallant Jester four-seven. Over."

A few seconds later: "Gallant Jester, go ahead Four-seven."

"We are in place and ready to rumble. Over."

"Negative on the rumble, Four-seven. Events in CONUS have delayed your counterparts. Remain on-site and observe the target. Will update you Alpha-Sierra-Alpha-Papa. Until then keep eyes on the prize. Over."

"Four-seven, roger that. Out."

"What the fuck!" Hanrahan said. "We've been put on the back burner. Something happened back in the states."

"What?" Major Dick Badger, the team leader said. "Rodriguez, do you have your multiband radio?"

"Yeah, Major."

"See if you can raise a local radio station. Maybe they're talking about it here. It's hard to imagine anything usurping this mission."

Rogers pulled a small gray radio from a BDU pocket, switched it on and rotated the tuning dial. It didn't take long to find a station with an announcer speaking in a hurried and excited voice. "*Cientos han muerto de terroristas suicidas en los dos aeropuertos bombardeadas cerca del Aeropuerto Nacional de Washington DC. Reagan no ha sido atacado.*"

"Jesus! Suicide bombers at BWI and IAD. This guy says there are hundreds dead. Apparently, Reagan wasn't hit, at least not yet."

★ ★ ★

The hot afternoon sun had begun to fade when the *Angry Panda* slowed to a halt and dropped anchor. Within half an hour, the first mate and two deckhands pointed three sixteen-foot, gray Zodiacs toward *La Pesca*.

★ ★ ★

EIGHTEEN

"... thirty-one dead and that's just counting the bodies with enough left of them to check for a pulse. There are parts strewn around like scraps on the floor of a butcher's shop, Major." Costa pulled a handkerchief from a back uniform pocket and wiped his forehead. BWI's air conditioning offered nature little competition now that most of the terminal's windows were blown out.

"Yes, sir. We'll do whatever we can to assist and give you an update when we know more." Flipping his phone closed and slipping it into a shirt pocket, Costa turned to Grabowski studying something on the floor near one of the sets of automatic doors. "Sounds like things are a lot worse at Dulles. That device detonated in the middle of a large crowd.

"What have you got, Jim?" Costa said, looking over Grabowski's shoulder.

"Take a look," Grabowski said, setting his black felt-tip pen next to, then snapping a digital picture of, a blood-stained, stainless steel ball bearing. The pen would give perspective to the picture, in place of a police evidence marker. There weren't enough of those in the State of Maryland to cover BWI's crime scene.

"Looks like a half-inch," Grabowski commented, looking at the picture on the camera's LCD screen. "These went through people like a magnum round through a melon."

The ball bearing lay near the base of what had earlier been a glass wall. A few inches away, a passenger's early check-in boarding pass fluttered, then lifted in a slight breeze. Its slide across the blood-stained floor revealed a video camera enclosed in the fingers of a severed hand.

"Maybe we got . . ."

✱ ✱ ✱

Lucky.

Staring at the television screen – its audio muted – John Mallard watched a recorded shot from one of the many TV news helicopters circling as close to BWI as the FAA had allowed before forcing all aircraft back to the ground.

A little unexpected but very welcome chaos!

✱ ✱ ✱

Baltimore's Druid Hill Park lies in the city's Northwest Quadrant near the Reservoir Hill neighborhood. The park occupies 745 acres of rolling hills, grassy fields, and the Maryland Zoo. Within Druid Park, near the intersection of Lake and Duck Pond Drives, the playground had only two occupants – Monica Stevens, age eight, and her best friend, nine-year-old Rachel Rosen.

The girls were easily picked out through a 3 X 9 X 40 Leupold scope mounted on the .45-70 single shot, Ruger #1 rifle. The rooftop northwest of the intersection of Eutaw Place and Brooks Lane offered an unobstructed view of the playground. Equipped with a two-point mounted suppressor, the hand-casted, 550 grain round's spat could barely be heard on the street in front of the six-story building, much less the playground over two hundred yards away. The massive round sped toward its target at subsonic speed without emitting the typical rifle "crack" made by supersonic bullets.

Rachel fell first. The .45-70 round hit her in the chest with the force of a Union Pacific locomotive pulling into the station. The force flipped her small body backwards, feet over head, onto a slide built for younger children. Death claimed her body long before gravity could.

Monica watched her friend flip – just another of Rachel's frequent silly stunts, though the first somersault she could remember. But Rachel's body impacted the slide hard enough to make it bounce slightly. Surprised, Monica cocked her head slightly to the right, as the shooter slid another 550 grain round into the Ruger's breech and closed it. A moment later it smashed her spine at shoulder height, driving her into the ground face first.

✱ ✱ ✱

Less than two minutes later, Roberta Clever – a senior advisor to Senator Tasman's presidential campaign – slowed another bullet slightly before it exploded the right side of her skull. Gray matter, bone fragments, and blood peppered the windshield and side of her black Cadillac Escalade, parked outside a synagogue, near the corner of Eutaw and Chauncey Avenue.

✳ ✳ ✳

The .45-70 bolt action slammed a fresh round into the chamber. The camouflaged suppressor swung left quickly, then snail-like, tracking another target. The female jogger – obviously pregnant – moved easily along the winding trail next to the northwest tip of Druid Lake.

The first round struck the right side of her bulging belly, spinning her left, spraying blood and amniotic fluid across the trail and grass. She lost her balance, stumbling onto her right side. The second bullet tore through her back, right atrium, ventricle, septum and left ventricle before exiting her left side.

The shooter casually picked up five hot, heavy brass casings, dropping four of them into a breast shirt pocket. After carefully wiping the fifth, a gloved hand stood it upright on the short wall.

✳ ✳ ✳

After leaving Senator Tasman's campaign office, Morgan had called Baltimore's Chief of Detectives – Jan Richmond – with an update on their intention to assist at BWI. Knowing they would never reach the snarled airport in by road, Richmond directed them to go to Reagan National and wait for the department chopper.

Now the two detectives walked along the sidewalk near BWI's baggage claim area in search of the scene commander to offer assistance.

"Want to bet who'll be lead dog in the jurisdictional fight for control?" Morgan asked.

"Let's see. Who do I want to place a wager on? We'll have two DOJ dogs – the ATF because they cover explosives' regulation and the FBI because they cover terrorism – pissing on the same tree and *missing* it. And, Maryland's State Fire Marshal, police, and the Anne Arundel County police just for starters. These days, the EPA could find a reason to horn in too. But . . . I'm going to bet on truth, *justice* and . . . the FBI."

"Hey! Paleface!"

A cold shiver ran down Morgan's spine in competition with a mental grin growing in the back of his mind and memory. He stopped, searching the crowd's faces behind the fluttering yellow police tape to his left.

"Jesus, Morgan! If I was a VC you'd be dead and I'd have your gear and already be two rice paddies away!"

The face he zeroed in on, using the words as a direction finder, had a vaguely familiar look. The wide grin broke down the final barriers in Morgan's memory.

"*Small Deer?*"

"In the flesh, Paleface!"

✷✷✷✷

NINETEEN

The team of Army operators in Mexico watched helplessly as the stolen Stingers were transferred out of the warehouse, loaded onto Zodiacs and ferried to a ratty looking ship off shore. Dusk had turned to dark as the cases moved in groups of three and four per inflatable boat. Night vision equipment made it easy to keep an exact count.

When the last Zodiac did not return to the dock, the team leader knew it would be a long night. "Cat Man. What was your count?" Major Badger asked.

"Thirty-six, sir." SSG Bill Cheshire responded.

"Mine too. Shit! Okay, Hanrahan, call in the fact that the transfer to that garbage scow was twelve short of the total load. And tell 'em the *Angry Panda* is getting underway."

★ ★ ★

"I saw a man with a fishing case leave the building around that time." The apartment's building resident's hand shook visibly. Setting a glass of water on the kitchen table, he looked up at Hermann and Morgan sitting opposite him and his wife.

"A fishing case?" Hermann asked, clearly more interested in the conversation than he had been a few seconds earlier.

"Yeah. It had all kinds of stickers on it for rods, reels, all the big names. You wouldn't need anything that big to hold a rifle that was all broken down into pieces." The thirty-something man glanced at his wife wiping tears from her right cheek with a Kleenex.

"Sniper rifles only come in small cases and pieces in Hollywood," Small Deer injected from the corner of the kitchen near the door. "No sniper worth his salt would disassemble and reassemble his weapon for each use. It wouldn't be remotely accurate. And the fact that no one heard any shots says it was suppressed."

Morgan and Hermann both shot the Indian a "shut up" glance.

"Sorry."

"Suppressed?" the man asked.

"A silencer," Hermann answered. "What did this man look like?"

"I only saw the back of his neck as he went down the stairs. He was a pretty light-skinned Hispanic. Or maybe a black man."

"How about his hands and hair?"

"He had long sleeves, black leather gloves and a Navy watch cap pulled down low. I didn't see any hair."

"It's a little warm for a watch cap. The long sleeves and gloves make sense," Morgan commented.

"So he didn't leave fingerprints?" the resident asked.

"Yeah. And maybe to reduce the amount of GSR on his hands and arms."

"GSR?"

"Gunshot residue. You sure it was a watch cap and not a ski mask with eye and mouth holes?"

"It could have been a mask. I only had view of him for a fraction of a second."

Near 9 p.m. EDT, Hermann got to his feet wearily, closing his notebook and sliding the kitchen chair back a few inches across the hardwood floor. He reached into his breast suit pocket and pulled a brass business card case into view. After opening it, he dropped his contact information onto the kitchen table.

"If you think of anything else, give me a call on my cell, regardless of the hour."

✷ ✷ ✷

. . . killed by a hit-and-run driver in her Federal Hill neighborhood.

Mrs. Moses is survived by her husband, Gordon R. Moses, and her mother, Mrs. William D. French IV of Dundalk . . .

Dusty logged off her *Baltimore Mirror* ID and redirected her Firefox browser to a saved White Pages search link.

How many listings for a William D. French IV could there be in the state, much less Dundalk?

✷ ✷ ✷

"Gallant Jester-four, you are to search the location for any of the missing merchandise and if found, destroy it. You are authorized to use any force necessary to do so. Do you copy? Over."

"Roger that, Gallant Jester. Will advise soonest. Out."

"Major, they want us to check out the warehouse and see if the missing Stingers are there. If so, we're to destroy 'em. They've authorized us to use whatever force necessary."

✭ ✭ ✭

"You took a civilian to a crime scene?"

Anyone who didn't know Jan Richmond wouldn't have been able to detect any anger in his words. Morgan wasn't part of the unwashed. "I've told you about Small Deer, sir. He's an old Army buddy. The Indian saved my life in the Delta."

"I thought you saved *his* life."

Morgan ignored the contradiction. "Sir, when we got the call at BWI about the sniper victims, my first thought was that when pancreatic cancer claimed Bill Wagner last week, it took our ballistics guy too. Small Deer knows weapons and ballistics better than ninety-nine percent of the so-called experts. He was going to be stuck at BWI for Christ only knows how long and I thought it made sense to take him with us."

"So, how much help has he been?" Richmond asked.

"Well, so far . . . none. But I'd strongly suggest keeping him in the loop on this as an advisor to the BPD. At least in the short term."

"Morgan, you know I trust your judgment. But you need to play this very low key. If word gets out that we're using the owner of a string of gun shops as our ballistics guru, you'll find my pelt hanging on the wall at 601 Fayette Street."

"Understand, sir. One last question?"

"Yeah?"

"How do you want us to play the Moses murders?"

"Slide them to the back burner for the time being. This sniper has four bodies – five, if you count the fetus – on his score card, one of them a Tasman aide. Going after the senator under the best of circumstances will put us in a very exposed position. If you can find time to work it quietly in the background, go ahead. But the Druid Park cases are our top priority at the moment for the mayor, not to mention that we'll probably get sucked into the investigational vortex that's going to swirl around the BWI bombing."

✭ ✭ ✭

Getting off the roof of the Hotel *Desde el Embarcadero* proved to be far simpler than any of the Army's four-man team could have imagined. After attaching Knight's Armament suppressors to their M9 pistols and opening the unsecured hatch that provided roof access, they silently climbed down two flights of stairs and past the desk clerk – sound asleep with his head resting on his folded arms. One team member covered the man, the snout of his suppressor aimed at the clerk's head. The man would never know how close he had come to being killed if he so much as turned his head in his sleep.

In the warm night air, they worked their way to the warehouse less than two hundred meters away. Outside the building, the team quickly and quietly checked for alternate entry points. The only way into the building was at the front – not good news for their exit if they had been followed. After nearly two minutes listening for any sign of it being inhabited and hearing none, Sergeant Cheshire spoke. "Major, let me have that common man's lock pick."

Major Badger produced a medium sized bolt cutter and handed it to Cheshire, who snapped the cheap lock on the personnel entrance next to the large sliding doors. A mixture of stale urine and beer greeted their olfactory senses inside. A quick sweep of the building utilizing their night vision goggles proved no one posed a thread and . . . no sign of the missing twelve Stingers.

"Call it in, Hanrahan."

"Yes, Major. Gallant Jester, Gallant Jester, this is Gallant Jester four-seven. Over."

"Go ahead, Four-seven."

"We have negative, repeat negative missing merchandise. Over."

"Roger, Four-seven. Wait. Out."

Several minutes passed as the men silently hunkered down in an outward facing, tight 360° formation just inside the warehouse door. Finally . . .

"Jester four-seven, make your way to extraction point Bravo, repeat Bravo, the grassy area between your current location and your insertion point. Your ride home is inbound at this time. Echo-Tango-Alpha one-five mikes. How copy?"

"Four-seven. Roger that. Moving. Out."

✮ ✮ ✮

Just after 1 a.m., Samantha Morgan rubbed her eyes with balled fists. "Okay, guys. I've got to get some sleep. I have an early morning surgery scheduled."

"Hey, Sam. I'm sorry. I'll get out of here so you two can rack out," Small Deer said, pushing up and out of the overstuffed couch.

"What?" Samantha's eyebrows collapsed into a frown. "You're not going anywhere, Henry. You're staying with us."

"I appreciate that, Sam. But I've already paid for the hotel room."

Morgan chuckled. "I think I can get 'em to give you a refund in the morning. Besides, we're going to need your help with the Druid Park sniper. The chief of D's already put his stamp of approval on it."

"Well . . . if you let me waive my *consulting* fee in payment for room and board . . ."

"Board? Who said anything about feeding your ass?" Morgan said, glancing at Samantha. Her smile reflected his.

"I'll make sure there's a full pot of coffee and something to eat before I head to the hospital.

"It's so great to see you, Henry. But you look too thin. Thinner than you did in the Mekong Delta, as a matter of fact."

"I'm fine, Sam. Just burnin' more calories than I take in. Christ. You're a doctor. Don't you want people to be thin?"

"Henry, there's thin and there's *too* thin. Goodnight."

"Night," both men said in unison.

Samantha walked to Hunter, kissed his forehead, and then disappeared down a hall.

Small Deer dropped back onto the sofa.

"So, Redman. You may be able to bullshit her, but I lived with you for a long time. What's up with the weight?"

"Bladder cancer."

"Jesus! Are you all right?"

"Yeah. I think so. I got pretty good treatment at the VA hospital. Just have to get checked on a regular basis."

"Make sure you do that!" Morgan said, more strongly than he intended to. "As they say in New York City: 'I know you where you live.' No *Indian* medicine man stuff. At least not as a primary. Okay?"

"Yes, sir."

Morgan picked up a note pad from the coffee table in front of the couch. "The ME says it was a .45-70. One of the rounds they recovered from the playground was in good shape. So was the first one to hit the jogger. Anything you might be able to tell about the suppressor from the bullets?"

Small Deer smiled. "First off, whoever picked that size round probably did so because it's relatively slow. The suppressor disperses the gasses to reduce the sound of the firing of the shell. But, you'd still get the telltale 'crack' when the bullet traveled faster than sound, like a .308 round does, for instance.

"Also, that's a huge bullet – or boolit as those of us who cast our own say. You'd use something that massive to bring down an American bison . . . or a human quietly. If they're in good shape, you can probably at least narrow down the weapon to a manufacturer, if not the specific model.

"I only got a quick look at the brass casing found on the roof, but I noticed something that may be important." Small Deer waited for the obvious question.

"Yeah?"

"The head of the case had a vertical mark on it."

"You mean like a scratch?" Morgan asked.

"Exactly. Bolt action rifles push a cartridge into the chamber and then twist to lock it in place for firing. So, there's a rotational motion. There's another way to secure a round in place, known as a 'falling breech block system,' which uses a heavy piece of steel that rides up and down in a channel to open and close the end of the chamber. If that steel block were marred by something during its life – like slamming a cleaning rod into it from the muzzle with the action closed, dirt or a bit of rock accidentally trapped between the face and action during cycling or the slip of a tool during a repair – it would leave a vertical mark across the end of casings as it secured them in place.

"I've got no statistics to back me up on this, but I'd bet that less than two percent of rifles sales today use falling block systems, Winchester high walls, Meacham, and Ruger Number One probably leading the pack."

Small Deer drained the last of his Miller Lite, then added, "Get me a longer look at the shell casing left on the roof and I may be able to narrow down the possibilities.

"The suppressor is another kettle of fish altogether. Modern versions use a series of baffles made out of metal to reduce sound by diverting the expanding gasses from a fired cartridge into hollow chambers between them. They don't touch the bullet as it moves through the suppressor. Others use wipes or metal mesh. A metal mesh might mark up a round as it passes through, but the chances of matching the boolit to the suppressor would be remote at best, unless you could test-fire the weapon and do a comparison. Even then it'd be very iffy.

"If the suppressor weren't aligned properly with the weapon's bore, then it might smack the baffles and dent them. That would leave a mark on the bullet but, again, there'd be little chance of matching the bullet to the suppressor."

"That's all great information," Morgan said rubbing his forehead. "I'll talk to the lab rats in the morning to get you a peek at the casing.

"So, what do you make of all the crap that hit the fan today, Injun?"

"Remember in the Mekong Delta, when we operated with the *friendlies*, the VC were kicking our asses on every operation? We decided to run U.S. only operations because we knew there was a spy in our midst. You said a U.S. only operation would be very small and I told you, 'We don't need strength. We'll use the VC's own strategy against them. Like the medicine of the mole! We'll come out of the ground anywhere, anytime, to fight when the VC least expect it, in their own sanctuary.'

"I think that's what may be happening here. The chlorine spill, BWI and Dulles bombs, the sniper, all of them actions that can't be, or haven't been, part of the post 9/11 tightening of security. The question is: Are all three the work of the same group? Or, are we seeing the work of lone wolves?"

"On different missions?" Morgan asked.

"Maybe."

★ ★ ★

At extraction point Bravo, Major Badger listened for an approaching aircraft from the north-northeast. Standing about forty feet in front of the spot the chopper should land, he slowly spun an infrared Chem-Light tied to a piece of parachute cord.

Within two minutes, a Blackhawk settled into the knee-high grass and Badger ran to its left side, covered by the machine gunner, and waited for the ship's crew chief to approach and make contact. After ensuring Badger's ID, the crew chief returned to the chopper and the major signaled the other members of the team to come out to him.

The three men approached – their long guns slung muzzle down, pistols holstered.

Badger tapped each man on the shoulder, confirming them as friendly to the air crew, each man then ran to the Blackhawk. Badger brought up the rear.

Once all four team members were aboard, Badger eyeballed each man, then declared to the crew chief that all were accounted for. The crew chief boarded last while giving the pilot the okay to take off. Countless practice training sessions allowed the Blackhawk to lift off in less than twenty seconds – homeward bound.

☆ ☆ ☆

Dusty Rhodes sat alone in her living room. The ongoing television coverage of the preceding day's events had deteriorated to rerun footage and stories aired earlier.

Grabowski wasn't home and probably wouldn't be before sunrise at best.

Dusty had written her BWI story, as best she could without actually being able to get to the scene, and filed it from home via the internet. Now, sitting on the couch, staring blankly at the widescreen TV mounted to the wall, she felt exhausted.

Getting to her feet, she picked up the DVR-TV remote, pointed it toward the wall and put her thumb on the "Power" button. Glancing at the television, she noticed two men come out of Tasman's D.C. campaign headquarters just as the screen went black.

"What the hell . . .?"

After fumbling to power the unit back on, the screen lit up again. Dusty rewound the image with the DVR's "Back" button then pressed the "Slow Play" button. As the scene unfolded again, Morgan and Hermann slowly emerged from the building and moved out of the scene at near glacial speed.

☆ ☆ ☆

"I don't give a rat *fuck* about collateral damage, General. We've got a lot of '*collateral* damage' at BWI and IAD. We're going to send a message. You kill American men, women and children indiscriminately and yours have no place they can hide. I'm not going to dick around like we did after 9/11. We're going to kick some *ass*!"

The eyes of the men and women seated along the long sides of the White House Situation Room table were all aimed at President Rodney Thatch.

The Secretary of State, a POTUS favorite, broke the stunned silence. "Sir, we have no good intelligence that confirms al-Qaeda's claims of responsibility. In fact, it's highly unlikely they had anything to do with the chlorine disaster and the Baltimore sniper is likely not their work either. The world will condemn a disproportional response . . ."

"'Disproportional response'?" the Vice President shot across the table before POTUS could speak. "These assholes claimed the train wreck and its environmental catastrophe and murdering five – including two kids and a fetus – in Baltimore. What do you propose? That we destroy a couple of airports in North Waziristan, Paktika, or Helmand Province?"

POTUS held up his hand like a traffic crossing guard near a school, stopping any response. "Madam Secretary, this nation lies face down in the muddy ditch of dread. Hundreds of billions, if not *trillions*, of dollars have been or will be lost in the transportation sector alone. The people's confidence in our ability to keep citizens safe inside America's borders lies dying, if not covered by a white sheet. Taking these steps will renew confidence in the government.

"There are already reports of vigilantes killing Muslims in Baltimore, Atlanta, and New York City. Other *great* Americans are taking the opportunity to loot while the police are stretched thin ensuring security. In places you'd never expect, like a *Walgreens* in Portland, Oregon."

President Thatch turned to the Chairman of the Joint Chiefs of Staff. "General, huddle with the other members of the JCS and come back to me with a plan in *ninety* minutes. I want B-52 strikes that make Vietnam's Arc Lights look like popcorn farts! Put them on any target suspected of harboring al-Qaeda, any of its splinter groups, and the Taliban. That order includes any part of Pakistan.

"I want Tomahawk cruise missiles, five hundred, one and two thousand-pound JDAMS. If you can take out a target with a Smucker's Jelly jar, I want it thrown to ensure maximum probability of destruction.

"I want a list of major Iranian targets to be the primary candidates for the initial strikes. Those sons-of-bitches must have had a hand in this. God knows they've killed enough of our kids in Iraq and Afghanistan with their IEDs alone. Give me a list of ports, power plants, SAM sites. I want our Green Berets and SEALs kicking in the doors of the IRGC and lighting them up big time."

"Sir . . ." was the only word the JCS Chairman was able to say before the crossing guard's hand reappeared.

"I'm not done, General! Take the nation to Threatcon Delta. Lock down every military installation worldwide, even if it's just a mess kit repair center."

POTUS swung his gaze around the long table, looking each Situation Room participant in the eye, before continuing. "I want our borders locked down too. No one in, or *out*. Questions?"

The mild mannered Secretary of Defense cleared his throat. "Mr. President, the actions you outlined will draw enormous criticisms and possibly military response from Russia and China."

"I said, *'questions'*!"

Turning to the Secretary of State, POTUS said, "I want you to meet with the Russian and Chinese Ambassadors, face-to-face, in the next three hours. Tell them we are going to have major military responses to these attacks that are in no way intended to be a threat to their forces or sovereignty. Discuss our plans with *no one* else."

"Yes, sir, but this could drive the Russians and Chinese to strike back."

"When you talk to their ambassadors remind them how much they're going to rake in rebuilding those puppet states. But tell 'em to hunker down, 'cause things are going to go *boom* day and night!"

"Yes, sir."

"Get the Israeli Prime Minister on a secure line. I want to tell Ehud what's going to happen personally."

"Are you going to ask him to get involved?" the Secretary of Defense asked.

"No. I don't want any Jewish fingerprints on this anywhere. They'll get blamed anyway, but at least we'll be able to honestly say they weren't involved."

The several members of the assemblage nodded their agreement.

POTUS continued. "And I want those fucking poppy fields sprayed. If you can't spray 'em, put a few loads of napalm in. We're going to kill 'em physically and *financially*!"

"One last point." POTUS looked around the table again for emphasis. "If I hear a *peep* about any leaks regarding what was discussed in this room today before or after these strikes begin, I'm going to track down the person or persons responsible and publically

crucify them before letting them check-into Leavenworth for *treason.*
That goes for every member of your staffs and . . . each of *you!*"

✲ ✲ ✲

Ninety-seven minutes later, POTUS met with the Secretary of
Defense, the Assistant Secretary for Special Operations, the Director of
the CIA, and the joint chiefs in the Situation Room. Chairman McMillan
cleared his throat, then spoke. "Mr. President, you asked for a plan. We
have two hastily pulled together without a lot of detail. The first plan
would be impersonal with B-52 cruise missiles and naval gunfire
bombardments organized and executed quickly. The second plan would
be personal – a slap in the face – targeting discrete facilities that would
cripple for years to come, but those types of strikes will take careful
planning. We know you want the former. In our earlier meeting, you
mentioned singling out Iran. The question is, how personal *vis-à-vis* Iran
do you want to be?"

"Very personal, General. What did you have in mind?"

McMillan keyed in 29.235481° N 50.31° E on his open laptop
and hit 'enter.'

In a few seconds, an aerial view of an island appeared on a large
flat screen mounted to the wall at the far end of the long conference
table.

President Thatch let out a low whistle. "Well, General, if your
people can take *that* out, we're talking a *sap* in the face. But it looks
very exposed and I don't want to lose more people in this response if we
can't take it out with a high percentage of certainty and few – preferably
no – casualties. But make no mistake, I want to send a message that's as
personal as the death of each of our kids. They helped put American
flags on coffins. Let's make that the spot where the bill starts to come
due for their involvement in terrorism around the world."

The Secretary of Defense hadn't spoken to this point, but now he
cleared his throat and glanced at his Assistant Secretary. Rubbing his
forehead with his left hand, he said, "Mr. President, we need to tell you
about the Diogenes Agreement."

The Secretary of Defense felt a vibration in his breast shirt
pocket. He removed his smartphone and read the newly arrived text,
then muttered "Christ!"

POTUS glanced over and asked, "What's up?"

"Our team in Mexico reported that only thirty-six of the Stingers were loaded onto a ship – the *Angry Panda*. They searched the warehouse, but none of the other twelve were there."

"*Fuck*!" Thatch studied the backs of his hands folded on the table momentarily. "Well, that isn't a surprise, really. We knew at least six wouldn't be there, but it confirms the fact that there are still six unaccounted for and they are undoubtedly within our borders."

POTUS raised his gaze, his eyes sweeping down the meeting attendants until they stopped on the Secretary of Defense. "Make the *Angry Panda* go away."

The Secretary frowned with a very concerned look on his face. "Mr. President, I just want to make sure that you understand what a severe statement that is."

"Bob, they stole Stinger missiles within *our* national borders. I understand. A message has to be sent to these assholes, and anyone who assists them in stealing, transporting and/or selling them, which is: 'Getting involved in anything like this carries a *very* heavy price, with no guarantee of success.' If we don't find the six missing missiles . . . God help the country if we don't . . . we'll *all* pay a heavy price, but especially *everyone* connected with their theft and use. I don't care how and I don't want to *know* how. Just make that ship disappear.

"Now, what the hell is the *Diogenes* Agreement?"

TWENTY

The following morning BWI, Dulles, and every other civilian airport across the nation remained closed, which at least temporarily minimized the threat of the missing Stingers. Only various first responder vehicles had access to the airports. Bomb, criminal and evidence investigators from a variety of organizations – primarily federal – pored over the evidence collected in the last eighteen hours at the terrorism scenes.

External BWI security camera footage clearly showed the arrival of a black Chevy Tahoe – stolen less than an hour earlier – and a man in military uniform stepping out of it near a curbside luggage collection point. After removing a carry-on bag from the passenger-side back seat, the man then walked directly into the terminal, pulling the wheeled, black bag. Inside, BWI's yet to be completed security coverage of the fledgling airline's check-in counter and an inoperative camera offered no direct video of the bomb blast.

Grabowski and Costa – both bone tired – stood in a high-tech ATF command scene van – the Fed's usual arm's length approach to local first responders nowhere in sight due to the severity of the situation. A large LCD monitor bolted to the vehicle's wall played the tape taken from the video camera Grabowski had found the previous day. The recording advanced at two frames per second, allowing the four men and two women watching it time to see details that might have been missed at its normal speed – nearly fifteen times faster.

Norma and Bob Brewer stood facing the camera, smiles frozen on their faces. In a final wave, Norma's raised right hand resembled a schoolgirl asking to use the bathroom or a witness being sworn in court.

The advancing frames showed movement beyond the Brewers, outside the terminal. Over three dozen of them showed a man in desert camouflage moving along the sidewalk, beyond a curbside baggage claim kiosk, at a rapid pace. Then the person shooting the video dropped the camera without stopping the recording, bringing the Brewers' feet into frame. After nearly thirty seconds of footage, the image quickly swung right and captured the feet of people in line to check in at R&F's counter.

The camera angle shifted up slightly, showing the hands and arms of a black man pulling two carry-ons – one inside and one outside of the black tensabarrier strip. Finally, the scene started to swing back to the left. As the two bags moved out of frame, the video ended with a bright flash.

"There's your blast," Costa said quietly. "Can you go back a couple of frames?"

The ATF agent complied, rewinding the tape slightly by punching the left arrow key on her keyboard.

"Notice the larger bag is outside the barrier?" Costa said. "I'm betting the guy is holding it for someone."

"Let's go back to the footage of the couple," Grabowski suggested.

Again, a few keystrokes had the video back to the Brewers' faces.

"See the movement outside. Can you zoom in on that portion of the scene?" Grabowski said, bent over the back of the woman operating the console and pointing to the monitor.

The external portion of the video scene filled the large screen, but became very indistinct. Just large blobs moving across the image in jerky motions every two seconds.

"Can you enhance it?"

"Yeah, I can. But not like the *CSI* shows you see on TV. Even the geniuses at Adobe have yet to figure out how to put pixels where there are none."

With a few keystrokes the images became marginally sharper.

"Can you reduce the amount of zoom?" Costa asked.

At a three times magnification factor, the image revealed all it had to offer. The man in military garb moved past the curbside check-in kiosk and out of frame. The last frame showed a cocked knee, lower leg and foot.

"He's out of uniform," Grabowski said quietly.

"What?" asked a member of the MD Fire Marshal's EOD squad.

"He's wearing loafers," Grabowski answered. "He's in BDUs. He should have on bloused combat boots. Those shoes wouldn't even be appropriate for a dress uniform, much less BDUs."

"Between this and the external airport security footage we saw earlier, I'll bet that's the perp. But, without an image of his face, that's not much help," Costa pointed out.

"Yeah," Grabowski agreed. Looking at one of the ATF agents he asked, "What do we know about IAD?"

"The last I heard an hour ago was that they'd analyzed all the security video frame by frame too. It showed a young black man park in the daily lot, get a large, wheeled suitcase out of the back of a Toyota 4-Runner, then walk into the terminal at the west-most entrance.

"Inside, he walked up the ramp and turned right at the bottom of the escalators, then patiently worked his way into the middle of the arrival hall crowd. Two hundred seventeen dead outright, forty-seven more pronounced at nearby hospitals as of zero-eight-thirty with another couple of dozen or more not expected to survive."

✯ ✯ ✯

Nine time zones east of Washington, D.C., *Judgment Day* – a Boeing B-52H – cruised at 31,000 feet. The aircraft, casually known by Air Force pilots and crew members as a "BUFF" for Big Ugly Fat Fucker, rather than a "Stratofortress," carried a crew much younger than itself and three GBU-31, 2,000-pound Joint Direct Attack Munitions or JDAMs in its bomb bay. On the side of one, scrawled in day glow orange paint, a ground crewman had sent a message: "For BWI and IAD!"

"Ahab-51, this is Wretched-Rabbit-09, requesting three bombs, impact fusing, on Butternut to be in effect for fifteen minutes. Final attack heading is three-five-zero, plus or minus fifteen or one-eight-zero, plus or minus fifteen." The voice via encrypted radio transmission sounded hollow and more distant than it was in reality.

The BUFF pilot keyed his radio's microphone. "Ahab-51 copy, three bombs, impact fusing, three-five-zero or one-eight-zero, plus or minus fifteen. In effect for fifteen minutes."

"Ahab-51, Wretched-Rabbit-09, good read back. Call in with direction."

"Ahab-51, in from the south heading three-five-five."

"Ahab-51, Wretched-Rabbit-09, cleared hot."

"Ahab-51 copy, cleared hot." Then he said into the aircraft's intercom, "You get all of that, Bouncer?"

Below the cockpit, on a windowless deck, the radar navigator acknowledged the target request, triple-checked the coordinates input into each weapon, and then told the pilot they were good to go. "Five, four, three, two, one, bombs away."

On the radio, "Ahab-51 weapons away, impact 55 seconds."

"Wretched-Rabbit copy."

The pilot turned the BUFF hard to port. "Well, that ought to be a real crowd pleaser," he said to the copilot. "Let's go find the tanker, get some gas, and head for home."

"Fine by me," the copilot replied. "Weird mission. Never had eyes on the ground in Pakistan before."

Three minutes behind Judgment Day, a second BUFF carried an identical load of JDAMs with instructions to deposit them on Butternut's three overlapping kill zones – the Air Force equivalent of a "double tap" on a high value target.

✲ ✲ ✲

The strategist rose to leave the bearded man for the evening and opened his mouth to speak. Outside the mud house, the JDAMs impacted at various points in and around the center of the small village, vaporizing each of its forty-two inhabitants and all eight structures. The second load of JDAMs made the surface of the moon look like a tropical paradise compared to the spot the village had occupied.

✲ ✲ ✲

A platoon from SEAL Team 2 – based on the amphibious assault ship USS *DeRemer* (LHD-11) for training operations off Puerto Rico – had a real-world standby mission to assist the DEA if and when necessary. As a result they had a full complement of firearms, ammunition, and explosives at their disposal. Because of the training aspect of their current activities, two team members were away on specialty training, leaving eighteen men aboard.

During a situational briefing, which included *no* one from the ship's crew including the captain, it was decided that recovery of the Stingers could create other real problems afterward if their serial numbers were somehow linked to those stolen. When POTUS said: "Make the *Angry Panda* go away," the Secretary of Defense and Chief of Naval Operations took him literally and passed that order to the

SEALs through the Navy's most secure means of communications. Under the best of circumstances any attack on the *Panda* would be classified as piracy, if it became public knowledge. However, that risk seemed minimal compared to dozens of military and civilian aircraft attacks if the Stingers remained in the wrong hands.

As the *DeRemer* headed in the general direction to find the *Panda*, the SEALs prepped their gear and built demolition charges – incendiary for the Stingers and 20-pound charges for the *Panda*'s hull.

The Navy's Special Warfare Combatant-craft Crewmen – generally known as "Boat Guys" – is a group that maintains and operates an inventory of small craft used to support special operation missions, especially those of SEALs. SWCC are highly and specifically trained in craft and weapons tactics. As the SEALs organized their equipment, the Boat Guys checked the preparation of a Mark V Special Operations Craft – for covering fire in case of problems – and two 11-meter Ridged-hulled Inflatable Boats. Once complete, they determined the intercept routes the small boats would take to ensure a deep water grave for the *Panda*.

Within forty-five minutes of POTUS being informed of the *Angry Panda*'s cargo, the Navy launched a Northrop Grumman E-2 Hawkeye airborne early warning aircraft from the Pensacola Naval Air Station to find and track the ship. It didn't take long before the *DeRemer* received the *Panda*'s position and heading.

✮ ✮ ✮

Baltimore's police commissioner, mayor, and other city officials looked uncomfortable at best in front of a mass of network and local news crews, reporters, and prominent area bloggers. Their faces reflected constant still camera flashes and the tension that accompanied an avalanche of questions regarding the sniper and bombings, while armed with only enough answers to make a snowball.

"That's all we have for you at the moment, ladies and gentlemen. We'll announce further briefings as the investigation warrants." The police commissioner stepped back from the podium with the BPD seal. A forest of microphones sprouted above its dark wood.

"One last question, Commissioner!" a woman's voice shouted.

"That's all . . ."

"Can you tell us why two Baltimore homicide detectives were seen leaving the Tasman for President Campaign headquarters in Washington yesterday?"

If the scene had been part of a late-night comic's featured warm-up video, chirping crickets would have been the only audio. The buzz that had begun when the group thought the news conference was over disappeared like a trailer park in a tornado.

⭐ ⭐ ⭐

Small Deer held the Druid Park sniper's shell casing in a gloved hand, turning it slowly. After peering through a jeweler's loupe for several seconds, he looked up at Morgan, Hermann, and Jan Richmond. "There's nothing unique about the striker. Only Glocks leave footprints in the snow."

"Striker?" Hermann said, glancing at Morgan.

"Firing pin," Small Deer said, before Morgan could respond. "You can always tell a Glock fired case from all others.

"The extractor is another story. From the width of the marks it left, I'm pretty sure your sniper has a Ruger #1. As I told Morgan, there aren't a lot of those around. Any gun dealer who sold one would remember."

Morgan shot Richmond an "I told you so" look under raised eyebrows, wrapped up with a grin.

Richmond acknowledged with a single nod. "Okay, check Maryland, Virginia, Pennsylvania, and West Virginia's records to see if a Ruger shows up."

"Might as well throw in North Carolina," Morgan added.

"If you find the weapon, it will be easy to match the markings on the brass to it. One thing is for sure. If I'm right about the Ruger, your sniper thinks outside the box."

Morgan frowned. "Why do you say that?"

"What's most people's idea of a sniper weapon?" Small Deer asked. Before any of his onlookers could answer, he continued. "That it has to be some heavy barreled, ultrafast, mega-optic laded, compensated, loudenboomer type gun. The Ruger is a single shot, premier sporting rifle, known for unparalleled strength, grace, accuracy, and beauty. It doesn't fit the sniper weapon's image."

⭐ ⭐ ⭐

With the *DeRemer* and *Panda* approaching each other, the time to intercept decreased dramatically. The operational plan had the *DeRemer* staying out of sight over the horizon to avoid detection by the other ship's radar, although the E-2 Hawkeye aircraft had reported that it was currently not operational. Still, the threat of it being easily activated dictated caution.

With the *DeRemer* nearing its operational position, the Hawkeye began jamming procedures across the RF spectrum eliminating the *Panda*'s ability to transmit anything – radio, satellite communications and mobile phones – once the mission began. The aircraft also kept watch for other ships that might enter the area before or during the operation.

At 2230 hours the *DeRemer* launched the Mark V and RHIBs into the darkness. All three craft swung in a wide arc, to avoid any visual contact from the *Panda*, until positioned off its stern. The Mark V carried two members of the SEAL team – snipers – for pinpoint cover fire if needed in addition to its own six-man crew. Each of the RHIBs sped across the dark water with eight SEALS, a deckhand to man a machine gun and a helmsman.

The RHIBs approached slowly, looking for any activity on any rear deck – glowing cigarettes or other movement. At 2315 hours, seeing none, the first RHIB approached the *Panda*'s starboard rear quarter aiming for the "sweet spot" between the bow wake and that coming off the stern where water flows smoothly along a ship's hull. The SEALs intended to board from the rear, since the pilot house-bridge is usually forward and mostly faces the bow of the ship. The stern is also noisy due to the engines, exhaust noise, wake, and churning propellers – an additional benefit. The timing – fifteen minutes after the hour – was designed to avoid changes in the watch so no one would see them come aboard.

Just ahead of the stern wake, the helmsman eased the RHIB's tapered port side nose into contact with the *Panda* and ran up the engine's rpm. This not only maintained contact with the ship, but also provided a very firm lock on the hull for his passengers' infiltration.

A man, next to the forward deckhand on the machine gun, used a lightweight pole to lift a grappling hook and attach it on a rail stanchion. After receiving a visual signal from the Mark V that the *Panda*'s stern was clear – and covered by his seven teammates – he climbed aboard. Once on the stern, he checked the area quickly and repositioned the grappling hook in a more secure location before giving the thumbs-up to the RHIB below.

The first man turned to cover the deck forward as the next two SEALs came aboard and covered the aft and port decks respectively.

The remaining team members quickly joined them and pulled up the demolition charges.

The second RHIB repeated the procedure – save the pole and grappling hook – then took up a covering position with the first. SEAL Team Two's members were now on board, the *Panda*'s crew completely unaware of their arrival.

Four SEALs took up deck positions – two port and two starboard side aft – to deal with any of the ship's crew flushed out during the takeover. All but two of the rest of the men formed up – similar to a SWAT team – and worked their way rapidly through the ship, eliminating the crew as they were discovered. Two went directly to the bridge to secure it and the communications compartment.

At this early hour only two seamen occupied the bridge. A single shot dropped the man at the helm onto the deck. The man on watch turned at the sound. His eyes went wide as he stared into a suppressor's muzzle. He lifted his hands in the air and watched the platoon's senior NCO descend a short stairway at the rear of the bridge to the captain's cabin.

Within a minute, the NCO returned with the clearly startled captain. "Where is the cargo you loaded in Mexico?"

"In the forward hold."

"How is it secured?

"It is not secured."

"No locks, no keys, no combinations?"

"That is correct, sir."

The senior NCO motioned for the man on watch to join him and the captain, then escorted them down the stairs to the captain's cabin. He returned moments later alone.

With the crew no longer an issue, one SEAL took the helm to keep the *Panda* underway at the slowest possible speed and maintain steerage. Two other team members established positions on the fore and aft decks in case any of the ship's crew had managed to escape.

A small, pyramid-shaped radar target was quickly placed on the fore and aft decks, easily seen by the Hawkeye, and a signal to abandon the RF jamming. Now the SEALs could effortlessly communicate with the Mark V, the RHIBs and the *DeRemer* – which got underway toward the *Panda*.

With the exception of the SEAL helmsman and fore and aft lookouts, the remainder of the team split with the majority moving to the forward hold, where they began uncrating the thirty-six Stingers. Incendiary charges were placed directly on the components.

The remaining SEALs got to work putting the 20-pound, timed demolition charges on the *Panda*'s hull near its water intake points. The charges were each primed with two ignition/detonation systems and were timed with a five-minute delay on the incendiaries and fifteen-minute delays on those designed to rip open the *Panda*'s hull, giving the SEALs an opportunity to get off the ship and ensure that all team members were present and accounted for.

During the fire in the forward hold, there were several smaller explosions as the Stinger batteries popped and their warheads exploded. Soon the fire began to involve the entire ship. Since heat rises, the charges set along the waterline did not experience premature detonation.

The RHIBs and Mark V had pulled back to a safe distance and were watching when the charges opened gaping wounds in the *Panda* and she began her last journey . . . to the bottom. In less than ten minutes, only a little debris on the surface offered any evidence of the ship's being there and that would scatter quickly in the Gulf's currents.

✱ ✱ ✱

Huber Heights occupies parts of Green, Miami, and Montgomery counties in western Ohio. Just off eastbound I-70, exit 38 is a Walmart open 24 hours, where Allison Martin worked the graveyard shift as a checker.

Ms. Martin had recently moved in with her boyfriend – Adam Kingsley – a Huber Heights uniform patrol sergeant. Kingsley's shift overlapped Martin's almost perfectly, and at the "new love" stage of their relationship, they communicated frequently via text messages.

Most of the customers in the store at 1:55 a.m. were taking a break from their east or west travels on I-70. The ginger-haired Martin had a clear view of shoppers entering or leaving from her register – the third from the north entrance and the only one open – and in the wee hours of the morning, she watched people come and go as a distraction to her boredom.

A white man entered with a long beard, a little lighter in color than Martin's hair, wearing sunglasses and a knit watch cap pulled down to his ears. He stopped, looked around, and since no "greeter" approached, walked to Martin's check-out lane.

"Where can I find electric hair clippers?"

"They're in the beauty department, that way," she said, pointing to her left-rear. "Look for the grooming section."

The man nodded and moved in the indicated direction.

He could pass for ZZ Top's Billy Gibbons, she thought.

In less than five minutes, the man returned to her register and paid cash for a Delaware Home Cut grooming kit.

"Where's the men's room?" he asked, shaking his head to refuse the receipt Martin offered.

"Straight back from here."

The man started toward the back of the store.

"I hope you're not going to shave that beautiful beard off."

"'Fraid so."

Martin watched until he disappeared down one of the runway-like aisles.

A few minutes later, the clean shaven man – now with an oddly two-toned face – walked out of the north exit.

Using the thumbs of both hands, Martin typed: "Just saw something odd. A guy with a beard that he'd clearly grown for years bought an electric hair trimmer. He went into the men's room and shaved it off. ILU! XOXOX"

"In the middle of the night? ILU2! XOXOXO," came the reply to her text almost immediately.

"Yeah. He had a long beautiful beard. And wait! Another man with a long beard just came in. He's going toward the men's room and he has the clippers in his hand. He's going to shave it off too, I bet."

"Sounds funny. Coming, 4 blocks away!"

★ ★ ★

Something in the back of Kingsley's mind tickled his memory. Two blocks from the parking lot, he radioed dispatch. "Central, Henry-thirty-three."

"Central, go ahead, Thirty-three."

"Wasn't there an APB from the feds put out recently?"

"Roger-that. Stolen Stinger missiles in New Mexico."

"Any description of the perps?"

"Negative, Thirty-three, but the California State Mounties took two of them into custody. A couple of Chechens."

"Were they bearded?"

"Hold on, Thirty-three." Less than thirty seconds later, dispatch responded. "Thirty-three, roger that, seriously bearded."

Kingsley drove into the Walmart parking lot a minute later, and turned off his headlights. With only three cars in the lot, the dark-colored Ford Explorer would have stood out even if its head, tail, and interior lights hadn't been on. He drove slowly to a point that allowed him to read the Nevada license plate and stopped the cruiser. Pressing the talk switch on the microphone near his left shoulder, he said, "Thirty-three. I'm in the Walmart parking lot, 7680 Brandt Pike, suspect vehicle Ford Explorer, four doors, black or dark blue in color. Nevada tag Charlie-Ida-Union-six-nine-four-seven. There appears to be a white male in the driver's seat. I have reason to believe another individual is in the store. Ten-sixteen, code-two."

"Roger. Ten-sixteen, Code 2, 7680 Brandt Pike."

Kingsley turned left and drove toward the rear of the SUV on a course that ran parallel to the driver's side. When the cruiser started to pass the other vehicle, he turned slightly to the left placing the nose of his Crown Victoria at an angle away from the side of the SUV. Putting the engine block between him and any potential trouble created a defensive position. After turning on the red and blue roof and take-down lights, Kingsley trained the car's exterior spotlight on the window of the Explorer. The bright lights ended any element of surprise but would serve as a beacon to his approaching back-up.

"Central, Henry-twenty-two. I'm en route to Henry-thirty-three's location. ETA two minutes."

"Central, roger that. Thirty-three, you copy?"

"Thirty-three, I copy."

As Kingsley opened the door to approach the SUV, a bullet shattered the cruiser's front passenger window. In the instant before Kingsley rolled to his left, seeking cover, he caught a glimpse of someone running into the store's north entrance.

A second and third shot broke the driver's side window, showering Kingsley with safety glass as he hit the ground with a thud. He pushed himself to a kneeling position, pulling his Glock 9mm from its holster. Scrambling toward the front of the cruiser, he keyed his microphone. *"Henry-thirty-three! Shots fired! Shots fired! Signal-thirteen!"*

The SUV's engine raced as Kingsley peeked over the hood. He rose slightly and fired six shots into the retreating driver's side window and windshield.

The Ford lurched backward with increasing speed and began a wide counterclockwise arc. Seconds later, it slammed into a shopping cart collection point, its engine still racing. The structure moved slightly until it came in contact with the dozens of heavy carts. At that point, the Ford's force lost the battle and its rear tires began to spin helplessly, creating heavy white smoke.

Kingsley rose cautiously, maintaining a two-hand grip on the Glock.

In the distance, the wail of a siren approached and moments later, additional red, blue, and take-down lights bathed the scene. Henry-Twenty-Two stopped in the same type of defensive position Kingsley had assumed and the driver took cover behind the vehicle's nose, Glock in hand.

Both officers watched cautiously as the SUV driver's door opened and the man behind the wheel tumbled to the asphalt. The .45 automatic in his left hand discharged on impact, sending a round into the right front fender of the newly arrived cruiser with a clang, as it a hit a spinning fan blade.

Kingsley ducked reflexively, but then rose slowly when the SUV driver lay motionless. "*You okay, Bennett!*"

"*Yeah!*"

Kingsley moved toward the still figure slowly. "I think I saw one run back into the store. Check out the vehicle, I'll see what's up inside."

"*Got it! Watch your six!*"

Inside the Walmart, Allison Martin had crouched behind her check-out counter when she heard gunfire erupt outside. Dating a cop had advantages, one being the drilling she received on what to do if someone attempted to rob the store or she heard shooting. As a result of her quick action, the SUV's second occupant didn't see Martin when he returned. He headed toward the back of the store in search of a rear exit, and unknowingly in the direction of more bad news.

The store's night manager – a retired Ohio State Trooper – heard the shots too. Normally, he would have been home asleep at this hour, but he had agreed to cover the usual manager's shift due to a new baby's early arrival.

The fleeing SUV occupant, pistol in hand, rounded the corner at the end of a housewares aisle and into the sights of a Sig Sauer P938 automatic equipped with a Crimson Trace Laserguard. Its red dot darted to his center of mass. His rising hand didn't get to waist level before two hollow point rounds dropped him to the floor.

Kingsley heard the shots and proceeded toward them slowly. *"POLICE! Drop your weapon and raise your hands."*

"I shot the guy! He's down and not goin' anywhere, officer."

"Who are you?" Kingsley shouted, in the direction of the voice.

"Store manager and retired state trooper!"

"Yeah? You need to let me see you and it better not be with a weapon!"

The manager gently laid the P938 on the counter of the gun department, raised his hands, walked toward and around the dead man and into Kingsley's line of sight.

"Where's your weapon?" Kingsley barked.

"On the gun department counter behind me."

Kingsley advanced cautiously, keeping the manager in view. As he passed the end of the aisle, the body on the floor came into his field of vision.

"Kingsley, I'm behind you!" Officer Bennett yelled. *"The driver is DOA!"*

"Okay. Did you call it in?" Kingsley said.

"I did."

Nodding in the direction of the manager, Kingsley said, "Where's your ID?"

"Right rear pocket."

"I need you back up against the wall and take it out with your right hand. Keep your left in the air. Understand?"

"Yes, sir!"

✫ ✫ ✫

Two hours later, the flurry of activity inside the store began to subside. The bodies were photographed, bagged and in transit to the ME's facilities.

The SUV's contents had been inventoried. After the Stingers were removed and placed in the care of a state EOD team, a tow truck pulled the vehicle to Huber Heights' impound lot.

The dead man in the parking lot required an officer involved shooting investigation. The shooting of the man inside required an investigation as well, but different.

The manager's Ohio concealed carry permit was inspected and his Sig Sauer taken into evidence. His OSHP retiree status afforded him more gentle treatment than the average civilian would have encountered.

☆ ☆ ☆

The President's Daily Briefing is a top secret document and the responsibility of the Director of National Intelligence. The PDB's topics are predominantly related to international intelligence and are an amalgam of CIA, DIA, NSA and FBI gathered information.

Later in the morning following the Stinger's recovery in Ohio, the topic opened the PDB.

"Two dead?" POTUS asked.

"Yes, sir."

"Any friendlies hurt?"

"No, Mr. President."

"Did we learn anything about them?"

"Yes, sir. They had directions from New Mexico to the Sleep-Inn at 15375 Rockaway Boulevard in Jamaica, New York."

"Jamaica . . . near JFK?"

"You could almost hit it with a rock from that address, sir."

"Hmmm. So that's eight down, four to go."

"Yes, sir."

"Okay. What's next?"

TWENTY-ONE

"Are you going to be out all night again, Jim?"

Grabowski stopped with his hand on the knob of the door to their garage. "Probably not. No sense throwing a lot of time into my career now that you've driven a stake through its heart!"

"Jim, I asked a simple question. I did my job," Dusty responded, defensively.

"Yeah, well, if you were married to a plumber or airline pilot, that wouldn't have made a difference. But you asked my boss's, boss's, boss that question in a news conference that had *national* network coverage. Do you think the Commissioner doesn't know who your husband is?"

* * *

"*No* one at Senator Tasman's Campaign headquarters had any discussions with the police from *any* jurisdiction." John Mallard's patience threshold had clearly been breached.

"Including Baltimore?" the Sunday morning talk show host asked. Getting Mallard for an interview – even one recorded before the show's usual air time – was a *coup* he intended to take full advantage of.

Mallard, seated in a high-backed chair, held his right hand out roughly two feet above the floor. "I thought you had to be at least this smart to host a Sunday talk show. *Even* at *Coyote News*! Was there a part of the word '*any*' that escaped you?"

* * *

"Senator Reynolds claimed she and her party had to dodge sniper fire when they visited the Middle East several years ago. Yet, video of her arrival shows no sense of urgency. In fact, the senator stopped at a podium and spoke for almost five minutes. Can you clarify the senator's statement, Miss Beaudro?"

Without batting an eye, Jackie Beaudro looked into the camera with no hint of emotion on her dark face. "Senator Reynolds misspoke. She had been traveling non-stop for five days with almost no sleep when she was asked about the incident. She has traveled extensively all over the world and in a moment of exhaustion, the senator misspoke. It's as simple as that."

"Well, ma'am. The record shows the senator 'misspoke' about it on three different occasions over a ten-day period. Were all those comments also all due to exhaustion?"

"With all the dead and maimed at two of our local airports and the resulting national emergency America faces, and a sniper on the loose in Baltimore, are the misspoken words of an exhausted presidential candidate the most important question you can ask?"

★ ★ ★

"I'm getting a lot of heat from the Editor's Office, Dusty." Jack Reigle's voice, usually upbeat, carried a genuine air of concern. "You've got to back off this Tasman story, at least for a while. Besides, there are two bombings and a sniper that are going to suck the air out of anything local, other than a catastrophe of even greater magnitude."

"Jack, this is going to be a blockbuster. I can feel it."

"Yeah? If you keep dogging it, you're going to get the *feel* of the unemployment office. You're a damn good journalist, Dusty. Don't push your career into the crapper again. You were lucky to resurrect your byline with the Simington story a few years back. There are some real big dicks playing for the White House. You don't want to be on the receiving end of one of their hard-ons."

★ ★ ★

"They've got a major problem, Morgan."

"I'm thinking I'd like to trade places with the SFM's EOD team if they're down to just one problem. Hermann and I have seven. Five in Druid Hill Park, Jordan Moses, and her old man."

"Well, your sarcasm aside, their problem may become yours too. The BWI and IAD bombers used old C-4." Grabowski paused for the question he knew would follow.

"Old?"

"Well, pre-1995."

"No taggants. Required after the OKC bombing," Morgan said matter-of-factly.

"That's right. With no way to trace the C-4 back to the manufacturer, we have no idea who received it."

✷ ✷ ✷

Dusty parked her car a few houses west of 231 East Churchill Street. Taking her digital camera out of the glove box, she got out of her 530i and walked toward the front of the Moses' residence. After snapping a close-up of the front of the building, Dusty moved across the street for a wide shot of the address and the homes on either side of it.

Exchanging her camera for a reporter's notebook in her purse, Dusty flipped through the pages to her transcribed notes from Gordon Moses' recorded phone call.

She was going to the neighborhood bank near our house.

Dusty looked to her left. There were no commercial buildings between her and Federal Hill Park. Glancing to her right, cars moved in both directions on Light Street, nearly two blocks away.

Her BMW chirped twice as its doors locked. Dusty walked toward the traffic.

✷ ✷ ✷

When Ayo Amoako opened the door of his D.C. apartment, a surreal image greeted him – as if a full length mirror had been installed in the hall.

"Good afternoon, my brother. I have come to liberate you," were the first words Ayo had heard from Dayo in years, and . . . the last of his life.

✷ ✷ ✷

Morgan, Hermann, and Small Deer stood in Druid Hill Park midway between the playground and the trail where the jogger died. The roof of the multistory apartment building on Eutaw Place to their southeast formed a straight line with the victims' park locations.

"That must have been like shootin' fish in a bucket," Small Deer said quietly.

"Yeah," Hermann responded. "And the body next to the synagogue lines up too. So, what are we doin' here, Morgan. We already know where the shots came from."

"Just trying to get a victims' eye-view of the crime scene, partner." Morgan answered. "The shooter picks out two kids and two women, one clearly pregnant. You have to believe that the top of that building would provide a target-rich environment. There must have been dozens of people in every direction. So, why four females, two of them young girls?"

"A homicidal maniac who hates the opposite sex," Hermann offered.

"Or, a religious fanatic who hates America *and* the opposite sex," Small Deer said. "In the last seventy-two hours, you've had train tracks sabotaged in Arizona that no one has taken credit for. A chlorine spill that al-Qaeda quickly claims responsibility for, but doesn't fit their MO. Bombings at BWI and IAD that *are* iconic of al-Qaeda's iniquitous acts, without a peep from anyone laying claim to them. And, a bunch of dead bodies in what looks like a very exclusive Baltimore neighborhood, that again aren't al-Qaedaesque if you're outside of Iraq or Afghanistan, which they do brag about.

"This has all the markings of the medicine of the mole, Paleface."

"Or, the four events weren't pulled off by the same person or persons," Morgan observed.

"Or that," Small Deer responded, with his signature grin.

✯ ✯ ✯

Dusty stood on the corner of Churchill and Light. Across the street the banner proclaiming Cornerstone's name change to Freeport Bank flapped in a slight breeze.

After a few seconds observation, she turned and started back to her car, knowing her next move. *No sense spending time here before I'm ready. Somebody might remember me.*

✯ ✯ ✯

Wearing a pair of latex surgical gloves, Dayo Amoako rolled his brother's body – encased in a sheet of plastic to prevent blood stains – into a 4' X 8' area rug without ceremony or emotion. As Ayo's identical twin, he mistakenly had no concerns about leaving DNA, but his fingerprints would lead an investigation back to Colorado and his prison record.

He wore Ayo's shoulder holster and SIG Sauer P229. The leather rig hung slightly loose on Dayo's frame. Clearly Ayo had eaten better or worked out more than his felonious sibling.

Dayo brushed his hands together, rose to his feet and turned toward the desk in the corner of the living room. A computer monitor displayed a Microsoft Office Excel spreadsheet with Ayo's work schedule.

Sitting down in a high-backed swivel chair, Dayo studied the sheet. Surveillance of his brother by other mosque members over the past weeks had mapped out the movements Dayo needed to mimic. The spreadsheet provided the times necessary to complete the choreography. He had been given strict instructions to act quickly. His assignment would be difficult to complete if his brother's fellow agents saw anything suspicious. Dayo didn't know the classmate hijinks, girlfriend break-ups, or war stories Ayo would be familiar with.

A black leather badge and ID case lay next to the keyboard. Dayo picked it up. Flipping it open, his brother's image stared back at him.

The cell phone on the desk vibrated, refocusing his attention. Unplugging the phone from its charger, Dayo pushed the smartphone's "Send" button.

"Special Agent Amoako."

TWENTY-TWO

Dusty Rhodes adjusted the brim of her sun hat, then pulled the door open and walked into the Freeport Bank branch on Light Street. Large aviation sunglasses covered her eyes. She removed them and slipped one stem into the outside breast pocket of a dark green, cheap, Sears jacket as she stepped into the air-conditioned lobby.

The view down the nose of any fashion conscious woman looking in Dusty's direction would have rivaled that seen by a Winter Olympic ski jumper sitting atop the long hill. Oddly, the exact reaction the reporter hoped for. The pants suit she wore – just hours before a frequently ignored item in a consignment store – had been out of style years earlier when first stocked by the nationwide department store.

A wad of paper towels taped inside the jacket, under the left sleeve, produced a bulge. Like the pants suit, her *sensible* black shoes wouldn't have looked out of line if worn by someone on the job in plain clothes.

Dusty glanced toward the four tellers' stations to her left, then started to take in the rest of the bank's geography when she heard her name called, and froze.

"Dusty Rhodes!"

A uniformed officer approached from her right. Behind him, a woman stood behind the customer service desk, looking in Dusty's direction.

"How the hell are you, Dusty?" the man asked, smiling.

She had a vague recollection of the man's face but not his name, until he was close enough to read the tag above his right breast uniform pocket: Douglas Seitz.

"Hey, Doug! I'm doing okay. How 'bout you?" Thinking quickly, Dusty realized this encounter could be put to her advantage. "What are you doin' here?"

"Just a routine business check. Freeport kicked all the Cornerstone employees to the curb when they took over. I'm just showin' the flag, so to speak."

Dusty laughed, louder than necessary, and slapped Seitz on the left arm. "Gotta win the hearts and minds! Right, Doug?"

Seitz smiled and said in a low voice: "Grab 'em by the balls and . . ."

". . . their hearts and minds will follow!" Dusty finished, laughing again, slightly louder than the distance between herself and the patrolman required.

"That's right. So, what are you doing here? This is way off your crime beat unless you know something I don't. Why aren't you up at Druid Hill Park?"

"The park area is my next stop, Doug. I'm just here gathering some info about that woman who was run down a couple of blocks away."

"Oh, yeah. Man, that was gruesome."

"Very," Dusty agreed. "Well, I've got to talk to the management and then be on my way. Good seeing you, Doug. Take care!"

"WILCO. You too. Tell your old man I said 'Hey!'"

Dusty patted the officer on the back as he headed for the door, then turned back toward the service desk. The woman who had watched Dusty's exchange smiled as the reporter approached.

A few feet before she reached the customer service desk, Dusty slowly reached into her inside, left breast pocket and pulled out her reporter's notebook, leaving her jacket open long enough to expose an old BPD "Pie Plate" badge hanging from her belt.

At the customer service desk, she reached into an inside right jacket pocket to retrieve a pen, displaying a set of handcuffs in a leather pouch also attached to her belt.

Addison Monti smiled from behind the desk. "Hello, Detective. How can I help you?"

Dusty smiled and looked at the woman's name tag. "Hello, Ms. Monti. I . . ."

"Please, just call me Addison. 'Ms. Monti' sounds so stuffy and formal."

"Okay, Addison. I just have a couple of quick questions I hope you can answer without me having to get a warrant."

"I'll do my best," Monti answered, the smile now gone.

"A woman named Jordan Moses was . . ."

"Oh! I remember *her*!" Monti said, shaking her head. "She was very cold and rude. Do you know she refused to shake my hand?"

Caught off guard, Dusty simply answered: "Really? Why?"

"She said all shaking hands did was spread germs."

"Hmm. I guess there's an element of truth to that. But it sounds very paranoid to me."

Monti nodded. "Absolutely."

"So, Ms. Moses came in and . . .?"

"She cleaned out her safety deposit box and left."

"How did she identify herself?" Dusty flipped open her notebook and clicked the end of her ballpoint.

"She had a key card for this branch – before it changed ownership – and a scan of her thumbprint matched the image captured when she subscribed to rent the box."

"So, no picture ID was required?"

A smile preceded Monti's answer. "Picture IDs can be faked. Not thumbprints."

✳ ✳ ✳

"There he goes, fishing stickers and all," Morgan said, pointing to the computer monitor. "That's a rifle case, probably custom-made to accommodate the sniper's rifle with a suppressor attached to it. I have to admit, the fishing stickers are a clever way to throw suspicion off the case. "

"That case would easily hold a single shot .45-70 rifle," Small Deer commented. "It could have a suppressor made for it and throw a very accurate boolit great distances and still be launched subsonic. Add a bipod and you could be off to the races."

Hermann – standing beside Small Deer – looked over Morgan's shoulder. "I'm no expert on sniper rifles, but I'd say you're right, Henry. The resident we talked to was right. If that's the shooter, I can't tell if he's black, Hispanic, white with a tan or . . . even a *guy*, for that matter."

"True," Morgan confirmed. "But, between the brass casing Proffitt's lab has and the slugs that are good enough for a ballistics comparison, they can easily make an ID if we ever give 'em a rifle to compare them to."

"The cartridge on the roof says the shooter is playing with you," Small Deer commented. "Five rounds fired, and four picked up. Leaving the brass says, 'I'm smarter than you cops.'"

✦✦✦

TWENTY-THREE

Mary Anderson looked up from her desk. "Well, hello, Ms. Rhodes! What brings you to Bluebell Cellular?"

"Hey, Mary. I need to ask Steve a favor. Is he in?"

"Oh! Why, yes, he is. I just got back from the ladies' room. Let me just make sure there's no one in with him at the moment."

"Thanks."

The executive assistant knocked softly on a mahogany door, then opened it slowly. "Mister Van Scoyk, Dusty Rhodes is here. Do you have a few minutes for her?"

Inside, a muffled, gravelly voice answered, "Absolutely! Send her in!"

Stepping into the CEO's spacious office, Dusty smiled and said, "Thanks for seeing me, Steve. How are you?"

"I'll always have time for you, Dusty!" Van Scoyk pushed up out of his leather swivel chair and rounded the desk.

Dusty extended her hand as he approached, but Van Scoyk pushed it aside, wrapping her in a bear hug. "It's great to see you! How are you, Dusty?"

"I'm good, Steve. How are you and the family?" Then before Van Scoyk could answer, Dusty added, "How's Steve Junior?"

Van Scoyk released the reporter and stepped back, looking down on her from his 6' 5" vantage point. "He's doing better, after many, many hours with therapists. I'm not sure he'll ever be a hundred percent after his kidnappers buried him in that box for seven days. But, he's alive – thanks in large part to you – so Linda and I continue to hold out hope that he'll eventually get back to his old self."

"Please give them both my best, Steve."

"I will. Now, what can I do for you?"

"I'm working on a story about a woman who was murdered. Her husband called me and was supposed to meet me the next day, but he never showed up. I'm wondering if your guys can tell me if his cell number is still in service and if so, where I might find the guy."

"So, you just need his address?"

"No, sir. I know where he lives and he's not likely to go back there. I need the location, or locations, of the cell towers he's been close to or called through recently."

"How recently?"

"The last week to ten days, if you would, please."

"This all sounds very cloak-and-daggerish. However, we'll see what we can find. But why didn't you just call me? Of course I'm delighted to see you . . . anytime!"

"Steve, I'm going to be totally honest with you. This story has the potential to be *very* explosive. I'll answer any questions you ask, but the less you know, the better off we may both be. In your office, we're the only people that know about my request. You never know who's listening to a phone conversation."

"Then say no more . . . that is, after you give me the cell number," Van Scoyk said, with a grin behind his short white beard.

☆ ☆ ☆

The .45-70 round drove the rabbi back into the doors of his synagogue with incredible force. The man slid a few inches toward the concrete stoop, then fell onto his left side. A crimson pool spread quickly onto the hard surface next to his body, began dripping onto the second step, finally inching across the middle of the sidewalk.

Ten meters away, an approaching female saw the blood pool first, then the rabbi's body. Her scream drew terminal attention.

The second sniper's bullet entered her forehead above her left eye just before removing most of the back of her skull.

☆ ☆ ☆

"Al Jazeera is reporting an al-Qaeda claim of responsibility for the Druid Park murders," Grabowski said. "But still not a peep about the BWI and IAD massacres."

"Rag-head radio! Fuckin' camel jockeys!" Costa responded angrily. "It's gotta be them, or some affiliate group. What gutless cocksuckers, walking into an airport, killing and maiming indiscriminately! Killing kids and pregnant women in a park!"

"And using C-4 that can't be traced to the manufacturer or where it went. They haven't had a lot of time, but the feds seem to be nowhere in their investigations so far – not that they'd spill their guts to us local *peons*," Grabowski said.

"I'm betting that C-4 came from a magazine somewhere on or near the East Coast. Remember how the feds asked us to identify any explosives manufactured prior to the legislation mandating the inclusion of taggants?" Costa asked.

"I remember you telling them to fuck off until they could come back with a warrant," Grabowski said, grinning broadly.

"And they never did." Costa stood up in the small office and walked to the coffee pot on a counter near the door. After filling his mug, he turned to face his partner. "Someone in the EOD business, civilian or military, who was less than honest when that legislation passed requiring taggants, might have foreseen the future value of explosives without them.

"Non-traceable C-4 could fetch a healthy price. There's probably any number of people who, for various reasons, would sell explosives thinking they would be used for legitimate purposes. Like the kid who gave old man Simington the Deta-Sheet a few years back?"

Grabowski nodded. "Yeah, the kid thought Simington was going to blow stumps with the stuff. I guess that's what the geezer actually intended to do with it . . . initially."

✳ ✳ ✳

Hermann lifted a fluttering strand of yellow police tape allowing Morgan and Small Deer to duck under it on their way to the front of the synagogue.

"What's the word, Doc?" Morgan asked a member of the ME's office, bent over the rabbi's body.

"Single GSW to the chest. Probably never knew what hit him. The woman on the sidewalk didn't for sure. Her brain is strewn a fair distance down the street."

Hermann looked at the synagogue's front door, noticing its blood stain. Stepping closer, he pointed to a hole in the wood. "Looks like it went through the victim *and* the door."

Small Deer stepped to Hermann's side. "Yeah, another real big piece of lead made that hole. Wherever it is inside, it's probably mangled too badly to get any markings off of it."

"One thing is for sure," Morgan commented. "Whoever the shooter is, he seems to have some issue with the Tasman presidential campaign. He killed Roberta Clever here and now the rabbi."

"If that's true, how do the little girls and pregnant woman fit in?" Hermann asked. "There's no connection between them and the campaign."

"Maybe they were meant to be a distraction," Morgan said. "If so, they are."

Hermann nodded. "Yeah. Let's check to see if there are any security cameras that caught these killings. One thing is for sure. He has one hell of a set of balls taking down two more people at the same spot as one of his earlier victims."

"Or, *she* has," Small Deer said.

⋆ ⋆ ⋆

Dusty looked up from her *Baltimore Mirror* desk to see Mary Anderson approaching with a manila envelope in her hand.

"Hello, Dusty. Mr. Van Scoyk asked me to bring this to you."

"Thanks!"

⋆⋆
⋆⋆
⋆

TWENTY-FOUR

The map on Dusty's desk showed a series of cell phone towers in the Baltimore metropolitan area, each identified with a red number next to it. A separate piece of paper listed the most recent calls, and dates, made from Gordon Moses' cell phone, with the last being less than eight hours earlier. A cluster of the calls – including the last –came from a modest Baltimore neighborhood.

At the bottom of the calls list, a handwritten note said:

Row house @ the west corner of Dillon and South Grundy Streets.

Dusty shook her head. *That makes no sense. If John Moses is there, it must be because he's hiding. He wouldn't go from Federal Hill to South Grundy for the cultural experience!*

✱ ✱ ✱

"Man, that's a huge boolit!" Small Deer said, looking at the evidence bag dangling from his hand. "That's 550-plus grains traveling at over 1,000 feet per second. Talk about overkill.

"This came out of a custom mold with damn near pure lead poured into it. It was probably originally intended for making stained glass. The ridges on the backend are for a lubricant to reduce lead being smeared on the barrel as the projectile passes through. Whoever cast this knew their shit."

"Yeah," Morgan commented, "we're lucky it's in pretty good condition, having passed through the soft part of the jogger's belly."

"It sure wasn't lucky for her," Hermann said, shaking his head.

"Based on the wounds of the last two victims, I have to believe they were hit with the same rounds, even though we haven't found 'em yet," Morgan said. "Do you agree, Red Man?"

"No doubt in my mind," Small Deer answered. "Listen, Paleface, I've got to be movin' on. We had a death in the family, on my wife's side, and she needs me to come home."

"I understand. Promise me something though."

"Sure."

"Let's not let nearly four decades go by before we get together again."

"Deal." Small Deer smiled. "I doubt either one of us has four decades *left*."

✳ ✳ ✳

"I need your help."

Peter Liu looked up from his desk. "Hello, Dusty. In my official *Mirror* capacity, or as your go-to-geek?"

"Yes . . ." Dusty said, with a nervous smile. "I need to borrow a camera and a telephoto lens. And, I need you to show me how to operate it."

"Wouldn't it be easier to just let me shoot the pics?"

"Easier, yes. Safer for you? No."

"Safe? You planning on getting embedded in a unit in Iraq or Afghanistan?"

"You don't have to travel that far. It's easy enough to hang your ass out right here. I mean 'safe' in the sense that I'm working on something I've specifically been told not to. If you take the pictures, you're going to get caught in the crossfire. And the subjects of these *portraits* may very well be killers."

"Well, I must say. You certainly have my interest, Dusty."

✳ ✳ ✳

"The composition of the C-4 used in the Dulles device is identical to BWI's." Grabowski looked up from the computer screen and glanced over at Costa.

"Well, at least we know all of it was manufactured at the same place, and probably in the same batch. But, no taggants leaves us . . . *nowhere*," Costa said, frowning.

✳ ✳ ✳

Dusty knocked on the front door of the row house on the corner of Dillon and South Grundy Streets. After nearly a minute without a response, she beat on the door with the underside of her fist several times.

Footsteps approached inside, and the door swung open. A short, balding, white man squinted into the bright afternoon sun with bloodshot, brown eyes. "Yeah?"

"Mr. Moses?"

"Huh?"

"Gordon Moses?"

"Who the fuck are you?"

"Dusty Rhodes. *Baltimore Mirror*. You were supposed to meet me. Remember?"

"You're a reporter?"

"Yeah, I am. But someone obviously gave me the wrong address. Sorry to have bothered you, sir."

The man leaned against the open door, watching Dusty retreat to the sidewalk, walk to her BMW and drive away.

"*Fuck!*"

☆ ☆ ☆

Dusty drove several blocks north on South Grundy to ensure being out of sight from the row house's porch. Turning right onto Foster Avenue and right again onto South Haven Street, within a minute she approached Dillon Street. After a third right turn, she pulled to the curb, got out, walked to a blue Toyota RAV4, and got into its front passenger seat.

Dusty's hand had yet to release the door's handle when the small man stepped onto the row house's porch. The afternoon sun lit him perfectly and Peter Liu's Nikon D-300, with its 70-300mm zoom lens, captured digital images at eight frames per second.

Stopping at the edge of the porch the man seemed nervous, looking left and right. Behind him, a platinum blond, with enormous breasts only partially covered in a tank-top made to look like an American flag, stepped onto the porch. Her left hand held a cell phone to her ear.

"I think I just stumbled into some serious shit, Peter."

"Like that'd be a first?"

"Probably *never* like this before. Gordon Moses' cell phone is in that house, but that guy sure as hell isn't anybody a bombshell like Jordan would marry."

Twisting the lens' zoom ring slightly, the viewfinder filled with a tight shot of the man's face. Liu depressed the shutter release again. "So, what's your guess about his companion? Stripper or hooker?"

"That depends on what her face looks like. You tell me."

Liu swung his camera a few millimeters to the right. Pressing the shutter release again, he said, "Her face looks like the surface of the moon, like she had a case of acne on steroids as a kid. I'd say stripper. That'd give her some distance from customers."

The couple took three steps down to the sidewalk, the man lighting a cigarette in flight, and to a white Honda Accord parked a few feet away on Grundy Street.

"Get a shot of the car," Dusty said.

"Already did. Maryland tags. 'BQQBS.'"

"What the hell does that spell?"

Liu punched a couple of buttons on the back of the Nikon, zooming in on an image he'd just taken of the license plate. After turning the camera so Dusty could see its LCD screen he said, "Pretty imaginative, if you ask me." Next to the breast cancer support ribbon, the pink Qs' tails resembled nipples.

"Boobs!" Dusty said, her grin indicating agreement with Liu's opinion.

★ ★ ★

On the sidewalk near 601 East Fayette Street Doug Seitz spotted Grabowski leaving police headquarters. "Hello, Grabowski! You're lookin' good."

Grabowski turned toward the voice. "Hey, Doug, how are you?"

"Not bad for a beat cop," Seitz responded. "I saw your old lady the other day. Did she tell you?"

"No. We've been swamped doing what we can to assist with the BWI and IAD bombings. I've only been home once when she was. Where was she?"

"Federal Hill Park neighborhood, I ran into her in the bank there. Used to be Cornerstone, but it got bought out and the name changed to Freeport."

Fuck!

★
★ ★
★

TWENTY-FIVE

"She was so smart and pretty. Her father and I just knew she would do great things in life." The painfully thin, elderly woman dabbed her eyes with a handkerchief. "Now she's gone."

"Mrs. French, we're very sorry for your loss." Dusty looked across the glass-topped coffee table at the frail woman. Jordan Moses' mother had clearly been a beauty in her own right decades earlier. "I certainly don't want to add to your grief. But, I'd like to ask you a few questions, if I might. It could help find the person responsible for her death."

"Are you with the police? You said you were a reporter."

Dusty shot Peter Liu, sitting to her left, a quick glance, then turned back to Mrs. French. "I am a reporter, working on a story about your daughter. My husband is a member of the Baltimore Police Department."

"Oh, I see. All right, I'll try to answer your questions."

"When I met Jordan, we talked about her having some very sensitive information related to this year's presidential primaries. We were supposed to meet again so I could see what she'd collected. I reminded her that holding information about a high stakes political race, especially one that decides who will occupy the White House, could be dangerous. And she said, 'I know. I have insurance.'"

"What did she mean?" Mrs. French asked.

"I don't know, ma'am. That's why I came to see you today. Did she bring you anything? Or, did you receive anything in the mail from her?"

"N . . . no. I hadn't seen or heard from Jordan in weeks."

"And nothing in the mail?"

"No."

"Okay." Dusty reached into her purse, removing a business card case. "Here's my card."

"I got something from that miserable man she married, but not Jordan."

"Oh? Where is it? May we see what he sent you?"

"I threw it away. Never opened it."

Dusty's heart sank. Another glance at Peter Liu showed his disappointment as well.

"It's in that trash can by the door."

Two sets of eyes bore into an overflowing, black, plastic trash basket beside a small table near the front door.

"May we look through it, Mrs. French?"

"I suppose so. It's just trash to me."

Peter Liu was out of the wingback chair, next to the trash can and about to reach into it before Mrs. French finished giving her consent.

"Wait!" Dusty said, loud enough to startle the elderly woman. "Sorry, ma'am. It probably makes no difference, but whatever's in the trash may be evidence.

"Do you have gloves, Peter?"

"In my bag." Liu turned quickly and bent over a large, green Gura Gear zippered camera backpack. Opening the left side compartment, he removed a pair of latex gloves and slipped them on.

"Mrs. French, while Peter is looking, can you describe your son-in-law?"

"Yes. He's worthless."

"I meant physically. Can you tell me what he looks like?"

"He's tall. Well over six feet. Very handsome. Dark, wavy hair, and almost aqua eyes. Jordan said that his eyes were what knocked her for a loop. They reminded her of the water around Bora Bora . . . her favorite place in the world. She collected pictures of it from the time she was six. She always said she was going to move there when she had enough money. It's apparently very expensive.

"She's gone now! She'll never get to see it in person . . ." Mrs. French buried her face in her hands and sobbed softly.

"I'm very sorry," Dusty said, moving to the couch next to the old woman and putting an arm around her.

Almost half of the trash can's contents lay on the floor when Liu removed an unopened, brown, bubble pack envelope, addressed by hand to the French's home. A printed return label in the upper left corner listed Gordon R. Moses' name.

"Got it," Liu said softly.

Dusty looked up. "Mrs. French. Do you mind if we open that envelope?"

"Just take it with you. I don't have any interest in what's in it. I'm tired. I want to lie down."

"Yes, ma'am. Is there anything we can do for you before we go?"

"Just clean up the mess."

"We will."

★ ★ ★

Addison Monti had a quizzical look on her face. "I explained all that to the other detective."

Hermann and Morgan exchanged glances.

"What other detective?" Hermann asked.

"The one who was with the police officer we see all the time. Officer Seitz."

"Did this detective show you his ID?" Morgan asked.

"*She* didn't actually hold up her ID card. Her badge was clipped to her belt on the left side, under her jacket. Number one-fifty-nine. She had handcuffs on the other side and a bulge under her left arm. I may be young, but I've been in banking long enough to recognize somebody wearing a shoulder holster."

"Hermann glanced at Morgan then back to Monti. "We'll need the security footage of the detective and of Mrs. Moses the day she emptied her box."

★ ★ ★

In the *Mirror*'s Lutherville office, Peter Liu looked on as Dusty opened the bubble envelope using a razor-egged letter opener and peeked inside. It contained a DVD, in a clear plastic envelope. "T²" hand-printed on the *disc*.

★ ★ ★

"Well, there's only one decent view of the woman impersonating Jordan Moses," Morgan said, in the BPD's AV room with Hermann. "Let's get Proffitt's crew to make some stills of her."

"Good idea," Hermann replied. "Let's see the make-believe detective video."

A technician punched a few keys and a second video appeared on the flat screen monitor. A woman in a white sun hat came into the bank and started toward the customer service desk, then stopped. She turned and had a brief conversation with a uniformed officer whom she appeared to know.

The officer departed the bank and the woman approached the service desk. The video clearly showed the woman pull a notebook from a pocket of her suit jacket. After a conversation with Addison Monti, the woman left.

"There's not a good view of her face," Morgan commented. "But it doesn't look like she ever flashed an ID, which confirms what Monti told us. Let's talk to Seitz."

✳ ✳ ✳

"The files are encrypted, Dusty. We need to talk to Gordon Moses to find out what the password is."

✳ ✳ ✳

"Hello, Ace, you got a minute?" Morgan asked

Proffitt chuckled. "Morgan, you're always nice enough to say that at the beginning of a phone call, but never take less than ten. Actually, I was going to give you a call. But what can I do for you?"

Morgan told Proffitt the reason for his call, then asked: "So, what did you want to talk about?"

"That answering machine tape Grabowski gave you. Did you listen to it?"

"No," Morgan said, beginning to feel uneasy at the mere mention of it.

"We went through the whole thing and did a non-scientific comparison of the voices on it to Senator Tasman's. We need a professionally collected voice sample to nail it down, but I don't think there's any doubt that it's the senator.

"But we have no idea who the other guy is."

"*Other* guy? You mean her husband?"

"Not likely. He sounds like someone she was doing before Tasman subscribed to her services."

"Really?"

"Yeah. I'll e-mail you a transcript of the tape and an audio file so you can listen to it yourself."

✲ ✲ ✲

"Homicide, Morgan."

"This is Officer Seitz. I got a call from my sergeant saying you wanted a word."

"Yeah, thanks. When you were at the Freeport Bank branch in Federal Hill a couple of days ago, did you see anyone you knew?"

"Freeport . . . Freeport on the corner of . . ."

"Light and Churchill," Morgan said. "The manager's name is Addison Monti."

"Yeah, Ms. Monti! Good lookin' babe!"

"I know, Seitz. I've seen her." Morgan didn't try to conceal the beginnings of frustration. "Let's try to stay on task here."

"Yes, Detective. The only person I can remember there was Dusty Rhodes. Now that I think about it, she seemed surprised to see me at first. Then I remember her talking like I was hard of hearing, which made no sense because we were only about two feet apart."

✲ ✲ ✲

"I've tried everything I know, Dusty. No luck," Peter Liu said.

"Okay, make a copy of the pictures you shot on Grundy. Can you copy the DVD? Or, do you need the password for that too?"

"I don't know. Let's see." Liu took a blank DVD and inserted it into his computer's second disc drawer. After entering a few keystrokes, the machine began creating the copy.

"Well, at least we don't have to give the only copy to Morgan and Hermann," Dusty said.

"They can probably get the feds involved to try and crack the encryption."

Dusty shook her head. "I don't think the feds are going to have any spare time for the foreseeable future, Peter.

"When you get done burning that disc, I'll take it and the pics to Morgan."

✲ ✲ ✲

"I don't *know*, Harley! I was asleep and this reporter came pounding on the fuckin' door! She thought I was Moses. Said we were supposed to meet. Said her name was Rhodes something or other."

"*Dusty* Rhodes?"

"Yeah, that's her. What should I do?

"Harley? Harley? You there?"

✲ ✲ ✲

"Grabowski."

"Morgan here, Jim. Your badge number is one-five-nine. Right?"

"Yeah."

"Do you have more than one badge?"

"Nope. Just the one I'm wearing."

Morgan let several seconds pass before speaking again. "You didn't ask why I want to know, Jim."

"Hey, Morgan! I'm not some *perp* you're trying to sweat. So, let's not do the BPD two-step. What's going on?"

"Sorry, Jim. You're right. I owe you better than that." Morgan paused for a moment. "It looks like Dusty impersonated a police officer at the Freeport Bank in Federal Hill. If she did, there's nothing we can do to protect her. We'll have to turn it over to the State's Attorney. Do you know anything about that?"

"*Christ on a crutch*! No! We've only been in the house together for a few minutes since the bombings, Morgan. And, I haven't talked to her since I chewed her ass on the phone for her question to the chief at the news conference. You want me to tell her to come in?"

"Nooooooo! I think you need to maintain as much distance as you can, Jim. You've skated on the fact that you two went to the Moses' residence . . . at least so far. The fact that you've been working almost nonstop, if she did this, will give you some cover. I'm going to call her now."

* * *

Sitting at the desk in his Chevy Chase home, John Mallard heard his cell phone vibrate and picked it up.

"Yes?" he said and listened for almost a minute before saying anything else. "It will be taken care of *immediately*."

* * *

Marine Major Brian E. Shipp – "Eddie" to his friends – stood on the sandy beach of Auhah Island, Kuwait, with the dark waters of the Persian Gulf lapping at his Danner combat boots. The mere spit of land – 800 meters long and 540 meters wide – sits 16 km southeast of Failaka Island, and 41 km from Salmiya on the Kuwaiti mainland. In April 1991, the island had been quietly leased for a hundred years by a CIA front organization – Nacogdoches Materials. Prior to the Iraqi invasion of Kuwait, it hosted a small heliport and a lighthouse. Now, four large, two-story, nondescript buildings – code named after Disney's Mickey, Minnie, Goofy, and Donald characters – covered the majority of the island in a diamond-shaped pattern with the open area between them covered in asphalt.

Shipp and his SEAL team had been chosen to perform a mission the U.S. military had been champing at the bit to pull off for years. Though the men who originated the idea for the Diogenes Agreement hadn't envisioned anything nearly as bold as what Shipp's team was about to attempt, they would certainly applaud the target . . . had they known about it.

Major Shipp took one last look at the few visible lights on Failaka Island, a little less than ten miles away, before turning and walking back to Goofy for the final mission briefing.

☆ ☆ ☆

Morgan printed two copies of the transcript of the answering machine tape received from Proffitt and forwarded the e-mail with the recording attached to an AV technician. Ten minutes later, he and Hermann listened to it in a soundproof room, following along with the transcripts. When they reached the last recorded exchange, Morgan blinked in surprise.

"I've heard that guy's voice recently, partner!"

"Who is it?"

"I'm not sure. Play it again, Sam."

The AV tech reran the audio.

"Jesus! Who *is* that?"

TWENTY-SIX

Dusty Rhodes sat in one of the BPD's interrogation rooms, facing Morgan and Hermann. The front legs of the straight-backed chair she occupied had been shortened slightly to tilt it forward. Questioning uncomfortable suspects had advantages, particularly in a place that held less charm than an angry repo man. Its gloss white walls reflected the harsh overhead light, making it uncomfortable to look anywhere except toward the interrogators for some small slice of relief.

"Why did you guys usher me in *here*? I came to help you! Do I need a lawyer?"

"Do you think you do, Ms. Rhodes?" Hermann asked.

"'Ms. Rhodes?' Suddenly, I'm *Ms. Rhodes*?"

"You are when you're suspected of impersonating a police officer," Morgan said flatly.

"I didn't do that."

"Well, that's an interesting denial, considering that we have a bank manager who says you did, and a cop who confirms you being in the bank and security camera images that will be the prosecutor's *coup de grâce*."

"Detective, I never identified myself as a cop. If she jumped to the conclusion that I was, I can't help that."

"According to Ms. Monti, you were wearing a badge, cuffs and a shoulder holster."

"The first two items are true. I was wearing a *badge* and handcuffs. The badge wasn't . . . isn't . . . hasn't been, an official BPD badge since the seventies."

"You were wearing Jim's old pie plate badge?" Hermann asked.

"I was, and he knew *nothing* about it. He hasn't been home and I've only spoken to him briefly on the phone since . . ."

"Since you outed Hermann and me at the press conference?"

Anger flashed in Dusty's eyes. "That's something *else* I didn't do, *Morgan*. I just asked why two BPD detectives were there.

"Look! I think I can help you on the Moses case, if you'll drop this silly impersonation bullshit."

"Yeah, how do you propose to do that?" Morgan said.

"I know where Gordon Moses is. Well, at least where his cell phone is. And if you look in that envelope I handed you before you strong-armed me in here, you'll see pictures of the guy who lives there, his girlfriend, and the license plate of their car."

Morgan looked at Hermann quickly before saying, "Where does he live?"

"The corner of Dillon and South Grundy."

"And you know this because . . ." Morgan said.

"I can't tell you *how* I know. But, I'd bet that's where Mr. Moses is."

"There's not much chance of that, Dusty," Morgan said, shaking his head. "Gordon Moses checked into a refrigerated unit at the ME's office the other day."

"*Shit*!" Dusty rubbed her forehead. "That makes the other item in the envelope pretty much useless then."

"What other item?" Hermann asked.

"The DVD that I got from Jordan's mother. John Moses mailed it to Mrs. French, but she never opened it. It's encrypted and I was hoping Moses could tell us the password. I'm sure it contains the 'insurance' Jordan told me about when we met."

"How do you know it's encrypted, Dusty?" Morgan said. "Tampering with evidence? That might put you in need of a lawyer."

"Come on, Hunter! I didn't *tamper* with it. I tried to see what was *on* it. I brought it to you, for Christ's sake! Get your geek squad to work and see if it helps you."

"You mean after *your* geek squad couldn't break the code?" Hermann interjected.

"Well . . . yes . . . sort of."

★ ★ ★

TWENTY-SEVEN

"It's your lucky day, Detective Morgan. We got the APB and five minutes later, we spotted the plate . . . which doesn't do the broad's jugs justice. They're like two railroad tank cars! Where do you want 'em delivered?"

* * *

"You're in a shitload of trouble," Morgan said. "What's the cell phone of a dead man doing in your possession?"

"I didn't have it, Penny did!" The small man squirmed in the chair with short front legs.

"So, she killed Gordon Moses? I don't think so. We have video surveillance footage of you and your big friend with the missing fingers going to Moses' house," Morgan said, hoping to bluff the man into a confession, or at least a mistake.

"I want a lawyer," the small man said.

Hermann chuckled. "You better hope O.J.'s dream team is available. Maryland hasn't executed anybody in a long time. But, you snuffed Gordon Moses, and when the lab gets done with your ride, we'll know you used it to run his old lady down in the street. How much mercy do you think a jury is going to have for the guy who did that, then climbed out of the car and took the time to cut off her thumbs?"

"They're not gonna find shit! 'Cause we didn't use . . ."

"Because you didn't use the Honda you were driving today to run Jordan Moses down," Hermann said.

"That's right . . ." Realizing his error, the small man looked down at the handcuffs and chain securing him to the gray interrogation room table.

"Penny had to have a fuckin' *smartphone*. Do you know what those things cost? And then every month . . ."

"Shut up!" Morgan snapped. "You said you wanted a lawyer and when you did, you took yourself out of any position to negotiate. So, unless you want to waive your right to counsel, we're not interested in anything else you have to say. I hope whatever you got paid was worth your life. 'Cause it's worth next to nothing now."

"I waive my, my . . . I don't want a lawyer. I'll talk."

"Who hired you to kill . . ." A quick knock on the interrogation room door preceded its opening.

"I need to see you two, right now," Jan Richmond said.

Morgan and Hermann exchanged a quick look before stepping into the hall. A uniformed officer entered the interrogation room and closed the door.

"Yesterday afternoon, Cappy and his partner fished a floater out of the Inner Harbor. She'd been capped twice in the back of the head. Two .22 rounds. I just got off the phone with Proffitt. The same gun killed Gordon Moses."

"No shit?" Hermann said.

Morgan glanced at Hermann. "I don't suppose she had anything that might have come from the Moses' safe deposit box on her."

"No," Richmond responded. "But, she's been IDed as a member of Tasman's Baltimore campaign staff. I'd say it's time to bring the boy wonder primary candidate in for a sit-down chat, as politically suicidal as that will be."

"We've already scheduled an interview with him," Hermann said.

"Where and when?"

"The end of the week at his D.C. campaign office. We could try to move it up, but their feathers are already ruffled, which might . . ."

Richmond cut Hermann off. "No, stick with whatever you have now. We'll take enough heat as it is."

Morgan nodded. "Okay. We had Proffitt make some stills of the woman claiming to be Jordan Moses at the Freeport Bank. We can compare them to the floater."

★ ★ ★

"Grabowski."

"It's me, Jim," Dusty said quietly.

"What can I do for you?" The warmth in Grabowski's voice wouldn't have melted the smallest snowflake.

"Jim, we've got to get past this. What do I have to do?"

"Dusty, I love you with all my heart. But when you do things like you did at the press conference, it makes things difficult for all of us, but especially me."

"How would you feel if I got angry with you for doing your job, Jim? I didn't plan it. The question wasn't part of some grand conspiracy to embarrass the BPD. I happened to see Morgan and Hermann coming out of Tasman's D.C. campaign headquarters. Why would they be there?"

"Dusty, you had met with Jordan and then talked to Gordon Moses before each of them was killed. You *knew* why they were at the campaign headquarters, and you asked the Commissioner anyway. That wasn't part of your *job*!"

Dusty didn't respond for several seconds. Finally she said, "That's a fair point, Jim. And, if it makes any difference, I took photos of the man found with Gordon Moses' phone and the DVD Peter and I got from Jordan's mother to Morgan and Hermann first thing in the morning. And, I'll help them in any way I can, going forward."

"Thanks, Dusty. I'm sure they'll appreciate it. And we'll *all* appreciate you not enticing people to jump to the conclusion that you're a cop."

"Jim, I promise I'll try to never do anything that puts you in an awkward position again. I want this to be over. I miss you terribly."

"I miss you too, sweetheart. It's behind us. Are you at the office?"

"Yes. I'm getting ready to leave. When will you be home?"

"I don't know, babe. I'm working with the ATF sifting through evidence. I'll try to be there before midnight."

"I'll be waiting!"

* * *

Dayo Amoako opened the left rear door of the black Crown Victoria and clicked the small LED flashlight on with his thumb. The bright, white light played on the end of the door, exposing its black, childproof switch. With a flick of an index finger, he threw it into the "on" position, preventing the door from being unlocked from inside the back seat.

After repeating the same process on the opposite rear door, Dayo returned to the driver's seat and started the Ford, then double-parked in front of the Willard Hotel.

✦✦✦

TWENTY-EIGHT

"Mr. President, I don't think we should continue down this scorched earth policy any longer. There are hundreds dead already in Afghanistan alone and probably more in Pakistan, Iran and Iraq. Only Israel is standing with us at the U.N." The Secretary of State paused for a moment. "This is causing even the British to question our actions. We are creating a great deal of international hatred for America and her people."

"They hated us to start with, Marge. In the next few minutes, I'm going to tell the country and the world, that this is just a taste of what will happen if there are any more attacks on us. We tried the carrot approach, spending trillions of dollars on aid. What did that get us?"

"Ten seconds, Mister President," a voice said from behind the bright lights in the Oval Office.

"Sir . . ."

"Not now, Marge."

"Five, four, . . ."

"Good evening my fellow Americans. Tonight, I want to share with you, and the world, what I ordered our military to do and why.

"Let me start by repeating the exact words President Reagan said on April 14, 1986, to America after the bombing of Libya: 'I warned that there should be no place on Earth where terrorists can rest and train and practice their deadly skills. I meant it. I said that we would act with others, if possible, and alone if necessary to ensure that terrorists have no sanctuary anywhere. Tonight, we have.'"

"Tonight we have, *again*. In response to the bombings at the Baltimore and Washington airports, American military forces have struck targets in Afghanistan, Pakistan, Iraq and Iran, using a variety of weapons and tactics. At my direction, our forces have inflicted many casualties on the elements that murdered innocent people here, have killed our military personnel overseas, and supported and *exported* terrorism around the world. We will make the battle damage assessments available to the Nation as soon as they pose no danger to the forces that performed bravely and with incredible professionalism.

"I realize this retaliation to the attacks on American soil may well be used for political purposes here and elsewhere. However, let me close by paraphrasing President Reagan's 1986 speech: 'We Americans are slow to anger. We always seek peaceful avenues before resorting to the use of force – and we did. We tried quiet diplomacy, public condemnation, economic sanctions, and demonstrations of military force. None succeeded. Despite our repeated warnings, Islamic extremists continued their reckless policy of intimidation and their relentless pursuit of terror. They counted on America to be passive. They counted wrong.'

"Good night and may God bless America and each of you."

✻ ✻ ✻

"Jesus fucking *Christ*!" Jackie Beaudro said, causing a dozen heads to turn away from a large monitor in the Ice Queen's campaign headquarters.

"Jackie!" the senator said under her breath before ushering the black woman into a small side office.

"Thatch just handed the election to whichever Democrat wins the nomination!" Beaudro said with no attempt to hide the glee in her voice. "If you win, you're *in*!"

"Jackie, the worst thing I could do at this moment would be to play politics."

"Of course, Senator. You don't need to. All we need to do is issue a statement saying that you fully support America's right to defend itself. All we have to do now is beat T-squared. The press will take care of the rest!"

✻ ✻ ✻

At 10:55 p.m., following a small fund-raising session, Senator Tasman walked slowly down the steps in front of the Willard Hotel, studying a sheet of paper in his right hand. A Secret Service agent held the back door of a black Ford Crown Victoria open for the senator, who nodded and smiled at the man as he eased himself into the car's back seat. "I'm ready to go home, Ayo."

"Yes, sir," the agent said, closing the door, and seating himself behind the steering wheel. A few seconds later, the Crown Victoria drove northwest on Pennsylvania Avenue, toward the White House. As it turned left onto 15th Street, Tasman heard the door's four locks click.

★ ★ ★

POTUS, the Secretary of Defense, the Assistant Secretary of Defense for Special Operations and the Joint Chiefs of Staff occupied the White House Situation Room. None of the President's staff had been invited to the briefing – raising a number of eyebrows, especially the Chief of Staff's.

President Thatch looked around the faces gathered at his end of the long conference table. "Okay, gentlemen, what have you got?"

General McMillan looked at the Secretary and his colleagues' faces for a moment before speaking. "Mr. President, it's your *sap* in the face of Iran. We believe our usual cruise missile response to this situation would be wholly inadequate. We all agree that the Iranians need to feel the sting of this for years to come in such a way that they can't ridicule our response to the world as 'business as usual.' Or use it to generate propaganda for their citizens it's just another sign that we are too weak and cowardly to show up and actually fight them. Our considered opinion is that you need to respond in such a way that induces doubt and fear into their decision making process for years, if not decades, to come.

"To say the military has been salivating for decades to do what we're about to outline would be an understatement akin to 'The Titanic hit an iceberg and had a bit of a problem.'"

McMillan hit a key on the open laptop next to him and the large screen at the end of the table came to life with a satellite view of the Northern Persian Gulf. Clearly marked were Iran, Iraq and Kuwait. A few keystrokes zoomed in on the western coast of Iran and two islands there, the smaller to the northeast of the larger – labeled "Khark Island."

"Sir, I know you're aware of the significance of this location from an economic perspective; however, it would also offer a huge morale boost to our men and women in uniform. Especially those maimed in Iraq and Afghanistan and the families of the fallen.

"We can give you as much detail as you like, sir, but the bottom line is this: in less than eight hours, Navy Seals supported by the

Army's 160th Aviation Battalion and the CIA are going to cripple Iran for years to come and hopefully drive its citizens to take their country back from the Ayatollahs."

"Just give me the big picture, General, and make sure this same group is assembled here when the operation begins. I assume we'll have live video."

"Yes, Mr. President, we will."

☆ ☆ ☆

Major Shipp stood next to a large map of Khark and Kharko Islands and in front of the assembled group in Goofy, a red laser pointer in his right hand.

"So, here we have Khark and its little brother Kharko to the northeast." The laser's red dot made circles in the center of the larger island.

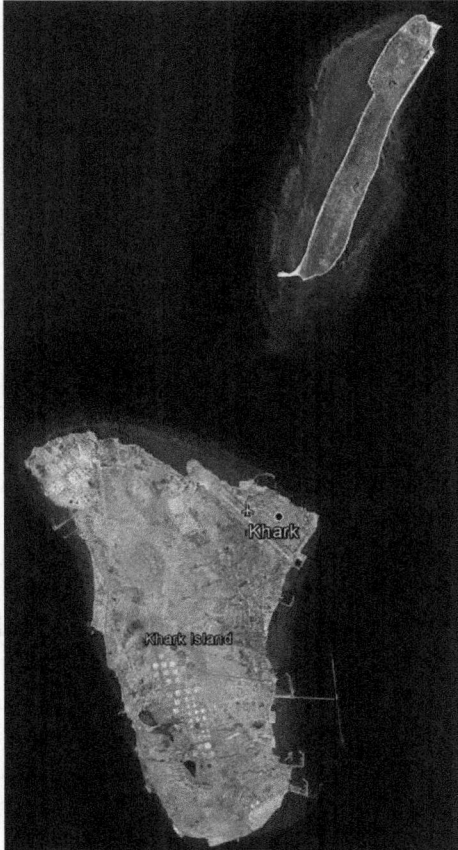

Khark and Kharko Islands

"This long oil terminal on the southeast side handles about 90 percent of Iran's crude oil exports. A little further south of it is a smaller liquid natural gas pier and storage facility near a few other volatile storage tanks. On the west side of Khark is a large docking pier – about 2500 feet offshore. You can see the pipes for material handling under-water here." The red dot moved across the water from the island to what looked like a long pipe above the surface with several knob-like bumps along its length.

"In the center of the island are three tank farms with forty-seven containers of varying size. The material handling locations and the tank farm are our primary targets.

"The Army's 160th *Night Stalkers* are going to get us in and out." A quiet groan went up following the word "Army."

"Fuck you squids and jarheads!" an anonymous voice said from the middle of the group, followed by a low chuckle from the other Army members of the assemblage.

"That's enough of that shit!" Shipp said sternly, followed by a wide grin. America's inter-service rivalries were alive and well. "We'll also have the support of two Air Force AC-130 gunships.

"The 160th will use CH-47 Chinooks to ferry our RHIBs and two heavily modified fast boats into position near the target area. For those of you old enough to remember *Miami Vice*, the fast boats are the same design as the one in the TV show's opening scene, but that's where the similarity ends. Ours will be carrying mines, four to a boat, strapped down two on either side. After dropping the mines near the three docking and transfer points, and in the three little harbors on the east side of the island, these boats will use their 25mm chain guns to unleash a barrage of armor piercing incendiary rounds and .50 caliber BMGs to ventilate the volatile tanks nearest the water."

A hand shot up from the group. "What kind of mines, sir?"

Shipp smiled before answering. "I like to call them, '*boutique*' mines. These little beauties have been built by CIA and Naval personnel. They're 500 pound, MK83, standard low drag bombs with modified fusing that's sensitive to ferrous metals. When the Iranians decide to rebuild what we've taken out, they'll get a little after-action surprise. The metal eyelets in their boots will set these things off, much less a steel-hulled boat. They'll be deployed at low tide –approximately 2200 hours IDT – 1730 hours Zulu – to make sure they're ready and waiting when the Ayatollah's boys show up.

"On shore, four Little Birds will deposit the ground assault teams within the main tank farm then they'll withdraw to Kharko Island to refuel from a Chinook and wait for the extraction signal. The four teams will attach demolition charges in the form of large magnetic clams to the volatile storage tanks. There will be several incendiary charges with timers to ignite the fuel as it flows out of the tanks.

"The rigid-hulled inflatable boats are equipped with dual .50 caliber Bushmaster chain guns. Their 500 rounds per minute will respond to any Iranian patrol boats lucky enough to escape the AC-130 gunships. They'll also serve as support for the assault teams' backup exfiltration vehicles – the fast boats – in case anything goes wrong with the Little Birds waiting to bring 'em home.

"But the SWCC boy's primary mission is to sweep in near the shipping facilities. If they draw fire from shore, the gunships can wipe 'em out quickly. That'll give the fast boats time to lay their mines without being hassled. If the RHIBs don't draw fire, they'll create a diversion by turning their chain guns on the tanks close by.

"We'll be dropped in between the tanks and start placing the venting charges and ignition devices while working our way south. Based on the satellite images, we should have enough to cover most of the major storage units. Any we can't set charges on will give the gunship crews something to light up.

"We'll have three Joint Terminal Attack Controllers on the mission. One wet for the RHIBs and fast boats, call sign Viper-Strike-four-one. One dry for the ground mission, call sign Viper-Strike-eight-six. And one in the sky, call sign Pee-Wee-seven. He's an Air Force JTAC to provide any necessary coordination between his counterparts below, the gunships, Chinooks and Little Birds. He'll be in in a Uniform-twenty-eight-Alpha.

"You may be wondering why we don't put one of our own SEAL JTACs in the sky. It's simply a matter of fuel economy. We want that Uniform-twenty-eight to be on station as long as possible if things go sideways. A second JTAC, depending on weight, could burn up to two and a half hours of fuel."

Another hand rose from the group. "Major, that looks like a nice housing area between the southwest part of the tank farm and the coast. Is it fair to say that's military security?"

"You read my mind, marine. The backup exfiltration for the main assault team will run just north of that housing. So we've pointed it out to our Air *Farce* friends for a healthy dose of their *attention* as the mission gets underway."

Shipp trained his pointer on a grassy area across from the housing area. "The primary extraction point is this soccer field. The gunships can make sure the Iranians' heads are down while we get out of Dodge."

"Sir, won't the 130's come under Iranian anti-aircraft fire, sir?" an anonymous voice asked.

"If there's any left after the earlier air strikes. The Navy pounded them pretty well. We've got satellite eyes on them, and they don't appear to have had time to rebuild or rearm yet. But just to make sure, we'll have some fly boys out of Aviano to make sure they keep their heads down. Plus, the CIA and Navy will send up a number of weather balloons with timers set to go off as we commence the operation. They'll dump boxes of chaff to sucker any active AA missiles to blow their wad at what appear to be aircraft on the Iranians' radar screens.

"And, of course the AC-130s will be puking flares themselves, if they sense any SAM threats."

"Sir, how do the fighters and gunships overfly Kuwait without them raising a stink and drawing attention to the operation?"

"They've been instructed to disregard any overflights since the beginning of the air campaign against Iran. They'll ultimately bitch about it publically, but privately they're cheering since Iran is a major threat to them too.

"Any more questions?"

No one raised a hand or spoke.

"If not, let me give you one more piece of information. Some of you may be wondering why there's a ground and amphibious element to this op when we could easily destroy the island without setting foot on it. A twenty-four cruise missile strike. A load of 2000-pound JDAMS followed with a wide bomb pattern of anti-personnel cluster munitions. Then the icing on the Ayatollahs' cake could be cluster mines dropped around the shipping facilities as a last laugh to relief or repair missions."

Shipp paused, but still no one spoke. "What I'm about to tell you comes directly from the President through the Sec. Def. and down the chain of command.

"Cruise missile strikes aren't unique. Our enemies mock us for not showing up and doing it like men. Pretty much the same if we use

JDAMS. Everyone knows we drop a few bombs and call it even. Just another day in Islamic Asia.

"Well, not tonight. President Thatch wants to make this a personal slap in the Iranians' faces. It'll be an easy message to understand. 'You have been fucking us directly or indirectly since Ayatollah Khomeini took over. You or your proxy states are responsible for hundreds, if not thousands, of American deaths. Tonight we're kicking your ass on an island. Any more bullshit from Iran and the next time we will be on your mainland.' Questions?"

No one spoke.

"Okay then. Let's gear-up. Synchronize watches. On my mark it will be 1525 hours Zulu. Mark!"

***"HOOYAH*!"**

* * *

The airpower headed toward Khark Island would have been enough for a major air show in most American communities. Eight Chinook – MH-47G – helicopters designed for Special Operations Aviation flew in two groups of three, separated by a quarter mile with the seventh and eighth Chinooks a half-mile behind. One of Major Shipp's RHIBs hung below each of the six leading choppers. The trailing Chinooks ferried two fast boats.

Four MH-6 Little Birds choppers flew in formation two miles behind the Chinooks. Each MH-6 carried four SEALs – two seated on platforms on either side above their skids. The operational plan called for the Chinooks to deposit the RHIBs and fast boats before the SEALs deployed to provide supporting fire and alternative extraction vehicles if needed.

A ninth Chinook trailed the Little Birds, its mission to refuel them on Kharko Island before they extracted the SEALs, since the 224-mile round-trip flight would come uncomfortably close to their 267-mile range.

Above the mass of rotary wing aircraft were layers of the fixed wing variety. Two AC-130U Spooky gunships, each carrying 25, 40 and 105mm weapons, circled at a classified altitude over the Persian Gulf within a short flight of the target area. To the west, at a higher altitude over Saudi Arabia, a KC-135R took up an orbiting station to refuel the Spooky gunships and the E-3 AWACS Sentry Airborne Warning and Control System. The E-3 would control all the fixed wing aircraft below it in a delicate dance, ensuring no mid-air collisions.

The Chinooks and Little Birds flew under the control of a specially designed Pilatus PC-12 with the Air Force designation: U-28A, piloted by a qualified Air Force JTAC – call sign Peewee-7. As outlined by Major Shipp, he would provide assistance if necessary to the "wet" and "dry" SWCCs and SEALs and coordinate the Chinooks and Little Birds' movements and communicate directly with the Ground Force Commander – Major Shipp, call sign Viper Strike Actual – if necessary.

The Swiss manufactured low-wing U-28A flew silently above 1,000 feet due to its propeller and special exhaust system. After taking off from a dirt airstrip outside Khafji, Saudi Arabia, it traveled northeast to rendezvous with the Chinooks and Little Birds carrying the SEALs and their boats. Modified with night vision capabilities similar to the Spooky gunships' the U-28A would coordinate the SEALs insertions and extractions and monitor their movements in the tank farm and shipping areas. Also on board were highly sophisticated satellite communications systems capable of transmitting live video feeds from the Spookys' surveillance and targeting systems back to Special Operations Command at Florida's MacDill AFB and the White House Situation Room.

The weather balloons released by the CIA and Navy had deployed their aluminum chaff earlier near the western coasts of Khark Island and the Iranian mainland without drawing any response. Either no surface to air missiles remained after the previous strikes or the Iranians recognized the ruse for what it was. In either case, any number of Russian SA-7 MANPADS, or their Chinese or North Korean variants, could be waiting on the island for the choppers and Air Force fixed-wing craft overhead.

✱ ✱ ✱

The phone on the *Resolute* desk buzzed. POTUS looked at it over the glasses hung near the point of his nose and pressed the intercom switch. "Yes, Karen?"

"Sir, they're ready for you in the Situation Room."

"Thank you. On my way."

✱ ✱ ✱

With all the fixed-wing aircraft in place, the Air Force major piloting the U-28A did a quick communications check with the AC-130U gunships named *Death's Kiss* and *Angry Spook*, call signs Leper-16 and Spook-38 respectively. He then directed them to go to the command and control frequency to be shared by the wet and dry JTACs below, the SWCCs in their RHIBs and fast boats and choppers. Once the radio frequency change completed and Peewee-7 acknowledged all the assets' responses, the net became quiet.

Half a mile off Khark Island's West Coast, the six Chinooks fanned out to form a line running north-south. Each chopper had an access hatch in the cargo bay amidships. One member of each SWCC crew opened the hatch above their respective RHIB and dropped a rope. Within seconds, the crews slid down and took up their stations in the suspended boats. Once all members were on aboard, each Chinook's crew chief informed the flight deck and the RHIB made contact with the water. When "wet" the crews disconnected the four heavy straps supporting their crafts, started their engines, and sped toward their assigned Khark Island targets.

The now-empty Chinooks turned to the north and began a circuitous circular route to Kharko Island where they would land and wait – rotors spinning – for the call to recover their loads for the return to Auhah Island. Behind the now waterborne RHIBs and departing Chinooks, the fast boats and crews were delivered with the same speed and efficiency.

Each Army and Air Force flight crew had been extensively briefed on the mission and all wet and dry special operator elements. Now with the pieces of the operation inbound to their targets, the AC-130U gunships took up their assigned positions. Leper-16 would move to a point between Khark and Kharko Islands to cover the Chinooks and Little Birds on the ground, waiting to extract the SEALs, SWCCs, their RHIBs and fast boats. Additionally, Leper would monitor the northern portion of Khark, the town of the same name, and the runway outside of it for any Iranian response.

Peewee-7 laid out the ground rules for Leper-16, advising the pilot that a free fire zone existed 200 meters north of Khark Island's tank farm and 100 meters northeast of the waiting aircraft on Kharko Island.

Spook-38 orbited above the southern point of Khark Island covering the RHIBs and fast boats attacking the shipping facilities.

"Spook-three-eight, Peewee-seven. Fire mission. Over."

"Three-eight. Go ahead Peewee."

"Peewee-seven. On the east side of Khark. On the north side of the base of the large T-shaped shipping terminal, there is a small harbor.

In it are seven small boats in the lower right-hand corner and three larger patrol boats docked along the leg running to the northwest. Copy?"

"Three-eight. Seven small boats in lower right-hand corner. Three larger docked along leg running to the northwest."

"Peewee-seven, good read back. Consider all those craft active targets. You are clear to engage."

"Three-eight, roger that. We have them in sight. Confirm all friendly boats are marked by infrared strobes."

"Peewee-seven, roger that. All friendly boats marked with IR."

Inside the AC-130U, the fire control officer (FCO) had monitored the previous transmissions and within a few seconds spoke to the pilot via the aircraft's internal communication network.

Guns on the AC-130U are referred to by number from front to back of the aircraft.

"Pilot, you have IR, gun two, trainable, channel A. FCO is ready."

The navigator confirmed the target location.

In the cockpit, the pilot checked the sight lines in her Heads Up Display and, satisfied, responded: "Arm two."

"Two's armed."

The pilot raised the consent switch to the "on" position, giving the crew the final safety check in the firing sequence.

The term "trainable" in the FCO's communication indicated that the sensor operator would fire the 40mm Bofors cannon rather than the pilot. Using a joystick, he carefully aligned the sights on the cluster of small boats identified in the corner of the harbor and fired.

The Bofors spat six 40mm high-explosive grenade rounds in less than four seconds. On board, the air crew watched their monitors for the few seconds it took for the shells to impact the docked craft below.

The six 40mm rounds impacted in and around the center of the cluster, quickly obscuring their images on the black and white screens in a boiling mass of fire and smoke. Several secondary explosions followed when a number of fuel tanks exploded as well.

The exploding 40mm, high velocity, armor-piercing, incendiary projectile and fuel tanks ended any element of surprise. Black dots began scurrying on the docks, many toward the three larger craft Peewee-7 had identified.

"Excellent, Spook. Looks like they're going to try to get the three big boats underway. You are free to engage. Over."

"Roger that, Peewee. They're next," the pilot responded.

The FCO spoke on the internal network again. ""Pilot, you have IR, gun three, trainable, channel A. FCO is ready."

"Navigation confirms."

"Arm three."

"Three armed."

The sensor operator moved his joystick, centering its crosshairs on the first boat in the line and fired a high explosive shell from the 105mm Howitzer. A few seconds later, it impacted the rear of the lead boat. If the flight crew's view had not been obstructed on their monitors by another flash, fire, and smoke, they would have seen the rear of the craft actually lift out of the water as it disintegrated.

The same sequence of events took place eliminating the other two crafts in short order.

✳ ✳ ✳

POTUS, seated in the high-backed leather chair at the end of the Situation Room table, watched the scene unfold on the large flat screen. "*Jesus*, General McMillan! I wouldn't want to be on the receiving end of *that*!"

"No, sir."

"What's the plan?"

McMillan pointed to a second smaller flat screen mounted next to the first. The image obviously came from a higher altitude than the AC-130U's video feed. Six small boats moved toward opposite sides of the island in single file formations of three. A larger boat trailed a quarter mile behind the last RHIB in each group. "Mr. President, the six RHIBs you see here will sweep the island's east- and west-side shipping facilities to see if they can draw fire. If they do, the 130 gunship you just saw being employed will take out any on-shore resistance. That will allow the fast boats to come in and deploy the magnetic mines.

"If there is no resistance, the RHIBs will use their firepower to ventilate the tanks nearest the shore and ignite them. That will create a distraction drawing the Iranian security forces attention away from the tank farm and reduce the amount of work the SEALs have to do in the areas outside the RHIBs firepower." The JCS Chairman paused for questions.

POTUS nodded. "Okay, go on."

"The four Little Birds will insert the SEALs in the tank farm in four locations." McMillan's red laser pointer indicated the landing zones between the rows of massive tanks from north to south. The JCS Chairman went on to explain the other major details of the operation.

The assembled groups' eyes focused on the flat screen. As the lead RHIBs sped toward the south side of the large T-shaped shipping area on the east side of the island, streaks of light began to dart from the shore toward the lead boat.

✳ ✳ ✳

"Peewee-seven, Peewee-seven, Viper-Strike-four-one, we're taking fire from the East Coast, south of the big shipping terminal. Call contact. Over."

In the U-28A overhead, the JTAC responded. "Four-one, Peewee-seven, roger. I have the gun location in sight and your IR beacon. Wait, out. Break.

"Spook-three-eight, Peewee-seven, fire mission, Over."

"Three-eight, go ahead, Peewee."

"Peewee-seven, friendly RHIBs marked by IR strobes two hundred meters southeast of large T-shaped shipping facility on east side of island. Over."

"Spook-three-eight, roger, visual friendly location, go ahead."

"Peewee-seven, target is south of the bottom of the leg of the T, marked by outgoing tracers. Looks like a Russian or Chicom heavy machine gun, call tally."

Spook-38 read back the target's location, Peewee-7 acknowledged it as correct and gave clearance to fire. Inside the AC-130U, the fire control officer had monitored the previous transmissions and, within a few seconds, spoke to the pilot.

"Pilot, you have IR, gun one, trainable, channel A. FCO is ready."

"Navigation confirms."

The pilot responded: "Arm one."

"One's armed."

The pilot clicked her safety switch on.

The sensor operator trained his sights to the Iranian machine gun position. When number one – a 25mm Gatling gun – opened up, sounding like a huge, enormously flatulent bird, it would have frightened even the angriest of spooks. On board, the air crew watched their monitors for the few seconds it took for the rounds to impact the four Iranians huddled together in the target area. Without sound, a dozen small black clouds, eerily outlined in white, sprang up, around, and over the gun position, eliminating it as a threat.

★ ★ ★

The explosions and noise of Spook-38's fire drew the Iranians' attention all over Khark Island either directly or via phone and radio. Peewee-7 observed a number of people depart the large housing complex on the southwest corner of the tank farm and begin moving toward the shipping facilities. A quick call to Spook-38 eliminated many of them. Those still alive, with enough guts and ambulatory, moved forward at a snail's pace. Many sought shelter under something solid and didn't move.

As planned, the RHIBs fired hundreds of rounds into the storage tanks nearest the water. Sparks from the ventilated containers and tracers provided an ample ignition source for the tens of thousands of gallons of oil and gasoline gushing onto the island and toward the water.

The fast boats entered the major shipping facilities, taking no fire in the process, and laid the magnetic mines almost at the maximum point of low tide as Shipp had described. As they departed, not wanting to be outdone by the RHIBs, the fast boat SWCCs emptied most of their ammunition into the tanks and other targets of opportunity on the shore, then headed for open water. The RHIBs followed their faster brethren at top speed.

The Little Birds landing in the tank farm drew almost no attention in the shadow of the light and sound show going on to the south.

"Peewee-seven, Viper-Strike-Actual. We're on the ground and moving."

The JTAC overhead acknowledged Major Shipp's call and passed the information to both gunships.

Shipp and his men moved among the tanks, quickly placing their charges and ignition devices. Each group of four leapfrogged the other three groups as they completed their work in a given row of tanks. Shipp wore a video camera, capturing the activity and transmitted it to Peewee-7 where it was recorded and relayed back to the nervous eyes in Florida and the Situation Room.

Within a few minutes, having encountered no Iranian resistance, the SEALs laid all their charges and neared the primary extraction point. "Peewee-seven, Viper-Strike-Actual. We're one hundred meters from extraction point X-ray. Over."

Overhead, the JTAC had continuously tracked the amphibious and ground team's progress. When the fast boats and RHIBs departed the shipping facilities, toward open water, he alerted the Chinooks to proceed to recover them west of Khark.

Having also monitored Shipp's team's movement south, he advised the Little Birds minutes before – now refueled – to get airborne in the direction of X-ray. With no aircraft left on Kharko Island, Leper-16 could discontinue the covering flight and move south to assist Spook-38 with any needed support. Before departing however, Leper-16 requested, and was granted, permission to riddle the runway outside of the town of Khark with 105mm Howitzer fire, making it unable to receive flights. Reinforcements and repair materials from the mainland would have to arrive by helicopters and boats – and the latter were in for some nasty surprises.

"Peewee, roger that, Actual. Birds are inbound. X-ray-two, mike's out."

On the soccer field, Shipp's team formed four, outward-facing groups twenty meters apart to allow for simultaneous extraction. Shipp barely heard the arriving choppers over the roaring tanks ablaze nearby. His eyes swept the housing facility to the west and the flagpole in front of it. "I'll be right back, top."

Master Chief Pridemore started to speak but before he could, Shipp raced across the edge of the field, pulling something from his right cargo pocket. Behind him the SEALS who could see what he had in his hand broke out in a cheer. ***HOOYAHHH***!

In the Situation Room, the assemblage watched the grainy, greenish, bouncing image from Shipp's camera as he ran toward what looked like a mound of earth surrounded by benches and four floodlights pointed up at sharp angles.

"What the hell is he doing?" POTUS asked, shaking his head.

McMillan blinked several times, trying to steady the picture in his mind. "I honestly don't know, sir."

Within seconds, the bottom of a flagpole became visible. Shipp's hands came into view as he unwrapped the halyard and pulled it down. An Iranian flag came into view. Shipp unclipped and replaced it with the Stars and Stripes, ran it up, re-secured the halyard around and over the cleat. He stepped back, saluted the colorful object, turned and raced back to the LZ.

Cheers erupted in the Situation Room. POTUS shook his head. "Son of a **bitch**! General, when that young SEAL gets his feet back on CONUS, you make sure you personally ream him a new asshole!"

McMillan, a smile still on his face, nodded. "Yes, Mr. President."

"And after you do, you tell him I think that was the *best* sap in the enemy's face for what happened to us on nine-eleven."

* * *

The Little Birds settled onto the soccer field as Major Shipp arrived back with his group. The pilot of the chopper closest to the flag-pole held out his right fist and Shipp bumped it lightly as he turned and sat on the already rising platform. As the ship climbed out, his video camera caught clear images of the American flag. It stood out straight in the rotor wash and mild sea breeze.

Shipp leaned forward and watched the tank farm recede in the distance. The ignition devices began going off at the first insertion points and the conflagration began its march toward the soccer field. The SEALs *HOOYAH*s were drowned out by the Little Birds' noise.

The gunships waited for the Little Birds to clear the area and, once they were over open water, began firing on the storage tanks closest to the soccer field.

Two Iranian gunboats – inactive until now – rounded the northeast point of the Khark Island and headed out to sea in pursuit of the departing choppers – a useless, fatal mistake.

"Leper-one-six, Peewee-seven. I have a couple of watercraft moving away from the island. I doubt they're a threat to the extraction activities, but there's no reason not to smoke 'em. You're cleared to engage at will."

"One-six. Roger that. Have them in sight. Appreciate the farewell gift, Peewee."

In less than a minute, flaming debris on the water marked the final casualties of the evening.

Hovering Chinooks dropped rope ladders over each secured RHIB and fast boat, and the SWCCs scrambled up and into their cargo bays. The twin rotor ships lifted their cargos, dipped their noses and followed the *Little Bird*s. The SEALs and boat guys flew toward Auhah Island without a scratch.

TWENTY-NINE

Fort Marcy Park – originally part of the system of fortifications around Washington, D.C., during the Civil War – sits about one-half mile southwest of the Potomac River in Northern Virginia. It is most well known in recent history as the spot where White House Counsel Vince Foster's body was found in July of 1993. The entrance to the park is off the northbound lanes of the George Washington Parkway, just after crossing a creek known as Pimmit Run.

The National Park Service patrol car eased down the access road at just after midnight. Though posted as closed at 10 p.m., the small parking lot and hiking trails were often frequented by amorous individuals and partying under-aged drinkers.

The driver noticed a dark lump in the last space of the parking lot. Swinging the car's spotlight onto it, a dark sock and the sole of a man's left shoe came into view. Within less than thirty seconds, the officer felt for the rhythmic throbbing of the common carotid artery.

★ ★ ★

"Prince George's County 911, what is your emergency?"

"We just found a body."

"What kind of body?"

"A dead one! You know, one *without life*."

"No need for the attitude, sir."

"Well, do you think I'd be calling if we'd found a dead parakeet or goldfish?"

"Your name, sir?"

"Drew Springer. I'm with BEST Recycling in Beltsville."

"It's 1:10 a.m. How did you come to find a body at this early hour?"

"We run a transfer station. Trucks show up between 5:00 a.m. and 4:00 p.m. One came in with a roll-off from a construction site in Northwest D.C. at closing time yesterday. The security guard's dog kept diggin' at the pile and uncovered a hand. The guard called me, I called you."

"So, no one noticed the body yesterday?"

"If they had, we'd have called you *yesterday*! Whoever murdered this person must have put the body in the roll-off when it was nearly empty, 'cause he was near the top of the pile when the dog found him."

"How do you know the person was murdered?"

"Wow! That's a tough one. Because when most people die, their corpse doesn't wind up rolled *up* in a rug in a roll-*off*."

✳ ✳ ✳

"Mr. President, I'm sorry to wake you, but there's an urgent call from the Secretary of Homeland Security."

POTUS blinked several times, trying to focus on the White House staff member's face before taking the offered phone.

"This is the President. What's up, Bob?"

"Sir, we've had a major security breach. It appears that Senator Tasman was murdered by his Secret Service driver. We . . ."

"What the *fuck*, Michael! How could that happen?"

The President's outburst brought his wife to a sitting position. "Rodney!"

"We had peeled off most of the senator's detail to cover other issues related to the bombings, sir. He was simply being driven from the Willard to his residence.

"The vast majority of my people have worked the last seventy-two hours straight without a break. There was no other way."

"There's *always* another way, Michael! Jesus! Not only a *senator*, but potentially the first black man to sit in the *White House*!

"You better have tighter cover on the Ice Queen and Desert Fox than the plastic on an Italian's sofa! My God! Just when you think it can't get any worse . . ."

"It already did, Mr. President. We just discovered postings on several white supremacists' websites claiming responsibility for Senator Tasman's death."

✮✮
✮✮

THIRTY

Almost five days to the minute after the bomb detonations at BWI and IAD, the nation's airlines began to function slowly, trying to move millions of travelers. With the exception of *Coyote News* the Stinger missiles' theft received virtually no broadcast or cable coverage. Newspapers and bloggers reported – in many cases, wildly exaggerated and unverified – stories ranging from assigning blame to ultra-rightwing Americans, to the "theft" being a hoax to terrify the flying public, driving down airline stock prices so greedy Wall Street corporate raiders could snap them up for a fraction of their actual value. In the case of the Fifth Estate, precious little "circulation" took place due to a lack of newsprint. America's transportation issues prevented resupply and most of the stories printed sat on loading docks.

Riots spread in cities large and small across the country as stranded passengers were pushed out of airport facilities for security reasons. Hotels were immediately booked solid, with many of those who couldn't be accommodated squatting in their lobbies, meeting and banquet facilities.

Restaurants quickly ran out of food when deliveries slowed to a mere crawl. Looting and shoplifting at grocery and convenience stores emptied most of their shelves in less than forty-eight hours.

Frustrated flyers descended on rental car agencies by the thousands, stripping them of anything on wheels in an attempt to get to their destinations – primarily home. The surge in motor traffic drained many gas stations' storage tanks and those with fuel had lines making the 1973 Arab oil embargo seem infinitesimal by comparison. Price gouging in several locations across the country resulted in mobs murdering station attendants. Two men in Illinois were soaked in gasoline and burned to death. City streets, state roads and interstate highways were littered with vehicles' fuel gauges pointing below "E." Carjacking incidents became rampant.

Gun stores had to post armed guards to prevent theft, resulting in a number of deaths. In Los Angeles, Chicago, and New York, handguns were selling on the black market for fifty times the usual rates. In Missouri, a mob broke into a military armory and emptied it of everything light enough to be carried off, including a 155mm mortar and 30 rounds of 90-pound HE munitions.

✮ ✮ ✮

At 300 East Madison Street, in Baltimore's Central Booking and Intake Center the short man handed a Corrections Officer a yellow Post-it note with a phone number written on. The CO looked at the number and then the man's face. "Is this the number of your lawyer?"

"No, my friend."

After dialing the number the CO held out the pay phone's handset to the prisoner.

"Harley, you got to get me out of here!"

"You stupid *motherfucker*! You called me on *this* line!"

The small man's voice cracked. "I got to get out of here, Harley. I knew you'd answer this line."

"Callin' your old lady never crossed your mind?"

"She's jammed up too, man. She had some blow on her when they picked us up. You're the only one can help me."

"Who have you talked to?"

"No one! I swear, Harley! *No one*!"

"You make motherfuckin' sure you don't before I can get someone to you. You hear me?"

"I won't say a word to nobody. I swear!"

✮ ✮ ✮

"We know he drove from the Willard to Fort Marcy Park based on the tracking chip in the car. He's there less than three minutes. At 2316 hours he heads up the GWP to the inner loop of the beltway. He crosses the American Legion Bridge into Maryland, takes the spur up to I-270, goes east on I-370 and continues on the Intercounty Connector across Montgomery and Prince George's Counties. The EZPass system recorded his paying the toll when he gets onto I-95 North at 2348 hours.

From there, we tracked him to Pier Side Drive near Baltimore's Harbor. At 0038 hours the tracking chip went dark."

Looking up at the Secretary of Homeland Security, the Secret Service duty officer paused for questions.

"You say you reviewed Amoako's service record and background investigation with a microscope. What jumped out at you?"

"Not a thing, sir. On paper, he's as clean as they come."

⋆ ⋆ ⋆

"You okay, Cappy?" Holcomb asked with a white-knuckled grip on the phone handset.

"Yeah, Major. He just winged me."

"So, take me through it."

"Well, not much to tell, really. We see a guy on Pier Side Drive get out of a dark car and lean back inside. The engine races and he must have put it in drive, 'cause it shoots off the end of the pier into the harbor. Then he climbs down a ladder and into a cigarette boat and off they go toward the Chesapeake Bay and God only knows where after that.

"We were just lucky enough to pinch 'em off just as they got to the bend near the Pump House. They fired four, maybe five shots at us. One of which nicked my arm enough to need a Band-Aid. Pike took one in the leg but I didn't know it at the time. He took the guy at the wheel down with a single shot, even though he must have been in bad shape.

"A guy in a suit threw up his hands and I boarded 'em. Then it got weird."

"Yeah?"

"The suit is a Secret Service agent. ID says he's Ayo Amoako. Now why would somebody like that ditch a car in the harbor, run from and fire on police officers?"

"Because, according to the feds, he's wanted in connection with the murder of a United States senator and potential presidential candidate."

"Well, he's in custody for killin' a member of the BPD Harbor Unit. That bullet in Pike's leg hit his femoral artery. He bled out before I could get him to help."

"I'm sorry, Cappy. Pike was a damn good man."

"Yes, sir. He was." Cappy's voice cracked. "What now, Major?"

"The feds undoubtedly know where their car went and it won't take 'em long to figure out we probably have him. Is this SS agent at Central Booking?"

"No, sir. He's in the ER. There were some pretty heavy seas when we took him into custody. Then he resisted arrest when we got him on solid ground and the backup officers and wagon man had to subdue him."

"Thank God he didn't get *subdued* by the CID and cell block guys!"

"He hasn't had a chance to resist *them* yet, sir."

✫✫✫

THIRTY-ONE

"Morgan."

"It's Moxley at Central Booking."

"Hey, Mox! What's up?"

"That dweeb you were interrogating about the Moses murders."

"Yeah?"

"He's belly-up. Found him in the shower this a.m. Somebody stuck a shiv in both his eyes and scrambled his brains, assuming of course that he had any to start with."

"God *damn* it! Did he say anything before he checked out?"

"Not to any of the COs. He was gone when we found him. Sorry Morgan."

"Who was the last CO to have contact with him?"

"I was. He made a phone call to someone named Harley. You want the number he called?"

"Hell yes!"

Moxley read the number. Morgan wrote it down and read it back.

"Is the woman who was with him still in custody?"

"The woman with tits you could land small aircraft on? Yeah. She's still here."

"Get her into isolation, quick."

"I had her put on ice before we fitted the little guy for a rubber cocoon."

★ ★ ★

"Mr. President, there's more than a little confusion in terms of who killed Senator Tasman."

"Go on."

"The Baltimore Police say they have Ayo Amoako in custody for killing a BPD Harbor Patrol officer."

"Yeah?"

"The PG County ME says the prints on the body recovered from a major recycling company in Beltsville, Maryland, belong to Ayo Amoako and that's he's been dead for 48 to 72 hours."

"Great! What are the white supremacists saying?"

"All the groups that have responded so far say their sites were hacked. None of them want any responsibility for good reason. A black mob in Mississippi burned a known KKK member's house to the ground, killing him and his pregnant wife."

"Just what we need now! A race war!"

* * *

Dusty Rhodes approached the desks of Morgan and Hermann.

As she neared Morgan's desk, she overheard him say, "His call went to a burner. Moxley said someone named 'Harley.' I'll start the paperwork to see what we can find out."

"I just came by to apologize to you two personally for the heat I caused you. I've made up with Jim and I wanted to try to close the book on my error in judgment. I'm truly sorry."

"Thanks," Morgan said, looking up.

"What can I do to help you guys?"

"What makes you think we need your help?" Hermann asked.

"I wasn't trying to eavesdrop, Detective, but I just heard Hunter say something about a burner and paperwork? I have a contact that might be able to provide information in the next few minutes, rather than the next few weeks. If I can help you pull your case together, I will."

"As long as you get a story out of it?" Morgan said, doing nothing to hide the sarcasm in his voice.

"If I get a story, that's fine. I'm just offering to help, like I've done in the past."

Hermann glanced at Morgan briefly and nodded slightly.

Morgan nodded in return, wrote a phone number on a slip of paper and handed it to the reporter. "The senator is no longer an active suspect in the Moses' murders . . . Dusty."

* * *

Senator Reynolds, bathed in dozens of photographers' flashes, stood solemnly behind the podium and its bouquet of microphones and cleared her throat. "I . . . we . . . want to say how incredibly shocked and saddened we are at the death of Senator Tasman. Thaddeus was a fine man, a good man, husband, and father. Although he and I were heavily engaged in becoming our party's nominee for the Oval Office, I never lost respect or admiration for him. The best interest of the State of Iowa and the United States drove every action he took in the Senate. Thaddeus Tasman was a very bright light, snuffed out for reasons we don't yet know, but far too soon for America's or the world's benefit."

✯ ✯ ✯

"We're fucked!" Senator Fox said to no one in particular, shaking his head. "The President's bombing the shit out of half the earth wasn't bad enough. Now, with Tasman's death, the Ice Queen will get the sympathy vote too."

Fox's campaign manager shook his head. "Senator, you never know how these things will play out. There may be strong support for Thatch's response to the BWI and IAD bombings, especially if it can be tied to Islamic extremists. And, the murder of a presidential candidate could drive the law and order vote, even from Democrats, not to mention . . ."

"We're fucked!"

✯ ✯ ✯

Dusty Rhodes approached the *Baltimore Mirror*'s employee's entrance, dead tired. She was about to make her way to the parking lot when a voice called from behind.

"Hey, Dusty! You got a minute?" asked Pat Sherman, another reporter.

Turning to face Ms. Sherman, Dusty smiled. "Sure, what do you need?"

"My car's in the shop on the corner of Rosemont and Damen. Can you drop me off there?"

"Actually, you can do me a favor on the way. I need to pick up a prescription at the Rosemont Pharmacy. I love their service, but so does everyone else and you have to circle their parking lot like planes the night before Thanksgiving at O'Hare to find a space. So, you drive my car, and I'll run in and get it while you double park. Okay?"

"Sure, let's go."

Dusty reached into her bag, pulled out her car keys and handed them to Pat. "I'm right over here," she said as they pushed through the door. "Just push that little button nearest the key twice to unlock all the doors."

As they approached the BMW, it made two chirping sounds when the locks released. Dusty went to the passenger side, opened it and sat in the front seat, her purse in her lap. Pat opened the rear door on the driver's side and set her bag and an armload of papers on the empty back seat.

Dusty buckled her seat belt as Pat opened the driver's door. A second later, Pat fell into the BMW face down, the majority of her skull above her eyebrows gone. Blood gushed from the massive wound, drenching Dusty in seconds, and filling her mouth as she opened it to scream.

THIRTY-TWO

"Is Dusty okay?" Samantha asked Morgan.

"She's physically okay. Seeing a coworker murdered and then realizing you were the target will be with her forever."

"Survivor's guilt."

"Yeah."

"Any idea who did it?"

"I do. The bullet was recovered in the back seat of her car. It looks like it's in good enough shape to run ballistics tests on it. It's the same weight as used in the previous sniper murders."

"Do you think Dusty was just another random victim . . . well, the woman who died, that is?"

"That's too much coincidence, Sam. Dusty has been snooping around in the Moses cases. I think she stumbled into something people in high places didn't want her sharing."

★ ★ ★

"There's nowhere to run now, Dayo. The only question you have to answer for yourself is, 'Do I want a federal needle in my arm, or life in a Maryland State Prison?'" Morgan had lied to criminals for years without any hint of dishonesty. This instance was no different. He knew the feds would use their muscle to pull Dayo Amoako out of the BPD's custody faster than a hummingbird's beating wings. Morgan just hoped Dayo didn't know that.

The man sitting in front of the two detectives had certainly seen some bad road in the hours since his arrest. Dayo's battered face presented the tip of the proverbial iceberg in terms of the physical abuse he suffered. Had his orange jump suit been removed, little effort would be required to see the bruises on his dark trunk and legs.

"Look, son. I'm not going to waste our time talking to someone who isn't interested in saving himself. You've got thirty seconds to decide if you want to answer our questions. If you don't, I'll turn you back over to some members of the police department who are very anxious to *talk* to you for a few more hours before the feds come for you."

"*No!*" Dayo mumbled through swollen lips and a fractured jaw, before he began to sob softly. "Don't send me back to those *animals!*"

"Then start at the beginning and tell us everything. If we get any idea you're lying or leaving out details, you're going back into the meat grinder. Understand?"

Dayo nodded. "Do you want me to start with the explosives I received?"

"Explosives?" Morgan shot a glance at Hermann. "Where did you get explosives and when?"

"From a woman near Aberdeen shortly after I arrived from Colorado."

Morgan glanced at Hermann and smiled. *Thank God for fair-weather jihadists!*

★ ★ ★

"I'm getting a lot of heat from the feds, Jan. What's the holdup on turning him over?" The BPD Commissioner asked the question knowing full well the probable answer.

Richmond didn't answer immediately, searching the Commissioner's face for a clue to how to play the situation. After a few seconds, he went with his gut instinct and the truth. "Sir, beyond the fact that he killed a member of your command, it appears that he may have given us a lead that's much more important than the death of Senator Tasman. We just need twenty-four hours to chase it down. If he could remain *lost* in the system that much longer, I think you'll be in a very defensible position."

"He murdered a black United States senator, Jan. You see what's going on across the country as a result. I can't sit here and hold them at bay for another day."

"He murdered a black Baltimore police officer most recently, sir – a man in pursuit of Tasman's alleged killer. I don't think even the feds want to go on record saying our man is less important because he wasn't a member of Congress," Richmond said, knowing the next person to speak would lose.

The Commissioner eyed his chief of detectives for nearly thirty seconds, then said, "You better damn well make sure that the amount of hide I'm going to contribute is more than worth the *misplacement* of a prisoner."

✷ ✷ ✷

"That's the address where the phone has been for the last eighteen hours, Hunter. It still was as of the time I dialed your number."

"Thanks, Dusty. You ready to do a little more for the cause of truth, justice and the American way?"

"Could you be a little more melodramatic?" Dusty chuckled. "What do you need?"

"Can you work with your contacts at DA to find out the names of the EOD specialists in Maryland and Virginia? Anyone who's been assigned in the last couple of years?"

"What makes you think I have contacts at the Department of the Army?"

"You're a reporter. Been one for more years than I suspect you care to admit. I'll bet you have more connections than a spider's web that's been under construction for a hundred years."

✷ ✷ ✷

"Is it my imagination, or do you only call me when I'm at a function for one of my kids?" The exasperated *Washington Post* reporter asked. "You interrupted my son's birthday party a few years ago to get information on that crazy old man's family. Now, my phone rings in the middle of my youngest's Bat Mitzvah!"

"I'm so sorry, Joan. It's just *extremely* important . . ."

"Yeah, I'm sure it's a matter of *national* security."

"It is, and far more than I can take time to explain now or you have time to hear, Joan. But, if you can help me, I promise your reputation will soar if we're successful getting to the bottom of the airport bombings and Tasman's death."

There was no immediate answer from the *Post* reporter. Finally she said, "You have my attention. What do you need?"

✷ ✷ ✷

THIRTY-THREE

"So Mr. Chatsworth . . . or can I just call you Harley? What charge would you like to start off with?"

The large black man sat cuffed to the gray interrogation room table. His thick wrists barely fit inside Morgan's silver bracelets.

"I want a fuckin' lawyer. Dat's what I want to start wit, motherfucker!"

The slight grin on Morgan's face broadened into a full-fledged smile. "Oh, man! Are we going to have fun with *you*. We have you for abducting and killing Gordon Moses, for conspiracy to kill Jordan Moses and the last person to call you from lock-up wound up with severe vision problems shortly after your conversation."

"You got no way of tellin' I got called."

"Well, let's see about that, Harley," Morgan said, nodding to Hermann.

Hermann put two evidence bags on the table. One contained the disposable phone collected upon the black man's arrest, the other a yellow Post-it.

Morgan pulled his cell phone from a breast pocket of his suit jacket and flipped it open. "If I dial the number on that Post-it, Harley, where do you suppose it will ring?"

"You got no motherfuckin' right to take my phone, man!" Harley said, making a vain attempt to snatch the bag containing the phone before the cuff chain through the table's eye bolt stopped his deformed hand inches short.

"I suppose you lost those fingers gettin' 'em snapped shut in a book at law school," Hermann said.

Morgan dialed the Post-it number. Within seconds the phone in the bag began to chirp.

Hermann bent over the table. "Will you look at that? Detective Morgan of the BPD is calling your phone, Harley."

"I *want* a motherfuckin' *lawyer*!"

Morgan nodded. "Okay, Harley. We'll get you one. Meanwhile, we're going to put you into the general population here. Then we're going to call a good friend on the *Baltimore Mirror* and feed her a story about how you, and your now dead accomplice, are being held in connection with the Moses killings and the fact that Ms. Moses was apparently servicing Senator Tasman.

"How long do you think it will take the powers that be in D.C. to make sure you have the same kind of vision problems your little friend suffered?" Morgan said, pushing his chair back to stand.

"You can't do dat, man! You got to *protect* me!"

"Harley, the only thing everybody on this planet has *got* to do . . . is *die*. The choice *you* get to make for yourself today is *sooner* . . . or later."

✹ ✹ ✹

"Two E-5s, Harper P. Lowe and Richard L. Burt, and a newly minted E-6, Aamina Al Yami. Lowe is from California. Burt is from Michigan. They're both at Fort Lee. Al Yami is from Georgia and stationed at Aberdeen Proving Ground near you," Dusty said. "Al Yami's name rang a bell, so I did a little digging."

"What did you find on him?" Morgan asked.

"Her."

"Yeah? Okay, what did you find on her?"

"Her father was working for a defense contractor in Atlanta when a Saudi spy was discovered passing highly classified information back to the land of sand and oil."

"So, he was the spy?" Morgan asked.

"No. Apparently he was cleared of any wrongdoing, but the company cut him loose anyway. He killed himself shortly after being fired."

"How can I get a picture of this E-6?"

"I already e-mailed images of all of them to you, Hunter."

"Thanks. How did you come by this info so quickly?"

"A friend at the *Post* has a husband at the Pentagon – Under Secretary of the . . ."

"I don't need to know any more. Thanks, Dusty!"

✯ ✯ ✯

Hermann slid a six-pack of women's photos across the table, face down. "Turn that over and tell me if you recognize anyone."

Dayo Amoako, cuffed to the table, used his right index finger to flip the photos over. Within seconds he placed the same finger in the middle of Aamina Al Yami's image.

"Her."

✯ ✯ ✯

"She has . . . had . . . three kids, Jim! The oldest is ten! Now they're going to grow up without a mother!"

"You can't take on a load of guilt over this, Dusty. Even if she was simply another random sniper's target, it's not your fault."

"Do you think that's what happened? Some psycho that's targeted women primarily?"

"No, I don't and neither do Morgan and Hermann."

"You talked to them?"

"Just briefly this morning. Let's remember where you've been snooping around."

"The Moses cases."

"Exactly."

"But Senator Tasman is dead."

"Let's run through the sequence of events. You use your contacts to track down John Moses' cell phone, knock on the door and what did you say when the man answered?"

"I said I was Dusty Rhodes of the *Mirror* and I asked if he was John Moses. At the time I didn't know Moses was dead too."

"And Peter Liu takes pictures of the couple leaving along with the BQQBS license plate, all of which you turn over to Morgan and Hermann."

"Yes."

"So, they snatch up these two, and the man virtually admits to running Jordan Moses down."

"I didn't know about that," Dusty said. "The virtual confession, that is."

"And another thing you don't know about – and I'm speaking to my wife now, and *way* off the record to the *Mirror* reporter I married – the guy you met at Dillon and South Grundy Streets gets a back door parole shortly after checking into the hoosegow."

"He was *murdered*?"

"He was indeed, not long after making a phone call to a number you got an address for that helped Hermann and Morgan track down the other guy involved in killing John Moses. So, Tasman may be wearing a toe-tag, but whoever ordered the hit in jail on Jordan's killer sure as hell isn't, and I've got to believe that same person wanted you dead too."

"Jesus!"

"As my mother used to say: 'You better call on someone who knows ya!' Because the Son of God ain't gonna take a bullet for you.

"The next thing I tell you has to be strictly confidential. You can't even think about this after I tell you, much less talk about it. Agreed?"

"What would my other choice be?"

"Not hearing this interesting tidbit."

"Okay, what is it?"

"Hermann and Morgan said the guy that killed Pat Sherman is the same sniper responsible for the kids in Druid Hill Park and others."

"So what does that say?" Dusty said, shaking her head in disbelief.

"For starters, that the whacko sniper is connected to the Tasman campaign somehow."

"Or, that the whacko sniper simply happened to pick Pat . . . or me . . . for a victim."

"Yeah, let's go with that wild assed possibility. There's over 800,000 people in Baltimore County where your office sits and the sniper just happened to . . ."

"Okay, Jim. I get it!"

"I'm not sure you do yet. The people who wanted you taken out know they missed. You have to consider yourself a target until this gets wrapped up. I think that means staying home and out of sight with round-the-clock protection."

"I can't hide, Jim. A colleague is dead. I'm going to do my job."

"Even if it gets you killed?"

"Making sure I don't is the BPD's job."

THIRTY-FOUR

Many of the first Sunday editions of American newspapers printed and actually delivered after the airport bombings carried the same color photo, above the fold, on their front pages. Reminiscent of the image of three firefighters raising the American flag over ground zero after 9/11, the picture brought tears to and cheers from readers."

Bright flood lights silhouetted the back of a lone individual, rendering a hand salute, below a red, white, and blue American flag waving in front of a dark building. The caption read: "*SEAL*ing the deal. An American Special Operations Force member salutes the flag he raised over Iran's Khark Island petroleum storage and shipping facility."

The story below the fold went on to describe the Defense Department spokesman's response to dozens of questions about the raid and many concerning the picture surfacing on *Coyote News* the previous evening.

"'Based on the proximity of the camera to the subject and flagpole, the DOD can only speculate on who took it. It is our understanding that the image, obviously of fairly high resolution, showed up on an assistant producer's desk late yesterday afternoon on a small USB drive. To our knowledge no service member has claimed credit for it.'"

"When asked if there would be disciplinary action taken if the photographer's identity were discovered, Rear Admiral Vernon Allison answered: 'Absolutely not.'"

★ ★ ★

"What did I tell you, Senator Fox?"

"You're going to have to give me more to go on than that. Tell me *when*?"

"After the President went on TV and announced military action in response to the airport bombings."

"I have no idea."

"You said: 'We're fucked,' and I told you that you never know how things might turn out. Well, that picture in the paper lit a fire. Hundreds of donations started pouring in this morning ranging from ten dollars to the maximum allowed by law. The SEALs and SWCCs kicking the Iranian's asses renewed Americans' national pride and energy to levels not seen since World War II. If we ever find out who took the picture, and how it found its way to *Coyote News*, you better damn well have the responsible party, or parties, sitting in the VIP section at your inauguration."

✯ ✯ ✯

On the other side of Capitol Hill, a very different conversation took place. "This will blow over, Senator," Jackie Beaudro said, with less conviction than the situation called for or that she had intended.

"What makes you think that?" Senator Reynolds asked.

Beaudro hesitated for several seconds.

"Yeah, that's what I thought. You've got *nothing*," the senator responded. "The Republicans are going to shout from the rooftops how Thatch's action shows their party means business and will keep the country safe. All we can say is: 'Thanks to the *brave* men and women of the armed services for their skill, dedication and courage under fire.'

"We're *fucked*, Jackie!"

✯ ✯ ✯

Since *Coyote News* had the only public copy of Major Shipp saluting the flag, each of the three major broadcast networks and *Coyote*'s cable competitors were bound by ethics to show the *Coyote News* logo when airing the image. An act more painful than ". . . a handful of kidney stones wrapped in barbed wire!" according to one network executive.

✯ ✯ ✯

At the *Baltimore Mirror* Dusty worked on one of her saddest stories since the series she'd won a Pulitzer for a few years earlier. Like the subject of her reporting then, Pat Sherman wasn't just a random name on a police report. Dusty had known her for years and admired her writing.

As she tried to write the story, the scene in her car kept interrupting her work. Finally, she took a break to work on something else.

With the murder of Senator Tasman now a major story, her editor had given her the green light to pursue it, but with a different pressure point. "Let's not kick this guy too hard now that he's down. No sense piling on."

"But Jack, there's a *pile* of dead bodies associated with him and even if he had nothing to do with any of them, we can't just sweep them all under the . . ."

Jack Reigle shook his head. "I said no piling on. Go easy."

His office door closing in Dusty's face made it pretty obvious that the discussion had ended . . . for now.

✦✦✦

THIRTY-FIVE

Morgan, Hermann and Officer Keith Mccaffrey of Maryland's Montgomery County Police stood on the doorstep of a large, expensive Chevy Chase home.

Morgan pushed the doorbell. Inside, chimes sounded as if they were playing in St. Patrick's Cathedral.

Within moments, a woman in a maid's uniform looked out one of the floor-to-ceiling windows on either side of the front door, then opened it. "Yes? May I help you?" the woman said with a Latin accent.

"We need to speak to John Mallard," Morgan said.

"Mr. Mallard isn't accepting visitors today. I'm sure you understand that after . . ."

"Ma'am, I didn't *ask* if we could see him. I'm *telling* you we're going to see him. Now, take us to Mr. Mallard or Officer Mccaffrey here will arrest you for obstruction of justice." Morgan jerked a thumb in the MCP member's direction.

The woman's eyes shot from Morgan's face to Mccaffrey's, which didn't show the slightest spark of sympathy. "Follow me, please," she said, spinning and walking back into the cavernous house.

They passed between dual winding staircases leading to the upper floor and into a library nearly the size of half a tennis court. Mallard sat on a leather couch, facing the windows that overlooked the back yard and pool. Between the couch and the windows sat a huge mahogany desk littered with papers. Mallard slowly stroked a fat chocolate point Siamese lying on the couch next to him.

"Mr. Mallard, I told the police officers you were not to be disturbed, but they insisted on seeing you."

Mallard waved his right hand above his head in dismissal. "It's okay, Amanda. I understand."

The detectives walked around the couch and stood between Mallard and the view. In Hermann's wake, the air's motion from his passage lifted a page off the desk and it fluttered to the floor. Officer Mccaffrey trailed a few steps behind the other men. He picked up the sheet, glancing at it briefly before setting it back on the desk.

"How can I help you gentlemen?" Mallard asked.

"I'm Detective Morgan." Pointing to his partner, he said, "This is Detective Hermann. Corporal Mccaffrey was assigned to accompany us today. What's the cat's name?"

"A. J. Fuck-face," Mallard said with no hint of humor.

"Must make it interesting when you take A. J. to the vet," Hermann said.

Mallard glanced at the detective passively with a slight nod.

"We have a man in custody in Baltimore who is accused of killing a man named John Moses and involved in the murder of his wife – Jordan Moses," Morgan said.

"What does that have to do with me?" Mallard's tone held not a flicker of concern.

"The woman was sleeping with your late presidential primary candidate."

Mallard shot to his feet startling the cat. "*Bullshit*! Thaddeus Tasman was a loyal family man. I won't have his name besmirched now that he's dead. What is this, some cheap political trick on the part of the opposition?"

Morgan stepped close to Mallard, their noses almost touching. "You need to calm down, Mr. Mallard," he said sternly. "We're doing this in the privacy of your home. If we were tools of any political party, we'd be standing in front of a few million dollars' worth of TV cameras and satellite trucks."

Mallard stepped back from Morgan's advance and dropped back onto the couch.

Morgan continued. "The man we have in custody says he made regular contact with someone high in the Tasman campaign organization. Was that you?"

"Of course not! Are you accusing me of conspiracy to murder?"

"Not yet, sir." Hermann answered. "But we have the suspect's burner records that show calls to only one number . . . another burner."

In fact, the call record on Harley's phone had been erased, but Mallard didn't need to know that.

"We're in the process of checking to see where the receiving pre-paid was for each call," Morgan said. "However, we already know where the last location was. Whoever answered the phone was in, or near, Tasman's campaign headquarters in the District."

"That's impossible!"

"That it could be a member of Tasman's team who was directing the hits?" Hermann asked.

"No, that you could have any idea about the location of the phone when it was answered. It's a given that no Tasman campaign member was involved."

Morgan chuckled. "Mr. Mallard, that's one of the great things about America . . . technology. In order to route cell phone calls, the receiving phone has to let the system know where it is. Then when a call is made, thanks to various pieces of legislation passed since nine-eleven, a record is kept of the location of the caller and the person called . . . if the phone has a registered user."

✯ ✯ ✯

Outside Mallard's mansion, Morgan and Hermann shook hands with Mccaffrey and were turning to their car when the officer stopped them. "I saw something interesting in there. That piece of paper I picked up off the floor was an explanation of benefits from Blue Cross, the same people who cover the MCP. The provider's name was P. Santini. He's an orthopedic surgeon who specializes in shoulder reconstructions."

"How do you know that?" Hermann asked.

"I didn't start out to be a cop. I was in the minors for a while – the Richmond Braves – and one of the other players went to Baltimore to have this doctor work on his shoulder. The guy's really good. Does lots of work for pros in the NFL, NBA, NHL, and so on."

✯ ✯ ✯

Dusty Rhodes walked down the hall toward the Baltimore Mirror's bullpen and her desk. Peter Liu came around the corner from a hall leading to the front door.

"Hey, Dusty! Did you drop off the Moses info to the long arm of the law?"

"I did. Not that it's going to do them much good without the password. What's goin' on in your world?"

"It's just another day in paradise. Same old, same old. Have a good one." Liu smiled as he headed for his own workspace.

"Yeah, Peter, you too." Dusty turned toward the bullpen, but then stopped dead in her tracks. "Paradise . . ."

* * *

"Major, Morgan here."

"What can I do you for you, Detective?"

"We have good information that the C-4 used at BWI and IAD came from Aberdeen Proving Ground through one of the EOD techs there. The guy who killed Cappy's partner – the one masquerading as his Secret Service agent brother and probably whacked Tasman – picked E-6 Aamina Al Yami as the person he took a delivery of C-4 and caps from in Aberdeen."

"Wow! Do the feds know this?" Holcomb asked.

"No, sir, not yet. The question is: Do we want to try to pull her in and charge her with the BWI attack before we tip the feds or do we leverage giving her up to the feds for something we want?"

"Like hanging onto the guy who shot Cappy's partner a little longer. I'd love to see that happen, but it's a decision way above my pay grade. Who else knows?"

"Just Hermann and me. I wanted to run this by you first."

"Let me get the Commissioner involved. I appreciate the heads-up, Hunter."

"Stay low, Major!"

"Roger that, man! You too!"

Morgan replaced the handset in the phone's cradle. It rang before he could release it. "Homicide, Morgan."

"Hunter, it's Dusty. Try Bora Bora or paradise as the passwords to the Moses DVD."

"Got it."

* * *

"We're in!" Peter Liu said, with a touch of glee in his voice.

"Let's see what we have," Dusty said over Peter's right shoulder.

The DVD player made a soft whirring sound, then an image appeared on the LCD monitor.

"Who's that?" Peter asked.

"Not Senator Tasman, that's for sure!"

After a few seconds a second scene appeared and the two watched in silence for nearly a minute.

"But, that sure as hell is," Dusty said quietly.

THIRTY-SIX

"Jesus Christ, Major!" the Commissioner shouted. "We have a *faux* Secret Service agent we've 'lost' in the system and now you want to withhold information about the dual bombings at BWI and IAD from the feds *too*?

"Sir, we just want to get a chance to interview this soldier before we pass the information on. We just need . . ."

"Let me guess, *another* twenty-four hours?"

✴ ✴ ✴

A soft whistle passed Hunter Morgan's lips. "Will you look at that? This case gets weirder by the minute."

"That it do, partner," Detective Andrew Hermann agreed.

On the computer screen, a man – not Thaddeus Tasman – was engaged in oral sex with a woman with a tattoo of a horseshoe and rose on her large right breast. Though his face was buried in her crotch, a scar ran diagonally across the back of his left shoulder.

✴ ✴ ✴

"I can't tell you that, Dusty."

"*What*? You got access to the stuff on the disc because of me, and you can't tell me what you found?" The anger in the reporter's voice could only have been missed if Morgan was deaf.

"It's an ongoing murder investigation. We can't give out details at this point."

"Morgan, do you think I'd turn over a potential blockbusting piece of information like that DVD without making a copy of it first?"

"Well, withholding evidence could get your *derrière* in a serious crack."

"I didn't 'withhold' anything. I gave you the exact disc we got from Jordan Moses' mother. And, I gave you the password that allowed you to see what's on it. I've seen it all. I just want to know what your take is on what *you* saw."

Morgan hesitated a moment before responding, but finally said: "Okay, Dusty. You can't print a word of this. Understand?"

"Of course I understand. *I* don't bite the hand that feeds me!"

"There was another man in Jordan Moses' life – apparently before Tasman – a white man. We can only see his back because his face is buried between her legs."

"Yeah, I saw that. The guy with the scar on his back. No way to identify him?"

Morgan hesitated for a long moment before answering. "Well . . . probably not easily."

"And is it your opinion that Tasman is clearly identifiable?"

"Oh yeah. This would clearly have knocked him out of the running for the Oval Office."

"Where do you and Hermann go from here?"

"We haven't decided yet, Dusty."

"Well, I have an idea."

"Yeah? What's that?"

"I'm going to do you a favor and . . . not tell you right now. If it checks out, I will. If it doesn't, and somehow it blows up down the road, you'll be able to honestly say you knew nothing about it."

"Jesus, Dusty! Be real careful where you stick your nose. We're buying toe tags in bulk these days and as much of a pain in the ass as you can be, I don't want your toe wearing one."

"I will, but you have to help me to help you."

"Yeah . . .?"

"Do you have anyone in custody for either of the Moses' murders?"

"We had two, down to one now."

Dusty ignored the obvious question and asked another. "Did either of them have cell phones in their possession? If so, give me the numbers, please."

"I can give you the number, but the phone's call records have been wiped clean. No record of who he actually communicated with."

Dusty chuckled. "Not in *your* possession."

✲ ✲ ✲

Joe Costa's cell phone buzzed in a breast pocket. "Costa."

"Joe, Hunter. I need a favor."

"Gee, I don't know. You're a *defective* now," Costa said with a slight laugh.

"It's serious, Joe."

"What can I do for you?"

"There's an initial review of the BWI and IAD bombings tomorrow, right?"

"Yeah, zero-nine-hundred at the Convention Center. Why?"

"Do you know if anyone from Aberdeen Proving Grounds is coming?"

"I don't think anyone from Aberdeen was invited. What's going on, Morgan?"

"We never had the following conversation. Right?"

"Okay."

"Joe, we have good information that the C-4 that was used at BWI and IAD came from Aberdeen. We need to get the EOD tech that supposedly provided it off federal property and into our jurisdiction. If I give you her name, can you call and invite her to attend?"

"Well, that might be a little obvious and she probably wouldn't want to see the results of her treachery. I've got a better idea. I know a senior officer at Aberdeen in her chain of command. Let me call him and ask to have the EOD staff attend. Make sense?"

"Completely. Give the guy a call."

✦ ✦ ✦

THIRTY-SEVEN

On Baltimore's West North Avenue, near Woodyear Street, a late model Toyota 4Runner several vehicles ahead of a BPD police cruiser made an illegal U-turn.

✲ ✲ ✲

"Detective Morgan, Paul Staron here."

"Hey, Paul, what's happenin'?"

"Guy made U-turn in front of 726. She does a car stop and sees a fire hydrant cap sitting on the passenger seat. He hands her an expired, no photo, international license from Argentina and has no other ID. She runs the tag, turns out to be registered to a 24-year-old woman. She cuffs him for the no verifiable ID. Cursory inventory before the tow turns up a big assed rifle in a fishing rod case. I seem to remember some chatter about a fishing rod case *vis-à-vis* the sniper investigation."

"Jesus Christ! Where is he now?"

"Central Booking."

"Thanks, Paul!" Morgan said and hung up the phone before hearing a response.

"Who's the duty judge today, partner?"

"Judge Sauer," Hermann answered.

✲ ✲ ✲

"That phone only made calls to one number, Dusty." Mary Anderson laid a brown envelope on Dusty's desk. "There's the list of dates and times."

"Thanks, Mary. Please tell Steve I appreciate this greatly and . . . I'll do my best not to bother you all again."

✲ ✲ ✲

Judge Robert Sauer eyed the application for a search and seizure warrant for nearly a minute. "So, you want to seize the rifle from the Evidence Control Unit and submit it to the crime lab and you want to seize and search the automobile. All of this based on the fact that the rifle was in a fishing rod case? That sounds like pretty slim probable cause to me, Detectives."

"Your Honor, ECU has confirmed that he was in possession of a .45-70 rifle. The same caliber that killed several of the victims. One of the building residents where the first shootings took place reported seeing an individual leaving the building that day with a fishing rod case." Morgan paused a moment and glanced at Hermann.

Hermann continued. "Your Honor, we just learned of the .45-70 caliber confirmation on the way here to see you. Otherwise, it would have been included in the application. Time is of the essence here, sir. If this man is released and allowed to collect what is currently his personal property, he will undoubtedly be in the wind."

The judge eyed both men for several seconds, then nodded and signed the application. Morgan and Hermann were out of Sauer's chambers before the ink dried.

* * *

Dusty took the pages out of the envelope and began to plot the received calls on a map of the U.S., carefully recording a number in each of the nine different geographic locations.

THIRTY-EIGHT

"Eduardo Garcia . . . or whatever your real name is, you're in deep shit, *amigo*," Hermann said. "The rifle in the back of your car is a match to the murder of at least three people. And thanks for leaving that brass casing for us at the first scene. That matched too."

"I'm not your friend," the man said with a slight Latin accent. "I want a lawyer."

"Oh, you'll get one. And now that you've asked for one, we can't technically ask you any more questions. However, there is one thing we're curious about. What the hell were you doing with the fire hydrant cover?"

"I found it."

"What?"

"It was lying in the street, so I picked it up so it wouldn't cause damage."

Morgan chuckled. "Well, aren't you the fuckin' civic hero? Keeping our streets safe after murdering at least four people – including two little girls, and a reporter who had three kids."

Hermann pushed his chair back and stood. "By the way, when your lawyer shows up, tell him that because of the ballistics match, we got a second warrant for the 4Runner you were driving. It seems the Johns Hopkins student who owns it has been in Buenos Aires for the last four months and has no idea who you are or why you were in her ride. So it, and all your personal belongings, including your burner are probably going to give us a lot of useful information."

"Burner?"

"Yeah, your disposable cell phone."

✳ ✳ ✳

"Hey, Paleface."

"You get home okay?"

"Yeah, no small feat. Managed to hop a ride with a friend of a friend who owns his own plane. What's up?"

Just wanted to tell you that you nailed it on the sniper's rifle. Nabbed a guy from Argentina on a traffic infraction."

"Hey, it's hard to be humble when you're the world's leading firearms expert."

Morgan could hear the laughter in Small Deer's voice. "Yeah, you haven't changed since the Mekong Delta! You're still that same shy, retiring guy. You've got to learn to open up!"

"I'll work on that. I read an article in the *Denver Post* about the sniper that was written by your reporter friend."

"Yeah, good piece, but I'd never hear the end of it if I admitted that to her. She just signed a syndication deal for a weekly column on interesting criminal cases. I hear they're going to call it *Slime and Punishment*."

✳ ✳ ✳

"Hunter, your suspect's burner only made calls to one phone number and I plotted the locations with dates and times of the calls. The number is 748-818-1945. The locations and dates seem to line up pretty well with at least three of the presidential primaries in Texas, Ohio, and Pennsylvania, not to mention several near the Tasman campaign headquarters. Does that make any sense?"

"Yeah, Dusty. It does. Thanks!"

Morgan hung up the phone, and swung around to face Hermann. "Well, partner, things just got a little weirder."

"How's that?"

"Two-Finger Harley's phone only made calls to 748-818-1945."

"That's the only number that called the *sniper's* phone! What the hell is going on here?" Hermann massaged his forehead with a large left hand.

"I don't know yet, but I think it's time to dig into what Mccaffrey told us in Chevy Chase. We don't know who had his face between Jordan Moses' legs, but we know he had a scar on his left shoulder. Let's get an image of that and see if we can get Dr. Santini to identify it as his work."

"I don't know, Morgan. All that HIPAA bullshit has gotten in our way before when we were trying to get medical information."

"I know. Maybe we can go through the backdoor this time."

☆ ☆ ☆

In the spring the wind often blows out of the Northeast at Chicago's O'Hare International Airport, designated "ORD." On the days and nights it does, Runway 4 Right is one of the departure points for many wide body aircraft, particularly those en route to international destinations with heavy passenger and fuel loads.

Runway numbers denote compass directions and drop the low order digit. Runway 4 Right therefore had a compass direction of 40° which on any given day allowed for takeoffs and landings into the wind.

U.S. Highway 45 snakes along the southeast side of ORD and at one point crosses less than two tenths of a mile from the end of Runway 22 Left – the opposite end of 4 Right.

A white, 2001 Chevrolet Suburban traveled northeast on Highway 45. Two tenths of a mile past the Lawrence Avenue intersection, it slowed and took the Balmoral Avenue exit.

A Jersey barrier runs alongside of the exit and extends onto Balmoral for a short distance. It ends in just over three tenths of a mile, allowing access to a dirt service road used primarily by county and state maintenance vehicles.

At the end of the barrier the Suburban slowed and made a sharp U turn onto the road. After a tenth of a mile, it circled an unoccupied service building, stopping halfway back to the barrier.

The driver tuned a radio to 121.9MHZ while the passenger got out and went to the back of the vehicle. He opened the right door to reveal an olive drab green Stinger missile case. Its contents had been removed. The assembled Stinger with its grip stock lay on top of the right case.

The radio transmissions were between ORD's ground control and outbound flights to various aircraft on assorted runways. Several Canadair Regional Jet flights from the major airlines were queued for takeoff on 4R. The pace moved as quickly as safety standards allowed with longer gaps for arriving aircraft that took priority over departures. However, after the airport bombings, air traffic had not returned to the usual heavy levels and today takeoffs far outnumbered landings.

The driver well knew the longer they sat there, the better the chances for discovery. But his instructions were to make a wide body aircraft the target of at least one of their Stingers. Finally, the ground controller transmitted the call he'd waited for.

"Speedbird-six-four-heavy, Runway 4 Right, position and hold."

"Speedbird-six-four-heavy, roger, 4 Right, position and hold," A British accented voice answered.

The driver quickly scanned the list of call signs and read: Speedbird – British Airways.

He shouted over his right shoulder: *"Next takeoff! ARM! ARM!"*

The passenger checked the Battery Coolant Unit in the handguard. It would shoot a stream of argon gas into the system – the chemical energy charge necessary to enable the acquisition indicators and power the missile. The Identify Friend or Foe system received its power from rechargeable batteries. The IFF would prevent the launch of the Stinger if it received a signal transmitted from a "friendly" target. Enemy targets transmitted no such signal, permitting the weapon's arming and firing.

A small ejection motor would push the Stinger far enough away for operator safety before the two-stage, solid-fuel sustainer accelerated it to over twice the speed of sound. Proportional navigation would provide the initial guidance to a non-friendly target before switching to either IR or UV mode that would guide the missile towards the target's airframe instead of any countermeasures that might be in use – of which virtually none existed for commercial aircraft.

Over two miles southwest of the Chevy Suburban, a British Airway's Boeing 747-400ER lumbered onto the end of 4R with 408 passengers and a crew of ten.

The passenger placed the weapon on his right shoulder, grasping the pistol grip with his right hand to support it and clicked off the safety, activating the BCU. In a few seconds he heard the missile system's gyro begin to spin up.

Using his left hand, he unfolded the antenna and removed the weapon's end cap, then raised and locked the sight assembly into position.

Moving his left hand forward, he grasped the uncaging switch used to lock the gyro onto the target, but did not press it.

✳ ✳ ✳

"Speedbird-six-four-heavy, cleared for takeoff, Runway 4 Right. Turn right to heading zero-five-five, climb and maintain 4000. Contact departure one-two-five-point-zero."

THIRTY-NINE

"Six-four-heavy, cleared for takeoff, Runway 4 Right, turn right to heading zero-five-five, climb and maintain 4000, contact departure on one-two-five-point-zero. We're rolling."

The captain pushed the throttle controls for the four General Electric CF6-80C2 engines forward and the aircraft began its journey to London.

☆ ☆ ☆

"Pasquale Santini . . . Pat. Yes, I know him. Hell of a surgeon," Samantha Morgan said.

"Sounds like a good *Irish* lad," Morgan responded, switching the phone to his left hand. "I just e-mailed you a picture. It's a bit racy. Would you give him a call and ask him if the scar on the back of the individual looked like his work?"

"Wow!" Samantha said, after opening the e-mailed image.

"I know, I know. HIPAA! Look, a person of interest is, or was, a patient of Dr. Santini's. We don't know what the man saw Santini for. This is part of our investigation into several murder cases. If Dr. Santini sees the picture and says: 'Yes, that the scarring typical of . . .' some procedure he performs, then we can either try to get a warrant to see the scar in person or get a warrant for the person's medical records in Santini's possession."

"I'll give Pat a call. I can't blindside him, though. I have to tell him the truth."

"Fair enough."

☆ ☆ ☆

"*IT'S COMING! GET READY!*" the Suburban driver shouted.

Within a few seconds, the passenger could hear the approaching aircraft's roar.

* * *

"Colonel Fallas, Joe Costa. How are you?"

"Joe! Good to hear from you! We're doing well. You?"

"I've still got a pulse. It's all downhill from there. Listen, I owe you a bit of an apology."

"For what?"

"Well, sir, with all the madness associated with the BWI and IAD bombings, the powers that be failed to invite any of your EOD folks to the initial debrief tomorrow at the Convention Center, One West Pratt Street at zero-nine-hundred. I know this is real last minute, and I'm sorry, but if you could send your folks, it will be a good investment of their time."

"I only have two. Can I send them both?"

"Yes, sir!"

* * *

After clearing the end of the runway and with enough air speed, the captain turned the aircraft's yoke slightly clockwise, bringing the plane onto the prescribed departure heading of 55°.

* * *

Speedbird-six-four-heavy roared five hundred feet over the passenger's head, in a slight right turn, climbing toward its cruising altitude. The passenger's hand shook slightly as he pointed the launcher toward the aircraft, looked over the aiming assembly, then through the Stinger's peep sight. He positioned the plane in the center of the range ring.

The steady, fast beeping indicated the IFF system had identified the Boeing jet as an unfriendly aircraft. He pressed the uncaging switch, allowing the system to track its target. Now the beeps changed to a steady tone with increasing volume. The IR system had locked on the Boeing's heat signature.

The passenger took a deep breath, held it, and squeezed the trigger. The Stinger shot out of the launcher toward its prey.

* * *

A Bell 206B-3 helicopter – one of two belonging to the Chicago Police Department – flew toward the Stephens Convention Center northeast of ORD, 1,500 feet above the Catherine Chevalier Woods.

A plume of white smoke shot up from a point near the end of Runway 4 Right, streaking skyward. Then at less than a thousand feet, the trail stopped and a silver object reflected the sun's rays as it fell into the soft green of the woods' budding trees. The former Army pilot's multiple deployment experiences in Iraq told him what he had witnessed.

He immediately radioed that he had just seen a failed Stinger missile attack on an unknown aircraft and he was changing course toward its point of origin.

Speedbird-six-four-heavy continued climbing. Its 408 passengers and crew would never know death had briefly nipped at their heels.

☆ ☆ ☆

On the ground, the passenger watched the missile stop climbing and fall out of sight. Knowing the authorities would arrive soon, he dropped the launcher tube, slammed the Suburban's back door and ran forward. Before he reached the open passenger door, the Chevy started moving toward Balmoral Avenue. He grabbed the door post and pulled himself into the vehicle.

The approaching chopper saw the SUV and began tracking it while calling for police units to intercept it.

CPD's dispatch put out the call and quickly notified O'Hare officials and Homeland Security.

☆ ☆ ☆

"Doctor Santini, Doctor Morgan is on the phone, line five."

"Thanks, Dee Dee." Santini lifted the handset and pushed the red blinking 5. "Samantha Morgan, how are you?"

"I'm good, Pat. You?"

"Fine as frog hair, and if you've ever inspected a frog up close, you know that's *pretty damn* fine."

Samantha chuckled. "I'll leave frog inspections to those more interested than I am."

"What can I do for you, Sam? Hopefully you don't need my specialty."

"I do actually, but not the way you probably think. If I send you an e-mail right now with an image attached, will you be the only one to see it?"

"Yeah, why?"

"This image is something you wouldn't want your family to see."

"Okay. What's up?"

"I just sent it. Hunter and his partner are investigating several murder cases. One of them involves a man engaged in oral sex as you'll see. His face isn't . . ."

"I got it. Oh! I see why this isn't 'G' rated."

"Right, anyway you can see he has a scar on his left shoulder. Hunter knows a person of interest in the investigation is a patient of yours . . ."

"How does he know that?"

"Because the officer who accompanied them to interview this individual in Chevy Chase saw a Blue Cross EOB that said you were the service provider."

"Okay . . ."

"My question is: Does the scar on the back of the man in the photo look like the result of a procedure you might have performed?"

✳ ✳ ✳

"Mr. President, there was a failed Stinger attack at O'Hare a few minutes ago."

"Failed? No one hurt, Bob?"

"No, sir. A CPD chopper pilot witnessed it. Sounds like the rocket failed shortly after takeoff and it fell into a nearby forest preserve. The pilot tracked the people that fired it. They were taken into custody without a fight and another Stinger recovered. CPD's EOD team has located the warhead. The area's been cordoned off, waiting for the Army bomb techs to recover and dispose of it."

"God, just when air traffic starts moving again this happens."

"Mr. President, we were lucky enough to get a notification from the CPD about the same time they told the officials at O'Hare. I called ORD's head of security and told her this had to be kept under wraps for national security reasons. They put a ground stop on operations saying there was a communications issue.

"Another CPD aircraft and a couple of Army gunships searched the area around the airport. When the word came that another Stinger had been recovered, and the air search turned up no other suspicious activity, they removed the stop and resumed normal operations. I also called the CPD Chief directly and told him we needed to keep a tight lid on what his pilot saw and did."

"You realize that if a commercial aircraft is shot down now, we'll be crucified because we didn't alarm the public, don't you, Bob?"

"I do, Mr. President. However, keeping this quiet will give us a better chance of finding the last two missing missiles. If we publicize what happened, not only will the public be panicked, whoever has them will undoubtedly go to ground."

FORTY

The sign-in desk for the debriefing of the BWI and IAD bombings the following morning had two bystanders who weren't bomb techs or investigators – Hermann and Morgan. Shortly before the scheduled start time, two Army members in camo BDUs approached the table. After they had signed in, showing their IDs, the pair turned for the door to the auditorium.

"Staff Sergeant Aamina Al Yami?" Morgan said.

The woman turned back toward the voice. "Yes?"

"May we speak to you for a few minutes?"

"Who are you?"

"I'm Detective Morgan, this is my partner Detective Hermann. We're with homicide. If you could just step over here for a few minutes, we won't keep you long."

SSG Yami turned to the E-5 with her. "Grab us a couple of seats, Boyd. I'll be there in a minute." Turning back to Hermann and Morgan she said, "Okay, where do you want to talk?"

★ ★ ★

"Commissioner, we know you have Dayo Amoako in custody. You need to turn him over to us forthwith." The big FBI agent stood with his feet apart, hands clasped near his crotch.

"We have a man in custody who shot and killed one of my men. We have no evidence he had anything to do with Senator Tasman's murder."

"Okay, Commissioner. If that's how you want to play it. It will take us about an hour to get a U.S. District Court Judge to issue an order directing you to release Mr. Amoako into our custody. Then, it's highly possible that there might be a leak to the press describing how uncooperative the BPD was in assisting in the investigation and prosecution of the murderer of a senator and potential presidential candidate."

"Let me tell you something, numbnuts! I was born at night, but not *last* night! You pull that kind of shit on me and there won't be a leak, I'll be standing in front of every TV camera and microphone I can gather to say that the FBI trivialized the death of a Baltimore police officer and refused to allow us time to process his killer. Tasman won't be any deader tomorrow than he is today. You'll have your man at 5 p.m., immediately after the State's Attorney's office has indicted him. And if you play nice, we might even include a little bonus that will make you look like a hero."

✳ ✳ ✳

SSG Yami sat on the short-legged chair in an interrogation room facing Morgan and diagonally across from Hermann.

Morgan took a picture of Dayo Amoako from his suit coat pocket and slid it across the table. "Do you know this man, Sergeant?"

"No. I don't."

"Well, he knows you. He picked your picture out of a photo array as the woman who delivered a shitload of C-4 and blasting caps to him in a parking lot near Aberdeen."

"I couldn't do that. It would be missed in an inventory."

"Sergeant, in my life before becoming a homicide detective, I was the lead bomb tech for the City of Baltimore. I know exactly how it would be done. You take twenty pounds of C-4 to the range, you blow ten pounds, but your records show that all of it was blown. But if Dayo Amoako is to be believed – and he seemed very sincere to my partner and me – this wasn't just garden variety C-4 that he took back to his Virginia mosque. You gave him C-4 manufactured before 1995. Do you remember what happened in 1995?"

"I was thirteen in 1995."

"The Oklahoma City bombing, April 19. Before that, explosives weren't required to have taggants. The C-4 used to murder hundreds at BWI and IAD didn't carry taggants. So, we have a direct link between you, Amoako and a mosque known to have extremist members."

"So, I'm being targeted because I'm a Muslim."

"No, you're being targeted because you're a traitor," Hermann said.

"I want a lawyer."

"Yeah, well, assuming you don't *disappear* when the FBI gets their hands on you, I'm sure they'll honor your right to counsel."

★ ★ ★

"Your Honor, Mr. Amoako is charged with first degree murder, attempted murder, first degree assault, using a handgun in the commission of a felony, theft of a federal vehicle and – though it sounds absurd – public littering." Celia Gray paused momentarily.

"Public littering . . .?" Circuit Court Judge Robert Cunningham responded.

"Yes, Your Honor. He dumped a Secret Service Crown Victoria in the Baltimore Harbor, which is why the Baltimore City Police Harbor Unit pursued the boat Mr. Amoako tried to escape in. During that pursuit, Officer Pike was shot in the leg and died before he could receive treatment. A second officer was also wounded during the apprehension of Mr. Amoako."

"Mr. Evans, how does your client plead?"

"Not guilty to each of the State's Attorney's charges, Your Honor."

"Ms. Gray, where are you on bail? I know it's a silly question, but I have to ask."

"We ask that Mr. Amoako be remanded, since he is clearly a flight risk as evidenced by his apparent attempt to evade other alleged crimes in the District of Columbia and Northern Virginia which brought him to Baltimore. As an aside, the Secret Service and the FBI are very anxious to talk to Mr. Amoako, as you might suspect."

"Yes, I'm sure they are. The defendant is remanded."

★ ★ ★

"Costa, you're a low life son-of-a-bitch! You played me so your dicks could snatch up one of my people!"

"Colonel Fallas, I'm sorry, but she was identified as the person who passed a load of C-4 and caps to a member of a mosque in Virginia with radical elements before the BWI and IAD bombings. If I'd played it straight with you, we'd still be wrangling with the Army just to talk to her."

"Where is she?"

"Probably in the back of an FBI Crown Vic on her way to D.C."

★ ★ ★

Interstate 395 North connects I-95 and I-495 – the Washington Beltway – from a point called the "Mixing Bowl" in Springfield, Virginia, to Washington D.C. It crosses over the Potomac River into the District via the 14th Street Bridge.

Just prior to the exit 10A for the George Washington Parkway South and Reagan National Airport, two plastic containers of 1.5 inch, smooth-shank connector, hot-dipped galvanized roofing nails bounced off the tailgate of roofing contractor's pickup after it encountered a large pothole. Both broke open on impact with the road scattering 1,200 automobile tire adversaries across all four northbound lanes.

* * *

The Baltimore City Police Commissioner stepped to the podium bathed in the TV camera lights and punctuated with still camera flashes. "I have a short statement. Following my comments, FBI Special Agent Roger Winters will also have a statement. We will take no questions."

The room's background noise quickly subsided with only an occasional digital camera's snap.

"Today the State's Attorney's office indicted Dayo Amoako on a variety of charges, including murder in the first degree of Baltimore City Police Officer Kenneth Pike. Mr. Amoako has been questioned by homicide detectives and made an important identification in the cases of the bombings at BWI and IAD. We have turned Mr. Amoako over to the FBI for questioning in the murder of Senator Tasman. We have also turned over the individual Mr. Amoako identified *vis-à-vis* the bombings. They are both on their way to FBI headquarters in D.C."

The Commissioner turned to a tall, black man in a blue pinstriped suit. "Special Agent Winters."

The FBI agent stepped to the podium. "As the Commissioner stated, we are transporting two individuals to Washington for questioning related to multiple crimes. In addition, this morning after obtaining a search warrant, a task force of federal agents raided the mosque Mr. Amoako attended. I am not at liberty to discuss the results of that search at this time; however, suffice it to say that a great deal of material was collected and several arrests were made. We will have updates for the press as warranted by the progress in these investigations. I want to take this opportunity to thank the Commissioner and praise the Baltimore City Police Department for their outstanding work and cooperation. Thank you."

* * *

"It's his work," Samantha said.

"He said that?" Morgan asked.

"Not in so many words, but I know Pat pretty well. He said that scar is very representative of one of his surgical procedures. He's a pro, Hunter. Even if I'd known the name of the man in the photo, Pat wouldn't have violated his ethics, not to mention HIPAA to confirm the identity."

"I understand. Thanks."

"So, do you have enough to get a court order for the man's medical records or a search warrant?"

"I don't know. We'll have to talk to the State's Attorney's Office. It's going to be very tricky at best. The only good news is that Dr. Santini practices in Maryland."

✳ ✳ ✳

Celia Gray, Morgan, Hermann, and two other men sat in a small interview room used for prisoner-attorney conferences. Handcuffs secured Harley's hands to the gray-topped table. His lawyer sat near the big black man.

"Mr. Chatsworth, you're in a heap of trouble," Celia Gray said. "You're looking at a minimum of two first degree murder convictions, and an accessory to a third murder and that's just what we know about so far."

"Are you here to make my client an offer?"

"I don't want no fuckin' *offer*! Dey got no proof, dis is all jus' bullshit!"

"Mr. Chatsworth, this is the place where you need to keep your mouth shut until I tell you to speak." The attorney shifted his gaze back to Celia and the detectives. "Do I need to repeat my question, Ms. Gray?"

"No, I heard the question, Mr. Daniels." Celia reached into her briefcase and pulled out a manila folder. In it were two pictures and several sheets of paper. She took the photos and turned them so Harley and his attorney could see them and slid the pair across the table.

"So, if it's proof you want, Mr. Chatsworth . . . here, you and your little friend are on your way to abduct and murder John Moses. Too bad you have that problem with your left hand, because it makes you easily identifiable even in a low resolution surveillance photo.

"Next, we have a statement from your partner seen here in the photo – before his demise – admitting to running down, killing, and removing Jordan Moses' thumbs. And who does he reach out to for help? You.

"So, yes Mr. Daniels, we're here to offer your client the opportunity to help himself, if he agrees to help us. How much he helps himself depends on the quantity and *quality* of any information he decides to share with us."

"What kind of help might he expect?" Daniels asked.

"For starters, not facing the excitement of a lethal injection," Gray answered.

Daniels chuckled. "The state will never conduct another execution. Everyone knows that."

"Yeah, that's what Wesley Baker's lawyer said too. Seems he was a little over-confident 'cause *his* client got the needle on December 5th less than three years ago," Morgan said. "So, the question is, Harley, as Clint Eastwood so eloquently put it in *Dirty Harry*: 'You've got to ask yourself one question. Do I feel lucky?'"

"How much time I lookin' at?"

It was Celia Gray's turn to chuckle. "Oh, Mr. Chatsworth, we're talking about taking the death penalty off the table. Make no mistake though, if we do, you'll never step outside of a prison for the rest of your life."

"I take my chances with a jury then."

Morgan shook his head and smiled. "Harley, if brains were dynamite you wouldn't have enough to blow your nose. Do you think that you'll live long enough to see the inside of a courtroom? Look at what they did to your little friend – which you probably had a hand in. Now that you're on the inside, do you think that the powers that be won't make sure you can't talk either?"

Daniels cleared his throat. "Mr. Chatsworth will require complete isolation before any sentence is handed down and special security in the assigned penal facility afterward."

"If Mr. Chatsworth gives us his full cooperation, we will ensure his safety," Celia Gray said.

Daniels leaned close to Harley and whispered in his ear. "I would strongly suggest you cooperate, Mr. Chatsworth."

Harley looked at Gray for a long moment. "Okay, what you want ta know?"

★ ★ ★

The announcement of Dayo Amoako's arrest sent various news outlets and bloggers scurrying for information. It took only a few hours for the first stories to appear in news reports and various websites that Dayo had a twin brother employed by the U.S. Secret Service.

The United States Secret Service (USSS) falls under the DHS, whose Office of Public Affairs spokesman had "no comment," when questioned about the Amoako brothers. However, a small investment – via the internet – in background checks provided Dayo's criminal record and Ayo's home address and phone number.

When Ayo failed to answer his door or phone, his apartment building neighbors began receiving queries. What is he like? When did you see him last? Is he a good neighbor? Does he have a girlfriend? It quickly became obvious that something had gone wrong when several residents mentioned that Secret Service and FBI agents had asked many of the same questions a few days before.

★★★

FORTY-ONE

"Wow!" Celia Gray said after Harley had been taken back to his cell. "That's one real bad man."

"We've got to get our hands on Mallard's medical records. There are just too many connections here for him not to be involved somehow." Hermann scratched the right side of his face. "So, we know they killed the Moses couple and Angela Bassett, the woman who impersonated Jordan at the bank after she turned over the DVD. What I don't understand is why the Tasman campaign would expose one of its own workers."

"And, didn't anyone in Tasman's Baltimore campaign office think it suspicious that a coworker was murdered?" Morgan added.

Celia Gray shook her head. "In answer to the first question, they must have been desperate to get their hands on the disc that would surely destroy Tasman's chances, not to mention his reputation."

Morgan nodded. "We need to interview some folks who worked with Angela Bassett. This is all tied together somehow. Harley's burner only called one number and our friend from Argentina only got calls from that same number."

"Let's do that. Who is Bassett's next of kin?" Hermann asked.

Celia Gray looked at her notebook. "Her mother. She lives in Westminster."

"Who caught her case?" Morgan said.

"David and Goliath. I'm sure they wouldn't mind you taking it off their hands, since we now have a tie-in to your three cases."

Morgan nodded. "I'll give 'em a call. Let's get back to Mallard's medical records." He glanced at Hermann and then continued.

"Remember Detective Tony Sacks, with the MCPD? We helped him on that pedophile case last year."

"Yeah, good guy," Hermann answered.

"Let's give him a call and see if he can get us into see a friendly judge down there to get a court order that allows Dr. Santini to confirm that the man servicing Jordan Moses is Mallard."

"Sounds like a plan."

★ ★ ★

"David and Goliath" were really Detectives David and Goodman. At 5'3" David could have been a jockey, if he hadn't become a cop. Goodman stood 6'5". The only part of the BPD he was restricted from was the helicopter unit, for obvious reasons. So, early in their days together, one of their thin blue line brethren had coined the nickname and it stuck.

"No, we've got no problem with that. Take the case. It's not like we're short of work," David said.

"So, you didn't recover any of her personal effects?" Morgan asked.

"No, but we were lucky though. Whoever tossed her in the water was in a hell of a hurry, or wasn't very bright, because they didn't weigh her body down. If they had, she'd probably still be listed as 'missing.'"

★ ★ ★

"My Angela was very devoted to Senator Tasman's campaign, that's why she quit her job and volunteered full time . . . more than full time, most days. I can't believe they're both gone," Veronica Bassett said, tears streaming down her cheeks.

"We're very sorry for your loss, ma'am," Hermann said. "We wanted to inform you that we have one of the two men who murdered Angela in custody in Baltimore. There's a strong chance that her death is linked back to the senator's D.C. campaign office. We're wondering if you have her personal effects from the Baltimore office. And if so, could we take a look at them?"

Mrs. Bassett looked stunned for several seconds. "You have her killer?"

"Yes, ma'am," Morgan answered. "He's confessed to Angela's and two other killings. As my partner said, we believe they all tie back to Tasman's D.C. election headquarters. So, if you have anything of your daughter's personal effects, we'd appreciate seeing them."

Veronica Bassett didn't answer, but pushed herself to her feet and left the room. When she returned she carried a cardboard box and handed it to Hermann. Inside were four items. A nameplate from her desk, a small pocket calendar, a cell phone and a handwritten note on "Tasman for President" stationery that read, "I'll take good care of you. J.M."

"That's all they brought over."

"Mrs. Bassett, may we take these items with us? We'll give you a receipt and I promise to return them as soon as we can," Morgan said.

"Yes."

"Do you have a recent photograph of your daughter that we might take as well?"

"Yes. Just make sure I get it back."

* * *

"J.M., as in John Mallard, I bet," Hermann said as they drove back to Baltimore.

"Yeah. Is that phone password protected?"

Hermann slipped on a pair of latex gloves and lifted the phone out of the box. After pressing and holding the "Off" button, the device sprang to life. "Let's see who's in her address book."

A few beeps later, the list of saved names appeared in alphabetical order. "There's our boy. 'John Mallard, *Mobile*.'"

"Does his number look familiar?"

"Nope, it doesn't. That doesn't explain why a lowly volunteer would have the campaign manager's personal cell phone number, but we now have links from our killers to Angela Bassett and Bassett to Mallard."

PART III
THE AFTERMATH
"Slime and Punishment"

FORTY-TWO

Montgomery County falls under Maryland's Sixth District Court on East Jefferson Street in Rockville where Morgan, Hermann, and Detective Sacks stood in Judge Matt McLaughlin's chambers.

"So, you believe this man with the scar on his back is John Mallard and you want me to sign an order directing Dr. Santini to turn over Mr. Mallard's medical records. Have I got that straight?"

"Yes, Your Honor," Morgan answered.

"And you got to this conclusion how again?"

"The woman in the photo – Jordan Moses – was murdered, as was her husband, John. They had video of Mrs. Moses and Senator Tasman in similar situations, as you see there. We have one of the men involved in the couple's murders in custody who has confessed to killing them, as well as a woman named Angela Bassett. Ms. Bassett was a full-time campaign volunteer for the Tasman campaign in Baltimore.

"Before she was murdered, Ms. Bassett impersonated Mrs. Moses and gained access to her safety deposit box at the Freeport Bank in Baltimore . . ."

"And you know this how?" Judge McLaughlin asked, holding up his hand as if in a swearing-in ceremony.

"We have surveillance video from the bank that shows Ms. Bassett there on the day and time the security system shows Mrs. Moses' safety deposit box being opened and the bank employee who served Ms. Bassett positively IDed her from a six pack Detective Hermann showed her."

"Very well, continue."

"My partner and I interviewed Ms. Bassett's mother, who gave us her daughter's items that were returned from the Baltimore campaign office. They included the note to her you see there with the initials J.M., and her cell phone which had John Moses' personal cell phone listed in its address book.

"We believe Mr. Mallard was also having an affair with Mrs. Moses and that he – or someone in the D.C. campaign office – was likely contracting for the couple's murders. We need to have Dr. Santini confirm that Mallard is the man in that photo so we can get a search order for Tasman's D.C. campaign office and Mallard's Chevy Chase home."

"And what's your link to the D.C. campaign office?" Judge McLaughlin asked.

"Calls to a disposable phone from the man who we have in custody. Cell phone tower reports show the calls were made to a number near the D.C. office, and to various locations where there were presidential primaries going on, each of which Mr. Mallard would have attended, Your Honor."

"How did you discover the link between Mallard and Dr. Santini?"

Morgan quickly explained the Blue Cross EOB seen by Officer Mccaffrey at Mallard's home.

Judge McLaughlin rounded up the various items of evidence on his desk and handed them back to Hermann, then signed the court order. "Good luck, gentlemen."

✦ ✦
✦

FORTY-THREE

Dr. Pasquale Santini studied the two photos on his desk with a magnifying glass – one from the video, the other taken in the O.R. at the conclusion of John Mallard's shoulder surgery. After more than a minute of back and forth comparison, he looked up at Morgan and Hermann.

"I firmly believe that the man in the photo with the woman is John Mallard."

"Thanks, Doc. Would you be willing to tell that to a judge?"

"I'll do whatever I can to assist you," Santini said, putting the magnifying glass back into his desk.

✫ ✫ ✫

"I hear the raid on the mosque rounded up some interesting people," Costa said to Grabowski as he filled his coffee cup.

"Through official channels?"

"No, of course not. The feds don't need us anymore . . . at least for the moment. I made a new friend with an FBI agent while we were at BWI. She told me."

"Yeah?" Grabowski responded. "She say anything about finding any C-4 at the mosque?"

"No, and I know where you're going with that. The numbers don't add up. According to Dayo Amoako, Staff Sergeant Al Yami handed over a container that weighed about thirty to thirty-five pounds. Even if you discount the weight of the container, the blast patterns at BWI and IAD would suggest no more than four to six pounds were used in each."

"Amoako said the container was plastic, so damn little weight there," Grabowski said.

"True. So, let's be conservative and say there was only thirty pounds in the container and each IED contained six. That means there's still eighteen pounds of C-4 out there."

✶ ✶ ✶

"Good evening, my fellow Americans." POTUS paused for several seconds. "I told you after the mass murder of our citizens that we would provide an update on our military actions in response to those heinous acts. There has been a great outcry abroad and domestically at what many call America's 'disproportional and brutal response.' They charge that world tensions balance on a razor's edge due to unprovoked attacks on foreign nations. They bemoan the world's economy has been driven to the brink of global bankruptcy. They cite the number of innocents killed.

"My goal, as Commander in Chief, was to send a simple message that could not possibly be misunderstood or misinterpreted: That America will no longer allow its enemies – foreign or domestic – to hide in the shadows or across international boundaries so long as I am in office.

"We will have an election in a few months, and the winner who occupies this office may well choose a different path. However, in the interim, Iran has paid a price for its decades-long involvement in spreading terrorism worldwide. Afghanistan has paid a price for flooding the market with drugs from poppy fields that lie smoldering as I speak. Pakistan has paid a price for harboring those who would see America destroyed.

"It is true, many innocent people died as a result of our attacks. I regret their losses greatly. On August 6, 1945, by order of President Truman, the atomic bomb dropped on Hiroshima where many innocent people lost their lives and others were maimed for the remainder of theirs. The Japanese government, incapable of believing, or accepting, what had happened did not surrender. Three days later, Nagasaki became a target.

"Here is my simple message to those who would do harm to America and Americans: Learn a lesson from the terrible price you have just paid, or seen others pay, for the airport bombings. Don't become a modern day Nagasaki.

"Goodnight, and God bless America."

☆ ☆ ☆

Jackie Beaudro turned the flat screen TV off and looked at Senator Reynolds. "You still have a shot at the Presidency, Senator. I believe there will be a groundswell of anti-Republican sentiment when the voters come to realize the enormity of Thatch's actions."

"That may be, but right now Americans are as fired up as they were after nine-eleven. The fact that neither the Russians nor the Chinese responded militarily suggests they didn't want to take us on. That renews America's superpower status around the world, but especially here."

"Perhaps they just see the opportunity to line their pockets rebuilding all the facilities Thatch had taken out."

"Maybe, but I don't know where Iran is going to come up with funds to pay them when their main source of revenue is out of commission for the foreseeable future."

The phone rang on a table in the corner of the hotel room. Beaudro walked to it and answered. "Yes?" She paused for several seconds, then said: "Thank you, good-by."

Jackie turned to Reynolds looking as ashen as a black woman could. "Chief Justice McKenna just died."

☆ ☆ ☆

"Good news, Mr. President. We've located the last two Stinger missiles," the Secretary of Homeland Security said with a slight smile on his face.

Seated behind the *Resolute* desk, President Thatch seemed to visibly shrink in relief. "Thank *God,* Bob! Where and how?"

"Do you remember that SNAFU on I-395 with the spilled roofing nails, sir?"

"I do."

"A couple of Metro police officers came upon an SUV on 14th Street, almost directly across from the Monument with three flat tires. The occupants were nowhere to be seen, but they left a disposable cell phone and a variety of documents behind in their apparent haste. The FBI is processing the vehicle for prints and anything else useful. An Army EOD team took possession of the Stingers. They're on their way to Fort Lee now."

"Can we keep the lid on this discovery too?" POTUS asked.

"I believe so, sir. Dana has been very effective in her stonewalling of the press during her daily briefings. We have the Metro Police Chief's word that she'll talk to the officers who made the discovery in person."

"Can we trust her?"

"I think so, Mr. President."

"If they were in the District, next to the Washington Monument, what do you suppose their target would have been? It seems Stingers would be more useful to terrorists in Arlington, near Reagan National."

"We think they intended to take down Marine One with you aboard, sir."

✯ ✯ ✯

Federal District Court Judge Debi Donaldson read the Search and Seizure request on her desk. Hermann had provided her with the same information given to Judge McLaughlin, and Dr. Santini had confirmed John Mallard's image appeared at the beginning of the Moses video.

Donaldson, a no-nonsense jurist who had served in the Navy before going to law school, shook her head. "I've heard everything ya'll have said but this looks pretty light on the probable cause scale to me. You have a picture of a guy you say is Mallard and you have a bunch of dots on a map that purport to be cell phone towers near to where Mallard might have been."

"Your Honor, those dots also represent where Senator Tasman *definitely* was on the dates listed. This application for a warrant could lead to information related to the senator's murder as well."

"The alleged murderer is already in federal custody. What's there to search for at the campaign headquarters?" Donaldson asked.

"We know there was Tasman campaign involvement, Your Honor," Morgan injected. "One of his volunteers in Baltimore impersonated Mrs. Moses at the bank and a note from Mr. Mallard to her was found in her personal effects after she was murdered herself. We believe it's natural to assume that there may be more evidence to be found in the D.C. campaign headquarters."

Judge Donaldson's steely eyes bored holes in Morgan's face for several long seconds. "Okay, Detectives. You've got your warrant, but you are *strictly* limited to the *interior* of John Mallard's office. If there's a signed confession lying outside his office door it's off limits. Got it?"

"Your Honor, with all due respect, we strongly believe that John Mallard is involved in these murders, but it could be another member of Tasman's D.C. staff."

"Detective . . . Morgan, you get Mallard's office or you get nothing. Which would you prefer?"

✮ ✮ ✮

"That was a nice story you did on Ken Pike, Dusty."

"Thanks, I only met him once, at a fundraiser for homeless veterans. He was really dedicated to their cause. You know he was in Vietnam too."

"Yeah, I did. He was one of Uncle Sam's Misguided Children."

"Some might say you were all 'misguided,' not just the Marines. So, can you bring me up to speed on the investigation?"

"Is this off the record?"

"Yes, *Hunter*! It's *off* the record," an exasperated Dusty Rhodes said.

"We found nothing in Mallard's D.C. office. Judge Donaldson limited the S and S warrant to his office only, so who knows what might be the rest of the building."

"What's next?"

"There's only one other place to look for the phone. Fortunately, he's a Maryland resident."

"Did you ever recover the gun used to kill Moses?"

"We did, and the knife used to collect his wife's thumbs. So, we've got at least one guy dead to rights."

"One guy? I thought there were two," Dusty said.

"There were, but one of 'em had a nasty accident in the slammer."

"Oh yeah, I forgot. Jim told me about it after Pat Sherman was murdered. Christ, Hunter! Can I write about *that*? I'm getting a lot of pressure from my editor to back off on all we know about Jordan and Tasman from the DVD. Reigle and the brass above him don't think it makes any sense to destroy a dead man's reputation. I know that's a bullshit excuse. They're worried about the *reaction* from a heavily Democratic readership and advertisers. I've been pushing back, but believe me, if I don't come up with a compelling reason to write the whole story soon, they'll snatch Tasman, the Moses couple, and Angela Bassett away from me quicker than a pit bull can take a pork chop from a baby. In fact, the only reason they haven't already is because I have the DVD."

"Wow! A reporter with a conscience!"

"Now, *that* hurt! Have I done nothing to assist you and Hermann on this case? Can I write it as 'an unidentified source within the BPD,' or some other fuzzy reference?"

Morgan paused for several moments before answering. "Okay, Dusty, you can say that a suspect in the double murder of Mr. and Mrs. Moses and the murder of Angela Bassett, a member of Tasman's Baltimore campaign office, was himself murdered."

"How?"

"Can't tell you that."

"Which one checked out?"

"Same answer."

"So, you tied the gun used in the Moses killing to Angela Bassett?"

"That would be a safe assumption, Dusty."

"Where was it?"

"We found it in the dead perp's house. Listen, when you write your story, *don't* mention Mallard or any reference to cell phone data. If by some wild chance he still has the burner used to give instructions in these murders, any reference to it in the news will make that disappearing pork chop you mentioned earlier look like it's in slow motion."

★ ★ ★

POTUS sat behind his desk in the Oval Office. Senator Emlyn Keith sat in a chair off the right, front corner of the *Resolute* desk, wearing an expensive yellow suit and a demure smile.

"Senator Keith, why in Christ's name would I do that? Why would I nominate a Democratic senator to be the next chief justice?"

"Mr. President, I can think of a couple of reasons. First, since my party controls the Senate, my confirmation would be almost a slam dunk. Second, it would allow you to keep Senator Reynolds from naming Chief Justice McKenna's replacement. And finally, I can assure you I'd be a much more moderate justice than Senator Reynolds will nominate when she's president."

"There's no guarantee Reynolds will be elected in November, Senator. In fact the Desert Fox has opened up a sizeable lead."

"Yes, Mr. President, because you kicked the shit out of a bunch of camel jockeys. We both know that races tighten up the closer they get to an election. I wouldn't be too quick to count the Ice Queen out.

"Please, Mr. President. The handwriting is on the wall. You're more unpopular than any president since Nixon, your recent favorable spike notwithstanding. You got the nation involved in not one, but *two* wars – neither of which has gone particularly well. You fumbled the response to a disastrous hurricane along the Gulf Coast.

"Jane Fonda has a better chance of becoming the National Commander of the Vietnam Veterans of America than the Desert Fox does winning in November. The nation will want a change and Reynolds will be sitting where you are now."

"Gee, Senator, you really know how to warm a guy up when you're asking for a favor. Why don't you just make your request to *President* Reynolds after the election?"

"Senator Reynolds and I aren't exactly . . . *simpático*."

"I guess not, not after you threw your weight behind Tasman."

✦ ✦
✦

FORTY-FOUR

The Montgomery County Police officer rang the doorbell of John Mallard's home. The same woman who had greeted Hermann and Morgan on their earlier visit opened the door.

"Yes, can I help you?"

Morgan stepped forward. "Good afternoon . . . Amanda, isn't it?"

"*Si*. How may I help you?"

"We have a warrant to search Mr. Mallard's home."

"Mr. Mallard is not home."

"He doesn't have to be home, Amanda," Hermann said

The diminutive Salvadoran native looked frightened. "I must call Mr. Mallard and tell him what is going on or he will fire me."

"No, you can call him when we're done. For now, take us to the kitchen, please," Morgan said. He didn't want to scare the woman in case they needed her assistance at some future point.

The three men followed the maid through the cavernous house to a kitchen filled with high-end stainless steel appliances. Morgan pulled out a straight-backed chair from a round kitchen table. "Have a seat."

"Do you have a cell phone?" Hermann asked as Amanda sat down.

"*Si*. Mr. Mallard gave me one."

"Why did he give you a phone?" Morgan asked.

"During the last part of Senator Tasman's campaign I had to be here eighteen to twenty hours a day. My sister had been watching my son, but she got a job and I had to hire someone. I could barely afford the cost, so I asked Mr. Mallard to pay me for the extra hours. He said he'd think about it. When the senator was killed, my hours went back to normal and Mr. Mallard said I could have the cell phone as a 'bonus.'"

"When was that?" Hermann said.

"Two, maybe three days after Senator Tasman was killed."

"Where is the phone now?" Morgan asked.

Amanda reached into her apron pocket and held the phone out in an open palm.

Hermann produced an evidence bag and held it out to Amanda. "For the time being, put the phone in here, please."

Amanda dropped it into the bag and Hermann turned and handed it to the MCP officer. "Hang onto this while we take a look around."

"Got it."

The detectives pulled on latex gloves and went back to the foyer. "That might be what we're lookin' for, Morgan."

"Maybe, but we've got a free pass to look around. Let's not waste it."

"Right-on, brother."

They started with the room where they met Mallard initially. His locked desk and cabinets presented no real challenge for Hermann's Southern Specialties set of picks. The men combed through all the expensive furnishings, looking for a paper trail to a disposable phone or anything else possibly associated with one. In one cabinet, Morgan discovered a stainless steel case with a four-digit combination lock.

Many people alter only one digit of a combination to make unlocking more convenient. Having done this himself, Morgan altered the last digit up and down one number without luck. He repeated the action on the first number and opened the box on his first try. Inside he found a yellow Post-it pad leaf and a leather-bound journal. The Post-it had two phone numbers printed on it.

"Hey, partner. Take a look at this."

Hermann walked over and Morgan handed him the box, then removed his notebook and flipped though several pages. "Read those numbers."

Hermann complied.

"The first one is for the phone found in the sniper's car. The second one is Chatsworth's. Let's go take a look at the phone Amanda had."

In the kitchen, Morgan retrieved his cell and punched in a number. A few seconds later, the phone in the evidence bag began to vibrate. Morgan looked at Hermann and took the bag from the MCP officer. "That's my phone number calling."

Hermann looked down at the maid. "You can call Mr. Mallard now, Amanda. But you'll have to use a house phone. This one just became evidence."

"Do you know where Mr. Mallard is?" Morgan said.

"He is playing golf. When will I get my phone back?"

"Probably not for some time. I'm sorry," Hermann said, dropping the Post-it into another evidence bag and the journal into a third. "Look, I don't want to scare you, but are you in this country legally?"

"*Sí.* I have a green card."

"We need to see it, please," Morgan said.

Amanda pointed to a counter across the room. "May I get my purse?"

"Yes. Please do."

* * *

"Are you threatening me, Dusty?" Reigle asked angrily.

"Call it what you want to, Jack. That's my story. That's *the* story. All of it we know about at this point, anyway. Run it or read it on my blog along with several thousand other local subscribers. We need to tell the whole truth, not just the part that's politically convenient and financially rewarding to the *Mirror*."

FORTY-FIVE

President Thatch stepped to the hastily erected podium in the Oval Office, bathed in camera flashes, and cleared his throat. Behind him stood the Vice President – looking none too happy – and Senator Emlyn Keith, her husband, and two daughters.

After a few seconds' pause, the deluge of clicking shutters trailed off to an intermittent drizzle and he spoke. "Good afternoon. With the recent death of Chief Justice McKenna, I wanted to move as quickly as possible to nominate someone with his deep reverence for the Constitution, his profound respect for the Supreme Court, and his complete devotion to the cause of justice. A person with a strong record as a jurist on the federal bench and a thorough understanding of the legislative processes' inner workings. So today it is my honor to nominate Oregon's junior senator, Emlyn Marie Keith, to become the seventeenth chief justice of the United States Supreme Court.

"I believe Senator Keith's direct appointment to the high court will be less disruptive than elevating and replacing an associate justice. I also feel it is important for the court and the country for the next chief justice to be in place by the beginning of the court's fall term in October.

"I know Senator Keith's nomination will draw raised eyebrows and criticisms from my party and probable suspicion from the other. However, the reality is, in a Senate held by a Democrat majority, the chances of Senator Keith's confirmation are much better than even.

"The nation will elect a new president in November. Leaving the chief justice's position unfilled until the results are known and any new members of the Senate are seated would be a disservice to America. I therefore urge the Majority Leader to begin confirmation hearings as soon as the law and logistics allow. Thank you."

★ ★ ★

Morgan and Hermann met John Mallard as he walked out of the Lincoln Links pro-shop accompanied by MCP officer Robert Elgar.

Elgar approached the campaign manager. "Are you John Mallard?"

"I am."

"Mr. Mallard, you're under arrest for conspiracy to commit and accessory to murder in the first degree," Elgar said. "Put your hands behind your back, sir."

"That's ridiculous! Murder who?"

"Well, alphabetically: Angela Bassett, John Moses, and Jordan Moses, your former lover," Morgan said.

Mallard complied and as Elgar cuffed him, looked over his shoulder at a stunned pro-shop staff member. "Call Saul Levy. Ward, Kline and Levy, they're in Gaithersburg."

"Yes, sir, right away, Mr. Mallard."

"Fancy law firm," Morgan commented.

"Yeah, and they're carnivores. They'll eat your State's Attorney alive."

★ ★ ★

"That *son-of-a-bitch*! He just sold me down the river!" Senator Fox screamed at no one in particular in his Senate office. "This will be taken as a clear sign that I can't win in November! *GOD DAMN IT*!"

"Sir, it might actually send a positive message that helps you," Fox's chief of staff said with less enthusiasm than she'd intended.

"How the *fuck* could *that* be?"

"This could be seen as a crack in the gridlock between the Oval office and Congress. You have an eleven-point lead, Senator. This nomination might swing votes *to* you. Maybe even some Democrats . . ."

"When was your last *fucking drug* test?"

★ ★ ★

"That fucking *bitch*! She *sold* him on it!" Senator Reynolds said to Beaudro a few blocks from Capitol Hill. "Thatch did this to take away one of the major pieces of my presidential legacy. And, you can bet your black ass that she'll grind her ax to a razor's edge and use it on every case that comes before the court that even whispers of any association with me."

"Well, Senator, as long as we be bettin' *my* black ass, I'd like to save a piece of it to wager dat da Desert Fox ain't da forty-fourth President of dese *U*nited States."

★ ★ ★

"Take me through the case, Detectives." Celia Gray sat at one the end of an oval conference table with Morgan and Hermann to her left and right.

Hermann spoke first. "You know Jordan Moses approached Dusty Rhodes to do a story about her involvement with Tasman. At some point before that meeting, she must have communicated with the senator or Mallard in an attempt to extort money or power. It apparently didn't work . . ."

"How do you know that?" Gray asked.

"Because she contacted Rhodes," Hermann answered. "If she'd gotten whatever she was looking for out of Tasman, it would have been stupid to make it public. The campaign would have sworn her to secrecy through an NDA."

Gray nodded. "That makes sense, and a corpse is the strongest non-disclosure agreement there is."

"Yeah," Morgan agreed. "So they put out a contract on Jordan, but she gets to Rhodes before the hit man gets to her. They snuff John Moses too, but again not before he makes contact with Dusty as well *and* sends a DVD to Jordan's mother – Mrs. French.

"So, the Moses are out of the way, but the proof Jordan spoke of isn't found on either body or in their home. Through phone taps or bugs in the house, the existence of the safety deposit box must have been discovered and the fact that it required biometric access. That's why they took Jordan's thumbs and she must have had a key card in her purse, because her husband still had one when his body turned up."

"Do you think the senator was involved in all this?" Gray asked.

Hermann answered. "We'll never know, Celia. He's got the ultimate NDA going for him too."

"So, how does Mallard get tied into this?"

"Because he's arrogant and cheap," Morgan said with a grin.

Gray cocked her head in a silent question.

"Arrogance – or maybe stupidity – caused him not to get rid of the disposable cell phone used to communicate with the Moses' killers. Being a tightwad drove him to give the same phone to his maid as a bonus for all the long hours she put in before Tasman was murdered. We'll get back to the phone in a minute."

"Okay, continue."

"So needing someone to play the part of Jordan Moses at the bank, enter Ms. Bassett. It appears from her personal effects and the contents of her cell phone that she and Mallard were close."

"Romantically?"

"We don't know. Her NDA is air tight too. She obviously knew too much to be left alive."

"How does Dusty Rhodes fit into the case, other than being contacted on separate occasions by Mr. and Mrs. Moses?" Gray asked.

"When the perps whacked John Moses, one of them kept his smartphone. Dusty must have maintained a good relationship with Steve Van Scoyk, CEO and Chairman of Bluebell Cellular, after she was instrumental in finding his kidnapped son a few years back.

"When John Moses calls Dusty at her office, she sees his number on her caller ID. Then he doesn't post at the place they're supposed to meet and Dusty can't get him on the phone. She and Grabowski go by the Moses' home and find the door open, the place tossed, and Jim finds a hidden answering machine tape that he takes into evidence and brings to us." Morgan motioned between Hermann and himself.

"Hidden? Sounds like he was executing a search. Exigent circumstances?"

"Exactly!" Hermann answered and nodded to Morgan to continue.

"Knowing Moses' cell number – and *not* knowing he's already dead – Dusty goes to Van Scoyk and gets a report of the cell towers handling recent calls and the actual location of the phone for hours at a time. She goes to the address with a *Mirror* photographer and knocks on the door. Having never met Moses, she tells the guy who answers her name, that she's a reporter, and asks if he's John Moses.

"When it becomes obvious that the man at the door isn't Moses, she takes off, circles around and gets the shutterbug to snap some pictures when the guy and a woman leave the house a few minutes later."

Hermann opened a manila folder and pushed two large, glossy, color prints toward Gray.

"She also gets pics of their Maryland tag – BQQBS. That's not particularly important to the case, but you can see how they arrived at that."

"Wow!" Gray said. "Legal problems and probably major *back* problems. At least they support breast cancer."

"Yeah. That's probably their only positive contribution to the planet. Anyway, Dusty comes to us and brings in the pictures. We put out a call and they're picked up within hours. My partner and I question the guy. He lets it slip that he ran down Jordan Moses.

"We put him into lockup and he asks a CO make a call to his 'friend.' The CO kept the number and remembered the guy's name: Harley. When the guy turns up dead in the shower, the CO calls and passes on the info about the phone call.

"You pretty much know Harley Chatsworth's story already. What you don't know is that *his* disposable cell phone only made calls to one number and they lined up with the Tasman Campaign Headquarters in D.C. and the states and dates of several Democratic primaries."

"I take it all that information came from Bluebell Cellular through Dusty Rhodes as well," Gray said.

Hermann nodded. "She saved us a ton of time, Celia."

"I'm sure she did. Let's hope a judge doesn't throw it out. Continue, please."

"About the same time, a guy gets picked up for an illegal U-turn. He has a BFD fire hydrant cover on the front seat and no valid license or ID. The officer throws the chains on him. They inventory the vehicle and, lo and behold, in the back there's a high powered rifle. The lab rats test it and it matches the casing he left near the Druid Hill Park sniper scene and several of the rounds recovered from victims' bodies – the most recent being the reporter the shooter apparently mistook for Dusty in the *Mirror*'s parking lot.

"He also has a burner and it only *received* calls from the same number Harley Chatsworth's phone *called*.

"We got confirmation from a surgeon that the second man in the video Dusty received from Jordan's mother is a patient of his . . . John Mallard."

"How did you link Mallard to the surgeon in the first place?"

"When we went to interview Mallard initially, we were accompanied by a Montgomery County Mountie. As we walk in, a piece of paper floats off the desk and the kid picks it up to put it back. He notices it's a Blue Cross EOB and the provider is a Doctor Santini. The officer played minor league baseball until an injury forced him to do something else. He knew of Santini's reputation with athletes for being the go-to guy for shoulder repairs. When we get back outside, he tells Hermann and me what he saw and who the doc is.

"We get stills from the DVD showing the back of the second man and Doc Santini confirms that it looks like his work. So we get a warrant to look at Mallard's medical records. The crime lab confirms that the guy in the video is Mallard, based on their comparison of the photos.

"That's the warrant Judge McLaughlin signed?"

"Correct. And, it turned out that the answering machine tape Grabowski discovered had exchanges between Jordan Moses and two *different* men. Tasman and . . . *John Mallard.*"

Hermann continued. "So, back to John Mallard the cheapskate. After we find nothing at Tasman's D.C. headquarters, we convinced Judge McLaughlin to sign a warrant for Mallard's home because in addition to everything else, most of the recent calls from the mysterious number went through a cell tower near his Chevy Chase mansion."

"You wrote the warrant for more than just the phone, right?"

Morgan frowned. "Come on, Celia. It wasn't our first rodeo. Of course we did."

"Sorry, I had to ask."

"Yeah, I know. So we arrive, accompanied again by the MCP, and his maid tells us he's not home. We take her into the kitchen. She says she has to call Mallard or he'll fire her. We ask her if she has a phone and she pulls one out of her apron.

"I put it in a bag and have the MCP Mountie hold onto it while we take a look around. In Mallard's office we find a lockbox and Morgan gets it open. Inside is a Post-it with the numbers of the burners we found on Harley Chatsworth and in the sniper's car.

Since we're there looking for a phone in the first place, we go back into the kitchen and Morgan dials the number Chatsworth *called* and the sniper-received calls *from* and *voilà*. The phone in the bag rings and it's displaying Morgan's cell number.

"The Salvadoran maid – Amanda Mejía – kept using it after Mallard handed it over and that led us to the jackpot."

Celia Gray let out a long sigh, then said, "Okay, gentlemen. I think we have a case. But the Blue Cross EOB worries me. If it gets tossed out, there goes your initial link to Mallard. Bluebell Cellular's assistance could be very iffy too, even though you got it indirectly. You never asked Dusty Rhodes to pursue that. Right?"

"We didn't ask," Morgan said.

Gray looked down at the yellow legal pad she'd been taking notes on, scribbled a final line and looked up at Morgan first and then Hermann. "Ms. Mejía's testimony is going to be crucial, as is Dusty Rhodes'. We need to quickly and quietly check on Amanda's immigration status. If Mallard is remanded until his trial, she'll have no income and could be working for someone else or just in the wind. If she's illegal, we need to make sure she understands that we're not concerned with her immigration status."

"We have her address. Of course, now she has no phone," Morgan said.

"She has a green card but fakes are pretty easy to come by these days. We'll check it out," Hermann said, standing up.

✶ ✶ ✶

"Sam, I need a favor."

"Okay, Hunter. Shoot."

"I need you to hire a maid."

"We already have someone who comes in once a week to clean. Our house isn't big enough to need a *maid*."

"Isn't the CEO of Jolly Maids a patient of yours?"

"She is. I delivered all four of her kids."

"Could you call her and see if she can put this woman on the payroll, at least temporarily?"

"Does this woman have a name?"

"Amanda Mejía. She's Salvadorian."

"I could if she's reputable and legal, but not before you tell me what this is all about."

"I'm sure she's very honest and we're checking on her immigration status now. She's worked for Mallard for years in a very high-priced home in Chevy Chase. If she hadn't done good work or appeared to be light-fingered, he would have fired her in a heartbeat."

Morgan explained the rest of the situation and said, "We can't lose contact with her. She's the link between the phone Mallard used and our case."

"Okay. Let me know her status. What's her phone number?"

"I'll have to give you that when I know her status, because we took her phone as evidence."

FORTY-SIX

"How does your client plead, Mr. Levy"?

"Not guilty of all charges, Your Honor."

"Where is the State's Attorney on bail, Ms. Gray?"

"Your Honor, we request the defendant be remanded. He has the financial resources and international connections to flee to any number of countries with which the U.S. has no extradition treaty. You may recall Mr. Liggett's escape in his private jet to the Maldives a few years ago, even though he'd given up his passport as part of the bail agreement. We believe Mr. Mallard is directly responsible for nine murders, as our case will prove, and must certainly be considered a flight risk."

"Mr. Levy?"

"Mr. Mallard is an upstanding citizen, Your Honor, and is anxious to defend himself against these trumped-up charges. He doesn't own a private jet or have the vast financial assets that were at Mr. Liggett's disposal. As you know, he was Senator Tasman's campaign manager and has a long and distinguished record of service in the public and private sectors."

"I'm inclined to agree with Ms. Gray. The defendant is remanded."

"Your Honor, considering the very high profile of this case, we request that Mr. Mallard be isolated until we can prove his innocence."

"So ordered."

The banging gavel signaled the start of a race from the gallery to on-camera and phone updates for the numerous media members in attendance.

✯ ✯ ✯

Hermann hung up the phone and smiled. "That was an ICE agent buddy I went to college with. He's working on the High Intensity Drug Trafficking Area. Amanda's green card is legit, Morgan. There *is* a God!"

"Good. I need to make a phone call. Then, we need to take a ride."

✯ ✯ ✯

A small boy answered Morgan's knock on the door. He looked up into the detectives' faces, but did not speak. His eyes dropped to the plastic Walmart bag Hermann held.

"Is your mother here?" Hermann asked.

"Mommy!"

The sound of footsteps came toward the door. Amanda Mejía placed her hand on the boy's shoulder and looked around the door. "Yes?"

"Ms. Mejía, may we come in? We have some good news for you," Morgan said.

"*Sí*. Come in, *por favor.*"

The detectives entered the sparsely furnished apartment's living room and sat on a stained, green couch. Amanda sat in a straight-backed chair opposite them.

The chocolate point Siamese the detectives had seen at Mallard's home lay curled up on the rug near Amanda's feet.

"You brought Mr. Mallard's cat."

"*Sí*. There is no one to take care of him there now. He would have starved. I changed his name too."

"I can understand that," Morgan said, smiling. "What is it?"

"Hickory."

"Oh," Hermann responded looking surprised.

"I am studying to be a citizen. A.J reminded me of President Andrew Jackson, Old Hickory."

"He was a tough man," Morgan commented. "Show Amanda what's in the bag, partner."

Hermann reached in and pulled its contents into view.

Amanda frowned, questioningly.

"This is a pre-paid phone to replace the one we had to take from you, Amanda. It has a thousand minutes on it. That's over sixteen hours."

Amanda's covered her mouth. Tears quickly filled her eyes before overflowing onto her cheeks and hands. "*Dios mío! Muchas gracias!*"

"You're welcome," Morgan said. "There's more. Later today, a woman named Erin Sundberg is going to call you on this phone to offer you a job. She owns Jolly Maids."

"To be a Jolly Maid?"

"No. To be Ms. Sundberg's maid here in Olney. The woman who works for her now has decided to move back to Guatemala and retire, but she'll stay on long enough to show you how Erin likes her house kept."

Amanda sat speechless for several seconds. Looking at the detectives, she questioned, "Why have you done this? You don't know me."

"Because we need you to testify at Mr. Mallard's trial about the phone he gave you. Will you do that?"

"*Sí, sí*! And the job?"

"You need one now. Mr. Mallard has no need for a maid."

✦✦✦

FORTY-SEVEN

Celia Gray laid out the State's murder case against Mallard without emotion before the seven women and five men in the jury box. Her well-rehearsed opening statement took less than fifteen minutes.

Mallard's defense council took even less time. "Ladies and gentlemen, you heard the State's claim of a solid case against Mr. Mallard. I won't waste your time with a longwinded rebuttal. Let me simply say it will become obvious to each of you very quickly that the charges against my client are wholly circumstantial and will leave you with an abundance of reasonable doubt. The State's Attorney will be unable to provide you with any *direct* evidence of my client's involvement in any of these tragic deaths. Thank you."

Judge Gina Marshall looked down at the prosecution's table. "Ms. Gray, is the State ready to proceed?"

"We are, Your Honor."

"Very well, please call your first witness."

"Thank you, Your Honor. The State calls Dusty Rhodes."

Dusty rose from the gallery and walked to the witness stand. A bailiff approached her with a Bible.

"Do you swear or affirm that you are about to tell the truth, the whole truth, and nothing but the truth?"

"I do."

"Please be seated."

Judge Marshall looked down at Dusty. "Please state your name for the record."

"Sharon Stella Rhodes."

A murmur came from the gallery.

"Very well, Ms. Gray. You may proceed."

Celia Gray approached a lectern standing between and in front of the prosecution and defense tables with a thick black binder. "Good morning, Ms. Rhodes. It seems the spectators were surprised to hear your actual name."

"Dusty is just a nickname I got in college, like Muddy Waters. I've always been glad they didn't tag me with that one. *Muddy* Rhodes would have been even less feminine."

Soft laughter came from the gallery, Celia Gray and Judge Marshall as well.

"Okay, Ms. Rhodes. You are a crime reporter for the *Baltimore Mirror*, is that correct?"

"Yes."

"Let's start with how you became involved in this case."

Dusty explained the call, and meeting, with Jordan Moses.

"And how did you learn of Mrs. Moses' death?"

"Her husband called me the day she was hit and killed by a car."

"And did you meet with John Moses as well?"

"No. We arranged to meet where his wife and I had the previous day, but he never arrived."

"Did you do anything to pursue the meeting elsewhere?"

"Yes, I went to his home."

"Did you go alone?"

"No. My husband accompanied me."

"And your husband is James Grabowski, a member of the Baltimore Police Department's Bomb Squad. Is that true?"

"Technically, he's a member of the Emergency Services Unit. He is a bomb technician, yes."

"Thank you for the clarification. When you and Officer Grabowski went to the Moses' residence, what did you discover?"

Dusty spent the next two hours recounting her involvement in the various aspects of the Moses murder cases, during which Celia Gray entered the answering machine tape and DVD into evidence.

"I have no further questions for Ms. Rhodes, Your Honor."

"Very well. Since it is close to the noon hour, we will recess for lunch and reconvene at two p.m. sharp," Judge Marshall said and banged her gavel.

As Dusty walked pass the prosecution's table, Celia Gray looked up and smiled. "Well done."

✷ ✷ ✷

A little over forty miles southwest of Baltimore, Dayo Amoako sat shackled in a conference room with his government appointed attorney and two DOJ lawyers.

The feds had taken the death penalty off the table in exchange for Dayo's confession to Tasman's murder and his testimony about the co-conspirators' involvement. Additionally, he would confess to his activities *vis-à-vis* the BWI and IAD bombings and testify as to how and where the explosives were obtained and his knowledge of the other members of the Virginia mosque who planned and executed the acts.

"Where will I be sent after I testify at the trial?"

One of the DOJ attorneys looked up from his notes. "That depends on if the State of Maryland extradites you to be tried for killing a Baltimore police officer. Either way, have you ever heard of Florence ADMAX?"

"Yes, when I was in Kit Carson. It's also in Colorado."

"*Florence ADMAX*!" Dayo's attorney said. "A supermax prison?"

"Yeah. Your client will get to rub elbows with people like Zacarias Moussaoui, Richard Reid, and Ramzi Yousef."

"Well, not actually rubbing elbows, since he'll be in solitary twenty-three hours a day for at least the first three years," the second DOJ man corrected.

"Isn't that a bit harsh?" Dayo's lawyer asked.

"Richard Reid didn't kill anyone and he's serving three life sentences plus one hundred ten years. Your client murdered a United States senator and conspired to facilitate the deaths and injuries of nearly nine hundred innocent people. Where would you suggest we send him? A Club *Fed*? Maybe Lewisburg?"

✷ ✷ ✷

Court reconvened and Dusty took the stand to be cross-examined. Judge Marshall looked at the defense table. "You may begin, Mr. Levy."

The somewhat rotund, middle-aged, slightly balding attorney rose and walked to the lectern with a binder of his own. "Thank you, Your Honor."

"Ms. Rhodes, I understand you've recently signed an agreement to become a syndicated columnist. Congratulations. Now, would you tell us how long you have been a reporter?"

"Almost forty years."

"And have you always been a crime reporter?"

"No."

"What other journalistic work have you done?"

"I covered medicine for a while."

"Why the change . . ."

"Objection, Your Honor! What is Mr. Levy's purpose with this line of questioning?"

"Your Honor, counsel opened this area by asking Ms. Rhodes if she is a crime reporter."

"Overruled."

"Thank you, Your Honor. Ms. Rhodes, do you recall my question?"

"Yes."

Levy smiled. "You don't intend to make this easy, do you?"

"I intend to tell the truth, Mr. Levy. You asked a question, I answered it."

"Very well. Why were you taken off the *Mirror*'s crime beat?"

"I lost my reporter's perspective."

"Because your father and grandfathers were members of the BPD?"

"That probably contributed to it."

"And how did you get your perspective back to become a 'blotter-beagle' as you once referred to yourself?"

"I happened to be in the office when an anonymous tip came in about a bombing at a prominent lawyer's home."

"That would have been Anthony Montgomery, correct?"

"Yes."

"You won a Pulitzer Prize for your series of stories about the bomber in that case. A Mr. Alonzo Simington, is that correct?"

"Yes."

"And in the process of covering the Simington case, you developed a strong relationship with members of the Baltimore Bomb, excuse me, the Emergency Services Unit, did you not?"

"Yes."

"And, as you testified earlier, you married one of its members, James Grabowski."

Dusty didn't respond.

"Ms. Rhodes?"

"Was that a question? If so, you already *know* the answer."

Levy ignored the slight angry tone and continued. "And when you were doing these Simington articles, who did Mr. Grabowski work with on the ESU?"

"He worked with a number of people, too many to count or name."

"Let me be more specific. Did Mr. Grabowski work with a bomb tech named Hunter Morgan?"

"Yes."

"To the best of your knowledge, what does Mr. Morgan do now?"

"He's a homicide detective."

"That's quite a change from bomb technician to the Homicide Squad. Do you see Detective Morgan in the courtroom today?"

"Yes."

"Would you be kind enough to point him out, please?"

Dusty pointed toward the left side of the gallery. "Detective Morgan is sitting on the aisle of the first row behind Ms. Gray."

Levy turned and briefly looked in that direction. "Yes, he is. And why is Detective Morgan here today?"

"He's one of the detectives who solved the murder cases your client is charged with."

"Move to strike, Your Honor. Until the jury renders a verdict, there is no proof that the cases are '*solved.*'"

"So ordered. The jury will disregard Ms. Rhodes' last response."

"Thank you, Your Honor. Ms. Rhodes, would you say you have a close relationship with Detective Morgan?"

"On and off. There are times we don't see eye-to-eye."

"When, for instance?"

"When he thinks I've done something that hinders an investigation."

"But any hindrances must have been minimal and infrequent or you'd have been charged and prosecuted. Correct?"

"'Minimal' is in the eye of the beholder, Mr. Levy, but I take your point. Yes."

"Now, you testified earlier about the answering machine tape your husband discovered at the Moses' residence. What did he do with it?"

"He put it in a Ziploc bag."

"And where did he take it?"

"To Detectives Morgan and Hermann."

"So Officer Grabowski went directly to the detectives. Wasn't it late in the evening?"

"It wasn't that late."

"Okay. Can you confirm that your husband delivered the tape to Hermann and Morgan immediately after you left the Moses' residence?"

Dusty hesitated.

"Your Honor . . ."

"Answer the question, Ms. Rhodes."

"No. Jim received a call about a suspicious package at a synagogue."

"And he took the tape with him to the call at the . . ." Levy checked his notes. "B'Nai Israel Synagogue at 27 Lloyd Street?"

"Yes."

"And it remained in his sole possession until he turned it over to the detectives?"

Again Dusty didn't answer immediately.

"Ms. Rhodes. Please answer my question."

"No. He left it in the car."

"And where was the car during this call?"

"I drove it to my office."

"Did you listen to it?"

"No."

"Be careful here, Ms. Rhodes. Perjury carries a stiff penalty, especially in a case as grave as this."

"I didn't listen to it."

"What did you do with it?"

"I had it copied."

"And you listened to the copy. Is that true?"

"I did, but not at that time."

"Who copied it?"

"The *Mirror*'s lead photographer, Peter Liu."

"When did it come under Officer Grabowski's control again?"

"Later that evening when he got home."

"And where was it at that time?"

"On the console of my car, where he'd left it."

"Your Honor, I move that the cassette tape entered into evidence earlier by the State be ruled inadmissible since the chain of custody was broken."

Celia Gray leaped to her feet. "Your Honor, there is no evidence that Ms. Rhodes tampered with or altered the contents of the tape."

Before Judge Marshall could rule, Levy responded. "Your Honor, she had it *copied*. How are we to know that the one in evidence is even the original? The chain of custody was not maintained."

"I'm afraid Mr. Levy is right, Ms. Gray. The tape is out."

FORTY-EIGHT

"Detective Morgan, how did you come to arrest Mr. Buckley?" Celia Gray asked.

"We received a photo of his tag number, put out an APB and he was arrested a short time later that day."

"You received the photo from Ms. Rhodes, is that correct?"

"Yes, it is."

"You and Detective Hermann interviewed Mr. Buckley, did you not?"

"We did."

"Your Honor, if it pleases the court, may we play the recorded interview?"

"Yes. You may proceed."

The lights dimmed and Celia Gray pressed the "Play" button on a DVD player.

The courtroom occupants watched and listened to Bradley Buckley's interaction with the detectives. Upon its completion, the lights came back up and Gray continued.

"Detective Morgan, how did your investigation continue following the interview we just watched?"

"Mr. Buckley was returned to the lockup where he asked to make a phone call. The CO asked if he was calling his lawyer and he said . . ."

"Objection, Your Honor! Hearsay!"

Before Judge Marshall ruled, Gray said: "Your Honor, we can call the CO to testify to this directly, if Mr. Levy's intention is to drag this trial out. However, I have a signed affidavit from him that corroborates what Detective Morgan is about to testify to."

"Let me see it, Ms. Gray."

Gray laid a copy on the defense table and handed the original to the bailiff, who passed it to Judge Marshall.

"This appears to be in order. Would you care to withdraw your objection, Mr. Levy?"

"No, Your Honor, I'd like it on the record as overruled, which I assume you're about to."

"Leaving a narrow crack for a possible appeal, are we? Very well, your objection is overruled. Continue, please."

"Thank you, Your Honor. Please continue, Detective."

"Since Mr. Buckley said he was not calling council and the CO overheard . . ."

Again Levy shot to his feet. "Your Honor, the defense strenuously objects to the inclusion of anything Mr. Buckley said. He could have . . ."

"Mr. Levy, *sit down*! Mr. Buckley spoke in front of the corrections officer and in doing so could have no reasonable expectation of privacy. The officer's affidavit clearly states the Mr. Buckley said: 'Harley, you got to get me out of here.' He asked for assistance in getting *out of jail*, not legal advice. Overruled."

"Thank you, Your Honor."

Gray returned her attention to Morgan. "Detective, what happened to Mr. Buckley while in custody?"

"He was murdered."

"By whom?"

"We don't know at this point. The investigation is ongoing."

"What did you do following Mr. Buckley's murder?

"We obtained the location of the phone Mr. Buckley called and arrested the man in possession of it."

"A Mr. Harley Chatsworth, the man Mr. Buckley called from jail."

"Correct."

"How did you get the location of the phone?"

"From Dusty . . . Ms. Rhodes."

"Did you ask her to use her connections to get information about Mr. Chatsworth for you?"

"We did not."

"Your Honor, I have no more questions for Detective Morgan at this point, but I respectfully request the right to redirect, if necessary."

"Granted. Mr. Levy."

"Thank you, Your Honor. I'll be brief," Levy said as he passed Celia Gray toward the lectern, binder in hand. "Detective, it is your testimony that you did not request Ms. Rhodes take any action on behalf of the BPD. Is that accurate?"

"It is."

"How did Ms. Rhodes know the number Mr. Buckley called and Mr. Chatsworth supposedly answered?"

"I gave it to her."

"Your Honor, I submit that Detective Morgan's answer just now proves an implicit request for assistance allowing the BPD to circumvent the need for a warrant for Mr. Chatsworth's phone information."

"Ms. Gray, I'm afraid I have to agree."

Levy looked back at Gray and winked. Then, turning back to the bench, said: "Thank you, Your Honor. I respectfully ask the court exclude the phone number and all the information that led the police to Mr. Chatsworth as evidence."

Judge Marshall took in a deep breath as she considered Levy's request. After nearly a minute, she spoke. "The jury will disregard Mr. Buckley's phone call to Mr. Chatsworth."

Celia Gray dropped her head, knowing what Levy would request next.

"Thank You, Your Honor. Since the State's case is built on illegally obtained evidence, the defense submits a motion that the charges against Mr. Mallard be dismissed with prejudice."

"It is late in the day, Mr. Levy. I'll consider your motion over the weekend and give my ruling when we reconvene on Monday. We're adjourned until then at ten sharp."

The banging gavel added an exclamation point to a case now awash in doubt.

★ ★ ★

Swift Justice, the nearest watering hole to the Clarence Mitchell Circuit Courthouse on the corners of East Fayette and Calvert Streets, took five minutes to reach, if a person had to spend three of them waiting for a traffic light to change. Gray, Hermann and Morgan sat in a horseshoe-shaped corner booth. A waitress delivered their order – beer for Gray and Hermann and a Diet Coke for Morgan – then returned to the bar.

"I'm afraid the judge is going to kick the case. If we're lucky, it won't be with prejudice," Celia Gray said, lifting her pint of Stella Artois.

"We can't let this dirt bag slip through a loophole, Celia," Hermann said. "If Judge Marshall releases him, he'll be gone faster than corn beef on Saint Patrick's Day."

Morgan looked at each of his table mates. "This is a classic case of 'Hope for the best but prepare for the worst.' We better figure out an answer for the latter before court convenes on Monday."

✦✦✦

FORTY-NINE

"All rise," the bailiff said loudly.

Judge Marshall took the bench. "Be seated."

"The Circuit Court of Baltimore is now in session."

"Mr. Levy, I have considered your motion and I am prepared to rule on it."

A momentary murmur went through the gallery.

"I believe the case against Mr. Mallard does hinge on evidence obtained illegally through Ms. Rhode's connections and is therefore inadmissible. I am granting Mr. Levy's motion to dismiss . . . *without* prejudice. The States' Attorney may refile if it obtains all evidence via legal means."

The gallery's reaction drew a bang from Judge Marshall's gavel. "*Order!*"

Levy rose to his feet. "Your honor, we request that Mr. Mallard be released ROR. He has spent considerable time in confinement and should not have to continue that incarceration any longer."

"Mr. Mallard, you are released and free to go."

"Thank you, Your Honor," Mallard said and got to his feet.

Spectators – almost exclusively members of the media – rushed out of the room. The banging gavel drew little attention and no decrease in the excited voices' volume.

Mallard shook Levy's hand, turned and followed the last of the gallery toward the dark double doors.

Levy walked to the prosecution's table and extended his hand to Gray. "Buy you a drink, Counselor?"

Gray ignored the hand, closed her briefcase and turned to face Levy. "It's a little early for me. And . . . I wouldn't start celebrating just yet."

☆ ☆ ☆

Mallard stood bathed in TV lights and strobes' flashes, his head slightly above a forest of microphones and recording devices. He raised his hands to quiet the din of rapid-fire, overlapping questions. "I just want to say that once again the American justice system has proven itself to be the hallmark of equity and fairness around the world. I took on the State of Maryland and won. Where else on earth could that happen?"

Behind Mallard the crowd parted Red Sea-like and Hermann's and Morgan's faces appeared above and on either side of the shorter Mallard. Neither man smiled as Morgan said: "John Mallard, you're under arrest for conspiracy to commit murder and accessory to the murders of Monica Stevens, Rachel Rosen, Roberta Clever, Ms. Cleaver's unborn fetus, Cheryl Greene, Rabbi Shlomo Polakoff, Fontanna Wisekoff, and Patricia Sherman. Place your hands behind your back."

☆ ☆ ☆

Several hours later Dusty looked down at Morgan and Hermann, seated at their desks. "*Jesus*! How did you guys pull *that* off? Mallard gets out of the soup, at least temporarily, on a technicality, walks out of the courtroom, is immediately rearrested for a slew of the sniper murders, goes to arraignment within the hour, and is remanded back into the slammer."

"We did the easy part," Morgan said, pointing back and forth between Hermann and himself. "Celia Gray did most of the heavy lifting over the weekend to pull it all together after my partner got the pleasure of letting Mallard borrow his set of matching bracelets for a while."

"But won't she have the same evidentiary problem with the sniper cases?"

"When the sniper got busted for the illegal U-turn, he had a disposable cell phone in his car. It never made any calls, it only received them. Mallard made all but one of them from the phone he stupidly gave his maid. But when he got word of you knocking on Bradley Buckley's door and asking if he was John Moses, Mallard panicked and screwed up."

Dusty screwed up her face and shook her head. "Screwed up how?"

"He must have been out of minutes on his disposable phone and didn't want to take the time to add more, because he called from his home office phone."

"Why would he be stupid enough to do *that*?"

"Panic makes people do irrational things," Hermann said and continued to explain. "After Mallard looked like he might get a second chance, we combed through all the evidence and realized the sniper had gotten calls from two different phone numbers. Celia popped her Haines *Criss Cross Directory* CD into her computer and found Mallard's home office phone listing in about a minute. Then Morgan and I scoot down to Judge McLaughlin's home and get him to sign a warrant for the Verizon LUDs for the land line number. My brother-in-law is a senior vice president there and greases the skids. He gets the request turned around in less than two hours and we have a legally bulletproof link between Mallard's office phone and the sniper's."

"I know I can't write about much if any of this now, but I have to ask. What could possibly motivate Mallard to be involved with a *sniper*?"

Morgan answered. "Jealousy. He felt betrayed by Jordan Moses when she took up with Tasman. When she came to Mallard to extort her involvement with the senator, it opened and exacerbated that wound, driving him off the deep end."

Dusty shook her head. "I don't get it. Neither of the Moses or anyone else associated with their murders was killed by the sniper."

"That's true, Dusty. All the sniper's targets – with the exception of you – were cover for his real target . . . Tasman."

"*What*?" Dusty dropped into the chair next to Morgan's desk. "I have to sit down for this! *Tasman*? Did the guy you have on ice cop to that?"

"No, he didn't know it," Hermann responded.

"Then how the hell do *you* guys know it?"

"When we executed the search at Mallard's home, we found a journal in a lock-box along with the phone numbers for Harley Chatsworth and Eduardo Garcia's disposable cells on a Post-it. We glanced through the journal and saw those numbers listed there, so we took it into evidence. It laid out chapter and verse about what he did and why. When Garcia got pinched, Mallard hadn't yet told him who the ultimate target was."

"But Tasman had a good chance of beating Reynolds and then Fox. Mallard would have been in the catbird seat. He could have had anything he wanted from *President* Tasman."

Morgan shook his head. "Mallard didn't really think Tasman could win according to several of the journal entries. They had polling showing Reynolds being more popular in the states that had to be won in November . . . Florida, Ohio, California. She'd won all those primaries handily.

"Their data also showed Reynolds would beat Fox pretty easily too."

"But if he wasn't going to win anyway, why kill off Jordan and John Moses, Angela Bassett, and Buckley?"

Hermann smiled. "That's easy. Mallard thought he'd backed the wrong horse. If he was going to have any future in politics after Tasman lost to Reynolds, he couldn't let his candidate's affair come to light and tear the Democratic Party apart, especially since he had been involved with Jordan Moses himself."

"But what if their polling showed that Tasman could beat Reynolds and Fox? Would he have still had his candidate murdered?"

Morgan shook his head. "We don't know for sure, but Mallard probably would have. They had data that said Tasman couldn't beat a white opponent. The early primary victories in the major states Reynolds had already won seemed to bear that out. The only place she stubbed her toe was on Super Tuesday."

Dusty covered her forehead with her left hand. "*Christ!* Talk about a bag of snakes!"

✣

FIFTY

In the following months, Dayo Amoako testified at nearly two dozen trials. Staff Sergeant Aamina Al Yami's court-martial began the parade. The young man impersonating an army specialist at BWI took a little while to track down. His federal trial came next and ended in a guilty verdict with a death sentence. Another twenty-one members of Northern Virginia's *Hazrat Ali* Mosque were indicted. Nineteen were convicted and received lengthy sentences in federal penitentiaries.

Maryland extradited Dayo, where he confessed to killing Officer Pike. He was sentenced to life plus ninety-nine years to commence upon his release from the feds' Florence ADMAX prison – not of much concern unless Dayo had nearly as many lives as a cat.

Mallard refused to take a plea for the sniper killings. Celia Gray's case played out just as she intended. Desperate to inject some shred of doubt in the State's case, Mr. Levy accused Amanda Mejía of being the mastermind behind the murders during his cross examination of her, bringing her to tears.

Eduardo Garcia – who had taken a plea deal – shattered that thin reed within the first five minutes of his time on the stand when Gray asked if during any of the calls he had ever spoken to a woman. "No. A man only, with the same voice."

The jury deliberated for forty-one, minutes before returning with a verdict of: Guilty. Mallard received the death penalty.

Celia Gray had every intention of retrying Mallard for the Moses, Bassett, and Buckley murders. However, during the sniper trial, Mallard's ultimate target came to light when Mallard's journal entries were entered into evidence. While awaiting the second trial, the former campaign manager's confinement security became lax by accident or intent. When the COs discovered his body, it contained countless stab wounds. No one was charged for the crime.

Dusty Rhodes won her second Pulitzer Prize for her series of articles on the conjoined murder cases. Her syndicated column quickly became popular, elevating her to a national figure. Regular invitations to appear on various talk and news programs made her face quickly recognizable – often to Dusty and Jim's chagrin.

The Senate confirmed Emlyn Keith's nomination to be chief justice in nearly record time, while Senators Fox and Reynolds hacked away at each other on the campaign trail. Fox's lead dwindled to fall within the poll's margins of error. Reynolds' past seemed to keep crawling out of the woodwork to create embarrassment – a Republican PAC's ad showing her falsely claiming to have been under sniper fire the most egregious example.

Morgan and Hermann retired from the BPD and started their own criminal investigation consulting firm – Last Resort Investigations, Inc. National media coverage of a number of their high profile cases quickly provided the two with more work than they could possible handle. Within a few weeks of their opening, LRI began to take on other notable investigators, including arson and bomb technicians. Grabowski put in his papers and joined the firm as a full partner. Costa followed suit shortly thereafter and bought into the partnership as well.

Samantha Morgan sold her share of the OB/GYN practice. In the following months, she used most of the proceeds to open several free women's clinics. A number of her wealthy former patients added funding, including a generous donation from Erin Sundberg.

Amanda Mejía so impressed Ms. Sundberg that she promoted her to supervise dozens of other employees. Jolly Maids' profit sharing program opened more opportunities for Amanda's son than she could ever have imagined. Proof that the American Dream could still be classified as: "Alive and Well!"

★★
★ ★
★

EPILOGUE

On Election Day, the coverage by the major media outlets began as the polls closed across the country. Few actual vote tallies were reported before 6 p.m. on the West Coast in an attempt to prevent eastern results from affecting voters' actions and the election in other time zones. However, scores of exit interviews conducted around the nation indicated a dead heat between Senators Fox and Reynolds.

As the evening progressed, two of the main broadcast television networks called Florida for one candidate, only to have to reverse themselves less than half an hour later. Obviously, the winner wouldn't be known until early – and possibly late – Wednesday morning. The turnout greatly exceeded expectations, causing countless pundits to come up with vastly different conclusions from the same data. After midnight, concern began to grow that the razor-thin leads that swung back and forth between the candidates might lead to recount calls, thus further delaying an announcement of the president elect.

A few minutes before 5 a.m., a bleary-eyed anchor looked into the camera and said with an obvious sense of relief: "With virtually all of the results now tabulated on the West Coast and a slight lead in Alaska, *Coyote News* is prepared to announce that the forty-fourth President of the United States will be Senator . . .

THE END

Glossary

Term	Definition
747-400er	Best-selling model of the Boeing 747 family of jet airliners. The "er" stands for extended range
10-16	Police code request for backup
AFIS	the FBI's Automated Fingerprint Identification System
AIDS	Acquired Immunodeficiency Syndrome
AKA	Also Known As
AP	Anti-Personnel
APB	All-Points Bulletin – Notification by police of all city, state and sometimes national law-enforcement agencies that a particular police department is searching for someone
ASAP	As Soon As Possible
ATC	Air Traffic Control
ATF	Bureau of Alcohol, Tobacco, Firearms and Explosives, a division of the Department of Justice
ATL	Hartsfield-Jackson Atlanta International Airport
AV	Audio Visual
AZTIC	Arizona Terrorism Information Center
BDU	Battle Dress Uniform AKA fatigues to earlier members of the armed services, particularly the Army.
BFD	Baltimore Fire Department
BI	Background Investigation
BMG	Browning Machine gun
BOLO	Be On the Look Out (similar to APB)
Boolit	Slang term for hand-cast bullets, usually made by competitive marksmen or serious hunters
BPD	Baltimore Police Department
B-roll	Supplemental or alternate footage shot to be intercut with an interview or documentary
BWI	Baltimore-Washington International Airport
C-4	Composition C-4, a plastic explosive that is "cap sensitive," meaning that a blasting cap is generally needed to detonate the material.
CBP	Customs and Border Patrol
CDT	Central Daylight Time

Term	Definition
CEO	Chief Executive Officer
CHP	California Highway Patrol
CIC	Criminal Investigation Command
CO	Corrections Officer
Code 2	Police term meaning "Urgent"
Code 3	Police term meaning the use of lights and siren
CODIS	COmbined DNA Index System
CONUS	Contiguous United States
CPD	Chicago Police Department
CRJ	Canadair Regional Jet
CSI	Crime Scene Investigation
DA	Department of the Army
DCA	Washington Reagan National Airport
DEA	Drug Enforcement Agency
DHS	Department of Homeland Security
District	District of Columbia - Washington, D.C.
DNA	DeoxyriboNucleic Acid
DOA	Dead on Arrival - originally the term applied to the "arrival" of a dead person at a hospital. Now DOA more commonly refers to a victim being dead upon the "arrival" of the police at a crime scene.
DOD	Department of Defense
DOJ	Department of Justice
DPS	Department of Public Safety
DVR	Digital Video Recorder
EMT	Emergency Medical Technician
EOB	Explanation of Benefits
EOD	Explosives Ordnance Disposal
EPA	Environmental Protection Agency
ESU	Emergency Services Unit
ETA	Estimated Time of Arrival
EVU	Emergency Vehicle Unit, the former name of Baltimore's Bomb Squad, currently known as the Emergency Services Unit
FAA	Federal Aviation Administration
FBI	Federal Bureau of Investigation, a division of the DOJ

Term	Definition
FCP	Fairfax County Police
Five by Five	Communications term indicating the quality of reception and signal strength of a radio communication from worst (1) to best (5)
COD	Cause Of Death
GFC	Ground Force Commander
GSR	Gun Shot Residue
GSW	Gun Shot Wound
GWP	George Washington Parkway
HAZMAT	Hazardous Materials
HE	High Explosive
HIDTA	High Intensity Drug Trafficking Area
HIPAA	Health Insurance Portability and Accountability Act of 1996
HIV	Human Immunodeficiency Virus
Hose Draggers	Firemen
HUD	Heads Up Display
Humvee	Actually HMMWV, High Mobility Multipurpose Wheeled Vehicle
IAD	Washington's Dulles International Airport
ID	Identification
IDT	Iranian Daylight Time - 4.5 hours ahead of Greenwich Mean Time (GMT)
IED	Improvised Explosive Device
IFF	Identify Friend or Foe, a system that stops the launch of a missile if the signal from a friendly target is received. Enemy targets transmit no such signal and the missile is allowed to fire.
IR	Infrared
IRGC	Iranian Revolutionary Guard Corps
JCS	Joint Chiefs of Staff
JDAM	Joint Direct Attack Munitions
JFK	New York's John F. Kennedy International Airport
JTAC	Joint Terminal Attack Controller
LAX	Los Angeles International Airport
LCD	Liquid Quartz Display

Term	Definition
LED	Light Emitting Diode
LUD	Local Usage Details
LRI	Last Resort Investigations, Inc.
LZ	Landing Zone
Mach 2.2	2.2 times the speed of sound
MANPADS	Man-Portable Air-Defense System, surface-to-air missiles
MCPD	Montgomery County Police Department
ME	Medical Examiner
MHP	Missouri Highway Patrol
MHZ	Mega Hertz (radio frequency)
MO	*Modus Operandi*, a Latin phrase whose approximate translation is method of operation
MSFM	Maryland State Fire Marshall's Office
NCIC	National Crime Information Center
NMSP	New Mexico State Police
NTSB	National Transportation Safety Board
NW	Northwest
OHP	Oklahoma Highway Patrol
OIG	Office of the Inspector General
OKC	Oklahoma City, Oklahoma
On the job	A member of a police force
ORD	Chicago's O'Hare International Airport
OSHP	Ohio State Highway Patrol
Perp	Perpetrator
PG	Prince George's (County)
PHI	Protected Health Information
PI	Police Interceptor
Priority Zero	A term meaning Dead On Arrival, no need for emergency medical services
POTUS	President of the United States
Puking Flares	Using decoy flares as an aerial infrared countermeasure used by a plane or helicopter to counter an infrared homing ("heat seeking") surface-to-air missile or air-to-air missile.
REX	Red-Eye Express
ROR	Released on Recognizance (no bail required)

Term	Definition
RV	Recreational Vehicle
RF	Radio Frequency
RHIB	Rigid-Hulled Inflatable Boat
Running Hot	Police slang for Code 3, respond with lights and siren on
RR	Road Runner
SAM	Surface-to-Air Missiles
SAP	A slang term for a blackjack; bludgeon: *Typically about five inches long, covered with woven brown leather - used to render a foe unconscious.*
SFM	State Fire Marshal
Signal 13	Police officer needs assistance (urgent)
SS	Secret Service
S and S	Search and Seizure
SFC	Sergeant First Class
SOA	Special Operations Aviation
SOCOM	Special Operations Command
SSG	Staff Sergeant
SWCC	Special Warfare Combatant-craft Crewmen (pronounced "swick")
T&PFR	Texas & Pacific Freight Railroad
Taggant	A chemical or physical marker added to materials such as explosives to allow testing and/or the identification of the manufacturer.
Take Down Bar Lights	Bright, white, forward facing lights used to illuminate the interior of cars before a police officer approaches it.
Ten-Sixteen	Police officer needs backup
Thin Blue Line	Police
THP	Texas Highway Patrol
TRP	Target Reference Point
USB	Universal Serial Bus
USCIS	U.S. Citizenship and Immigration Services
USDOT	United States Department Of Transportation
USSS	United States Secret Service
VA	Veterans' Administration
Vic	Victim

Term	Definition
VIN	Vehicle Identification Number
VIP	Very Important Person
WILCO	Will Comply
WMD	Weapons of Mass Destruction
Zulu	The military termination for Greenwich Mean Time (GMT AKA Coordinated Universal Time (UTC))

www.ingramcontent.com/pod-product-compliance
Lightning Source LLC
Chambersburg PA
CBHW031500270326
41930CB00006B/184